Organization Development Interventions

Organization Development Interventions

Executing Effective Organizational Change

Edited by
William J. Rothwell
Sohel M. Imroz
Behnam Bakhshandeh

Routledge
Taylor & Francis Group

A PRODUCTIVITY PRESS BOOK

First published 2021
by Routledge
600 Broken Sound Parkway #300, Boca Raton FL, 33487

and by Routledge
2 Park Square, Milton Park, Abingdon, Oxon, OX14 4RN

Routledge is an imprint of the Taylor & Francis Group, an informa business.

Library of Congress Cataloging-in-Publication Data
A catalog record for this title has been requested

ISBN: 978-1-032-04913-7 (hbk)
ISBN: 978-0-367-89397-2 (pbk)
ISBN: 978-1-003-01980-0 (ebk)

Typeset in Garamond
by MPS Limited, Dehradun

William J. Rothwell dedicates this book to his wife *Marcelina*, his daughter *Candice*, his son *Froilan*, his grandsons *Aden* and *Gabriel,* and his granddaughters *Freya* and *Marcelina*.

Sohel M. Imroz dedicates this book to his parents *Mdabu and Deena Waheed*, his wife *Bijoly*, and his son *Ashaaz*.

Behnam Bakhshandeh dedicates this book to his life partner, *Cindy Gillen Klenk,* for her unconditional love and support. Thank you for being a beacon of healthy body, mind, and spirit. Thank you for being an example of visionary, kindness, and positivity. And thank you for sharing your life with me.

Contents

Appendix A
Selected Resources to Support OD Intervention

Preface

William J. Rothwell, Sohel M. Imroz, and Behnam Bakhshandeh

Organization development (OD) is a planned system of change. It relies on behavioral science approaches to facilitate change in organizational settings, helping people to work together more effectively. An *OD intervention* is a planned change effort, taking the term "intervention" from psychology to imply that is long-term and not a quick fix. OD interventions purposely disrupt the status quo; they are deliberate attempts to change an organization or sub-unit toward a different, and more effective, state.

An effective OD intervention meets the needs of the organization and its people. To work best, it must address the root causes of organizational problems rather than the symptoms. Interventions lead to corporate culture change.

The Purpose of the Book

This book provides OD practitioners, managers, and other change agents with a comprehensive examination of OD interventions. It gives a step-by-step approach with example cases, practical tools, and guidelines for implementing different OD interventions at different levels.

It is noteworthy that about 60%–70% organizational change projects fail. One reason for failure is that the changes are not effectively implemented, and implementation of organizational changes is the focus of this book. Designed for use by organization development practitioners, management, and human resource professionals, this book provides readers with basic principles, practices, and skills of OD by featuring illustrative case studies and useful tools. This book shows how OD professionals can actually get work done and what the step-by-step OD effort should be. This book looks at how to choose and implement a range of interventions of varying scope.

The Target Audience for the Book

This book is written for anyone who seeks to implement change efforts. That would include:

- *Managers* and *workers* who participate in change efforts and often help to shape them
- *Teachers* or *professors* who teach about implementing change efforts
- *Consultants* who facilitate change efforts

The Organization of the Book

This book is organized in four parts. The chapters in **Part I** introduce OD interventions. **Part II** describes individual and small-group change efforts are implemented. **Part III** focuses on intermediate and large-scale change efforts, and **Part IV** focuses on the future of OD interventions.

Examined at a more granular level, the book consists of 14 chapters. **Chapter 1** opens the book, addressing the question "What is an OD intervention?" **Chapter 2** offers perspectives on different intervention models. **Chapter 3** offers a step-by-step approach on implementing OD interventions. **Chapter 4** looks at how instruments may be used to prompt individual change and help to guide its direction. **Chapter 5** reviews popular executive and management change efforts.

Chapter 6 looks at mentoring and sponsorship interventions, describing how they are carried out. **Chapter 7** examines small-group interventions, while **Chapter 8** examines team-building as an OD intervention. **Chapter 9** is about intermediate-sized interventions, which consist of those that occur inside organizations but do not affect the whole organization. **Chapter 10** explains what is unique about large-scale interventions, and **Chapter 11** moves beyond interventions limited by organizational boundaries to focus on change efforts spanning entire industries.

Chapter 12 discusses community development efforts that rely on OD methods. **Chapter 13** offers predictions about the future of OD interventions. **Chapter 14** describes unique issues frequently surfaced when implementing OD interventions.

Acknowledgments

The authors would like to thank all those who helped on this project. And that includes some appreciation expressed among ourselves, since this was a big group that required coordination and efforts.

William J. Rothwell would like to express special thanks to Sohel M. Imroz for getting the project plan put together and coordinating among the authors. Dr. Rothwell would also like to thank Behnam Bakhshandeh for stepping up during critical stages of the project. Finally, Dr. Rothwell thanks Farhan Sadique for his help in adding the Appendix and all the authors for their dedication over a long period to bring this work together.

William J. Rothwell
State College, Pennsylvania
November 2020

Sohel M. Imroz
Daytona Beach, Florida
November 2020;

Behnam Bakhshandeh
State College, Pennsylvania
November 2020

Editor and Author Biosketches

William J. Rothwell, Ph.D., SPHR, SHRM-SCP, CPLP Fellow, is a Professor in the Masters of Professional Studies in Organization Development and Change program and also in the Ph.D. program of Workforce Education and Development at The Pennsylvania State University. He can be contacted by email at wjr9@psu.edu. He has authored, coauthored, edited, or coedited 110 books since 1987. His recent books include *Virtual Coaching to Improve Group Relationships* (Routledge, 2021); *The Essential HR Guide for Small Business and Start Ups* (Society for Human Resource Management, 2020); *Increasing Learning and Development's Impact Through Accreditation* (Palgrave, 2020); *Workforce Development: Guidelines for Community College Professionals*, 2nd ed. (Rowman-Littlefield, 2020); *Human Performance Improvement: Building Practitioner Performance,* 3rd ed. (Routledge, 2018); *Innovation Leadership* (Routledge, 2018), *Evaluating Organization Development: How to Ensure and Sustain the Successful Transformation* (CRC Press, 2017), *Marketing Organization Development Consulting: A How-To Guide for OD Consultants* (CRC Press, 2017), *Assessment and Diagnosis for Organization Development: Powerful Tools and Perspectives for the OD practitioner* (CRC Press, 2017).

Sohel M. Imroz, Ph.D., SHRM-SCP, ITIL, is an Assistant Professor of Human Resources Management at the David O'Maley College of Business, Embry-Riddle Aeronautical University. Prior his academic career, he had almost 20 years of professional experience in HR and IT. He is interested in two broad research areas: Human Resource/Organization Development (HR/OD) and IT Service Management (ITSM). In the area of HR/OD, Sohel has completed many projects and conducted research on leadership development, competency model, social network analysis, and team-building. He is also interested in topics such as knowledge management, talent management and succession planning, employee engagement and retention, and data analytics in HR. In the area of ITSM, his past projects include various ITIL processes (e.g., Request Fulfillment, Incident, Problem, Change, and Asset Management), information security risk management, and professional online communities. His recent book is *Case Studies on Contemporary Practices in Management & HR* published by the International Association for Educators and Researchers (IAER, 2020). Sohel holds a Ph.D. in Workforce Education and Development with an emphasis in Human Resource Development and Organization Development from The Pennsylvania State University. He can be reached at imrozs@erau.edu.

Behnam Bakhshandeh, Ph.D., MPS-OD&C, is the founder and president of Primeco Education, Inc. (see www.PrimecoEducation.com). He is an accomplished business manager, known widely as a dynamic writer, speaker, personal and professional development coach, and trainer. Implementing his skills as a passionate, visionary leader, he produces extraordinary results in record time. Behnam brings his broad experience and successful track record to each project, whether it involves personal development, implementing customer-focused programs, integrating technologies, redesigning operational core processes, or delivering strategic initiatives.

Before designing Primeco Education technology, Behnam led educational programs and later managed operations for a global education organization based in two major US cities. During these seven years, Behnam worked personally with tens of thousands of participants. He was accountable for expanding customer participation, training program leaders, increasing sales, and improving the finance department's efficiency and management of the staff's overall operations and their team of over 400 volunteers, who together served an annual client base of over 10,000.

Behnam designed the Primeco Education technology in 2001. Since then, he and his team members have helped countless businesses and individuals achieve their goals and transform their thinking. His proven methodology and approach are based on his extensive experience in business and human relations.

Behnam had a Bachelor of Science Degree in Psychology and a Master of Professional Study in Organizational Development and Change. Recently, he completed his graduate studies for his Doctorate in Workforce Education and Development with a concentration on Organization Development and Human Resources Development at Penn State. Behnam enjoyed expanding into psychology as an addition to his already strong background in philosophy and ontology. He particularly enjoyed and was inspired by Positive Psychology and the Humanistic Psychology approach.

Behnam has worked in the personal and professional training and development industry since 1993. Since then, he designed and facilitated many coaching modules for individuals, couples, public, teams, and organizations, and published many books and audio/video workshops related to personal and professional development.

He can be reached by email at Behnam@CoachBehnam.com and by phone at 760-518-9804. He is at his office at 27 N. Main Street – Suite 202, Carbondale, PA 18407.

Marie Carasco, Ph.D., PCC, GPHR, SHRM-SCP, is an organizational behavior scholar-practitioner with international multi-sector experience connecting psychological principles to business and organization issues. Her research lies at the intersection of leader development and identity work, and she is interested in how people experience change. Marie is the Founder and Chief Social Scientist of Talent en Floré LLC (see www.talentenflore.com)—an executive coaching practice supporting individuals interested in personal or professional change. Her practitioner expertise is in high-potential leader development and appreciative approaches to managing change. As a former Director of Talent Strategy and Engagement, she has served as a trusted advisor to c-level leadership teams guiding task forces for large-scale global change initiatives and applied research projects in the aerospace, oil and gas, government consulting, and education sectors. Marie is also an Assistant Professor of Human Resources and Organization Development in the School of Business and Management at Azusa Pacific University (APU), and she teaches graduate courses at George Mason University, Schar School of Policy and Government, and the City University of New York (CUNY)–Brooklyn College, School of Natural and Behavioral Sciences. She is the co-author of The Essential HR Guide for Small Business and Start Ups (Society for Human Resource Management, 2020). Marie holds a Ph.D. in Workforce Education and Development with an emphasis in Human Resource Development and Organization Development from The Pennsylvania State University, and an MBA in Organizational Behavior and Coaching from The University of Texas–Dallas, Naveen Jindal School of Management. She can be reached at marie@talentenflore.com.

Norm Jones, Ph.D., has consulted with HR and Finance executives on increasing strategic diversity and articulating the bottom line around inclusive workplace practices. He has remarkable expertise in mid-management coaching and has worked one-on-one with dozens of high-potential employees who have been identified in the talent pipeline as "ready" for more senior positions within the organization. He has consulted both nationally and internationally and maintains research interests on topics such as trust development among senior teams, metacognitive approaches to student of color academic success, and inclusive onboarding in large organizational systems.

He has served in several senior diversity officer roles in higher education since 2001. As Harvard University's inaugural Associate Chief Diversity Officer and Deputy Director in the Office of the Special Assistant to the President, Norm helped establish the University's first office of diversity and inclusion while overseeing the day-to-day operations of several other offices, including Title IX, Affirmative Action and Equal Opportunity, and Disability Services. He currently serves as the inaugural Chief Equity and Inclusion Officer at Amherst College, where he oversees the Office of Student Diversity, Equity and Inclusion, the Office of Faculty Equity and Inclusion, the Office of Workforce Equity and Inclusive Leadership, and the Office of Academic Engagement and Student Success.

S. Ron Banerjee, MPS, CFS, CLTC, is a financial advisor specializing in the Tax-Exempt Markets for Voya Financial Advisors, Inc. He is currently a Ph.D. student in Workforce Education and Development with a focus on Human Resource Development at Penn State. He also holds a Masters of Professional Studies (MPS) degree in Organization Development and Change from Penn State University. Ron is a decorated veteran of the US Navy. He is an advocate for disabled veterans and serves the local and Penn State communities by holding Board positions in several organizations, including Meals on Wheels and the Penn State World Campus Alumni Society. He and his wife, Tara, sons Alex and Nick, and daughter Caroline live in State College, PA. He can be reached by email at srb4@psu.edu and by phone at 814-404-8578.

Leila Farzam is an experienced consultant with extensive human capital and organization development experience within global organizations, both private and public sectors. She is currently the Subject Matter Expert in Advisory Services for REI Systems. In addition, Leila is a Ph.D. Candidate (ABD) in Workforce Education and Development with an emphasis in Human

Resource Development and Organization Development at Penn State. Her research focuses on the employee engagement and retention factors needed for the millennial generation to be high performers in the workplace. As a student, Leila serves on the College of Education Graduate Student Council (CoEGSC) as Past President, and Workforce Education Graduate Student Association (WEGSA) as President. As an alumna, Leila serves on Alumni Council as an Elected Member on the Executive Board, Penn State Altoona Alumni Society Board of Directors as Past President, Penn State World Campus Alumni Ambassador Program as an Appointed Alumni Ambassador (OD&C Program), and Penn State Altoona Enactus Business Advisory Board as a Board Member. Leila holds a Master of Professional Studies in Organization Development and Change, and a Bachelor of Science degree in Business Administration with a concentration in Management and Marketing from Penn State. She can be reached by email at psualumleila@gmail.com.

MiJin Lee is a Ph.D. candidate in the Workforce Education and Development program at the Pennsylvania State University. She is a Human Resources Officer at an international organization. She can be reached by email at mul284@psu.edu.

Jamie Campbell is the 2013 Dr. James Robinson Equal Opportunity Award winner. This award is given to recognize a Penn State faculty or staff member who has contributed to the University by improving cross-cultural understanding. He has served as a panelist on topics ranging from social justice to students' issues and has served as a speaker for several leadership programs. Jamie also serves as an advisor to several student organizations within the Smeal College of Business such as The Black Male Leadership Symposium. Currently, Jamie is the Assistant Dean for Diversity Enhancement Programs at the Smeal College of Business. He is a 1995 graduate of Morehouse College, where he obtained his BA in Sociology. He obtained his M.Ed. with concentrations in Adult Education and Instructional Education from Central Michigan University in 2003. Jamie currently is a fifth-year Ph.D. student in the Workforce Education Program with concentrations in Organization Design and Human Resource Development at The Pennsylvania State University. His research focuses on Succession Planning as a form of Crisis Management. He and his wife Kimberly are the parents of three children (Grace, Vivian, and Lillian).

Advance Organizer

William J. Rothwell

Complete the following Organizer before you read the book. Use it as a diagnostic tool to help you assess what you most want to know about OD interventions—and where you can find it in this book *fast*.

The Organizer

Directions

Circle a *True (T)*, a *Not Applicable (N/A)*, or *False (F)* in the left column opposite each item. Spend about 10 minutes on the Organizer. Be honest! Think of OD interventions as you would like to practice them. Then, indicate whether you would like to learn more about OD interventions to develop yourself professionally as an OD practitioner. For each item listed in the center column, indicate with a *Y* (for "Yes"), *N/A* (for "Not Applicable"), or *N* (for "No") in the left column whether you would like to develop yourself in that area. When you finish, score and interpret the results using the instructions appearing at the end of the Organizer. Then, be prepared to share your responses with others you know to help you think about what you most want to learn about OD interventions. If you would like to learn more about one item below, refer to the number in the right column to find the chapter in this book in which the subject is discussed.

The Questions

Circle your **I would like to develop myself to**:
response
Chapter in the book in which the topic is covered:

Y N/A N 1.	Define key terms associated with efforts to implement OD change efforts.	1
Y N/A N 2.	List different OD interventions.	2
Y N/A N 3.	Describe the steps in implementing OD efforts.	3
Y N/A N 4.	Use instruments to guide individual OD efforts.	4
Y N/A N 5.	Use OD efforts with executives and managers effectively.	5
Y N/A N 6.	Use mentoring and sponsoring to facilitate change efforts.	6
Y N/A N 7.	Summarize effective ways to work with small groups in change efforts.	7
Y N/A N 8.	Use team-building.	8
Y N/A N 9.	Implement intermediate-sized interventions effectively.	9
Y N/A N 10.	Implement large-scale change efforts.	10
Y N/A N 11.	Use industry-wide change efforts.	11
Y N/A N 12.	Employ community change efforts.	12
Y N/A N 13.	Offer predictions about the future of OD interventions.	13

_____ **Total**

Scoring and Interpreting the Organizer

Give yourself *1 point for each Y* and *0 points for each N or N/A* listed above. Total the points from the *Y* column, and place the sum in the line opposite to the word **TOTAL** above. Then, interpret your score as follows:

Score

13-12 = *Congratulations! This book is just what you need.*
points Read the chapters you marked *Y*.

11-9 = You have great skills in OD interventions already,
points but you also have areas where you could develop professionally. Read those chapters marked *Y*.

8-5 = You have some skills in OD interventions, but you could
points still stand to build some skills in selected areas.

4-0 = You believe you do not need much development in
points implementing OD interventions.

FOUNDATIONS

Chapter 1

What Is an OD Intervention?

William J. Rothwell

Contents

Read the following vignettes. Take out a pen and a piece of paper, and indicate what you would do if faced with each one:

Vignettes

Vignette One

A large company is implementing a customer service improvement effort. The company hired an external consultant to survey a random sample of customers on Friday of each week. The surveys center around how customer service teams deal with those customers calling in for help. On Monday mornings each customer service team receives the results of the survey from Friday, and they use those results as a focal point to plan for improvement over the next week. The customer service manager is not, however, involved in any team meetings or survey efforts. A practitioner helps each team draw conclusions from the survey results and establish action plans for improvement.

Vignette Two

An organization development (OD) practitioner is offering help to a television station that is moving to self-directed work teams. The consultant meets each week with the television team that manages a television show. There are 10 teams. After each team meeting, the consultant has an "open door session" in which individual team members may meet with the consultant to discuss issues that influence them individually. When the consultant is not onsite, she stays in touch with the team members by videoconference, text messages, and phone calls.

Vignette Three

The manager of an HR department decides to act as her own OD practitioner. Each week she meets with her team online (and by videoconference) to discuss ways of helping the team work together more effectively. She began the effort by interviewing each team member about ways the team could improve its group dynamics and then fed back the results of the interviews to the team. The team members decided on what issues to improve and brainstormed on ways to improve in such areas as group decision making, group problem solving, and even group participation.

Vignette Four

The CEO of a large company recently decided to restructure his organization. He believes that a new structure will be more effective in helping the people of the organization design their efforts to achieve the organization's strategic objectives. On a Friday afternoon, the CEO hosted a broadcast on the company's intranet to reveal the new organization chart and to answer questions about it. He was overwhelmed with questions—some 4,300 in a few minutes. The CEO promised answers to the questions, but they were never offered. The CEO did not offer any other broadcasts or send out other messages.

Summary

The vignettes above provide short descriptions of what OD interventions might look like. Some of the vignettes describe good approaches; some, of course, do not represent good approaches but show areas in which OD practitioners can offer meaningful help.

What Is an OD Intervention?

Defined in simple terms, an *OD intervention* is a planned, participative change effort. It is, when regarded in context, the implementation phase of the Action Research Model (see Figure 1.1) or the implementation phase of the Appreciative Inquiry Model (see Figure 1.2). Carried out to solve organizational problems or to leverage organizational strengths, OD interventions are change efforts. Much has been written about them (see Bunker & Alban 1996 and 2006; Franz 2012; Walton 1969). Not all change efforts are OD interventions because many change efforts are neither planned nor participative. Many change efforts in psychology may be regarded as related to OD interventions, since OD and psychology share many values (see, for instance, Michie et al. 2014).

OD interventions are not the same as *ad hoc* change efforts. Unplanned change efforts are managed *ad hoc*, and managers tend to "make up the change plan as they go along." They make decisions as problems arise. Often, *ad hoc* change efforts consist of managers taking actions and then solving the problems the managers created from their own ill-planned efforts. As a simple example, managers change the working hours of a company. They then discover that the new working hours conflict with the times that employees must pick up their children from school. As a result of the problem created by

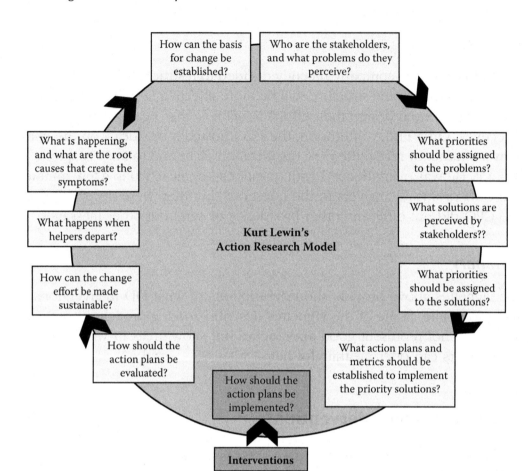

Figure 1.1 Kurt Lewin's Action Research Model (ARM) and Placement of Intervention in Context.

their efforts, they must change the working hours again. Workers then grow confused about the company's working hours, and some people are subjected to corrective action because they were never told about (or got the message about) the new working hours!

While OD interventions are not the same as *ad hoc* approaches to change implementation, they are also different from a project management-driven approach to organizational change. While change management is popular, it can mean project-driven approaches to change. When using that approach, managers will devise a detailed model to guide any change effort. Like all project plans, the change effort will have step-by-step implementation plans, time-based milestones and deadlines, staffing plans and responsibility charts, and budgets. Managers devise the plans and then implement them rigorously. If unexpected problems arise during implementation—which is often the case in modern

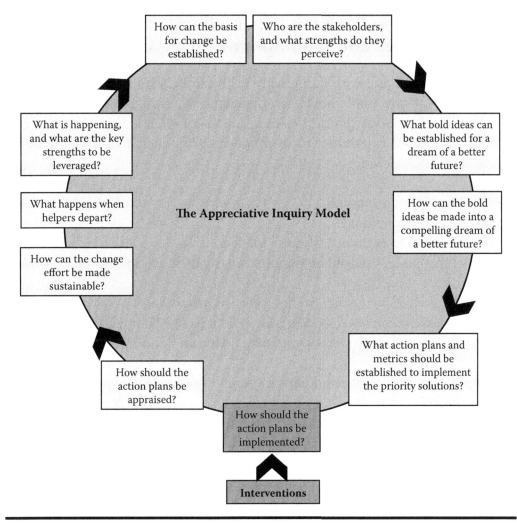

Figure 1.2   The Appreciative Inquiry Model (AIM) and Placement of Intervention in Context.

business—then managers decide whether to change the project plan or else force workers to abide by the original plan. In many cases the workers are forced to abide by the original project plan even when external conditions render achievement of project targets difficult or even impossible.

Change management generally places accomplishment of project tasks above stakeholder participation and shared decision making. OD, in contrast, generally places stakeholder participation and involvement above project accomplishment because of trust that keeping worker ownership in the change will ultimately lead to success—and perhaps to innovation to address dynamic business and competitive conditions.

OD Interventions Are Implemented in Ways Consistent with OD Values and Assumptions

OD interventions bring with them many values and assumptions, and change efforts using OD are implemented in distinctive ways that emphasize those values and assumptions. *Values* are expressions of what is important and not so important to the organization. *Assumptions* are beliefs that underlie actions. OD values include:

- Belief in human dignity
- Respect for individuals
- Belief in the importance of participation
- Belief that people should be mindful of how their actions can be perceived

Many other such values exist. In the book *Organizational development: Values, process and technology*, Margulies and Raia (1975) listed OD values that remain relevant to this day. To summarize, Margulies and Raia wrote that OD:

- Permits people to act as humans rather than play a part as mere economic resources
- Allows people to realize their capabilities
- Emphasizes effectiveness (doing the right things) over efficiency (doing things right)
- Builds a highly engaging and highly involving corporate culture
- Gives workers voice in decisions affecting them
- Pays attention to worker individuality rather than treating people using "one-size-fits-all" approaches

OD practitioners assume that:

- The best experts to solve problems in an organization are not external experts but rather the people within the organization.
- The biggest problem confronting an OD practitioner is that the stake holders do not agree among themselves on what are their problems, what are the priorities of problems deserving of action, what are the best solutions to problems, what are the priorities of solutions deserving of action, how to implement solutions, and what metrics will best focus on important issues.
- Perception is reality.

- Feelings are as important as facts.
- Group dynamics affect productivity.
- No group of people is functioning as effectively as it could be functioning.
- Full participation is a goal to be sought because the best ideas come from full involvement.
- While group consensus is desirable, it is rarely possible; therefore, many decisions should be based on the logic of the majority vote.
- When opinions vary from the majority, care should be taken to listen to the concerns of minority opinions, and steps should be taken to address them.
- While participation is desirable, nobody should be coerced into participating.
- Organizational leaders tend to have an unfortunate habit of devoting too much time and attention to task accomplishment and too little time and attention to group dynamics of workers carrying out the tasks.
- OD efforts, if they are to succeed, must have management support and keep that support over time.
- Changes in organizational corporate culture can take much longer than decision-makers expect, and often management expectations about the speed at which human change can occur are unrealistic.
- The ultimate tests of any change effort are whether the change works and is sustainable.
- Change failures are as important as change successes because both failure and success can change corporate culture, creating shared beliefs among workers about what works and what does not work.

OD Interventions Differ by Issues, Types, and Number of People Affected

OD change efforts are implemented using interventions, but many kinds of interventions exist. Just think about it: how many ways can managers effect change in organizational settings? While nobody has tried to count all the ways that management could try to change an organization or ways that external events force the organization to change, it would seem intuitively that the number would be a large one. A common way to conceptualize kinds of OD interventions is to organize them by:

- The issues to be addressed (problems to be solved or the strengths to be leveraged)

- The size (number of people) involved in the change
- The type of change effort or solution to be used

Figure 1.3 illustrates these categories and how they are related.

Interventions Organized by Issues

Change efforts can be carried out to solve a problem or leverage a strength. Many problems can exist. So, too, can there be many organizational, group, or individual strengths.

The challenge when OD practitioners help organizations solve problems is to isolate *root causes* and distinguish them from *presenting problems*, the symptoms of problems that lead managers to call for change. Presenting problems are the consequences or results of a problem. They tend to be what managers or workers notice. Root causes are not usually quite so visible; yet, a problem cannot be solved unless a root cause is addressed.

Consider a simple example. Managers call in an OD practitioner to help reduce excessive turnover. But turnover is a symptom of some other problem, the root cause(s). There can be, after all, many reasons why turnover exists. No solution will work to reduce turnover unless the real reasons for the turnover are addressed.

The same logic exists in medicine. A patient goes to the doctor with stomach pain. The stomach pain is a symptom of some problem. It is the doctor's job to find out what causes the pain. Only then can the doctor prescribe medicine or therapy to remove or reduce the pain by addressing the cause.

Leveraging strengths can also be prone to special challenges. If an organization is making much money, managers and workers alike may grow complacent, unwilling to change and to "fix what is not broken." Yet, inaction will tempt competitors in efforts to grow stronger in the same areas. Likewise, strengths are too easy to take for granted. When efforts are successful, managers may feel that their success is what they are entitled to—and not what has been earned by the organization's key competitive advantages. Note the issues identified in the model shown in Figure 1.3.

The Size Involved in the Change

How many people are involved in a change? That is a critically important question, since the time it takes to implement a change is affected by the number of people called upon to change. If the company is Coca Cola, which does business in at least 102 countries, we might well imagine that it would take longer to implement a companywide change than it would take in a small company. Note the levels of change shown in the model shown in Figure 1.3.

Types of Solutions

Solutions address the root cause of a problem or else leverage an organizational or group strength. Solutions are akin to the medicine meant to cure the illness. They can also refer to change efforts intended to build or leverage strengths by realizing a compelling dream of an ideal or highly desirable future. Note the types of solutions shown in the model shown in Figure 1.3.

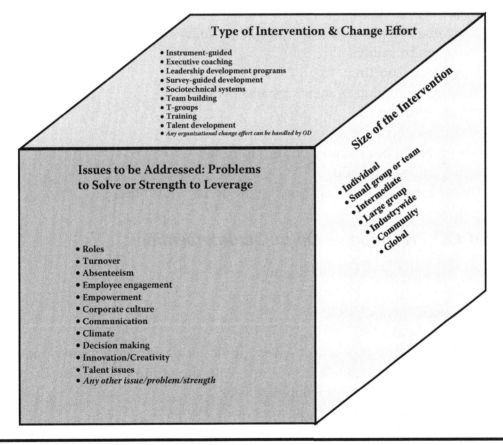

Figure 1.3   Issues, Size, and Type of Change. Adapted from the "OD Cube" in Schmuck, R. and Miles, M. (1971). *Organizational Development in Schools*. Palo Alto: National Press.

Roles of Team Leaders, OD Practitioners and Team Members in OD Interventions

What are, or should be, the roles of team leaders, OD practitioners, and team members in OD interventions? This section addresses this question.

What the Team Leader Does in OD Interventions

During OD interventions, team leaders or managers should:

- Introduce the consultant/helper/practitioner to the team or group
- Explain the role of the consultant to the team or group
- Direct discussions
- Take steps to draw in silent group members during problem solving or decision making
- Intervene when team members attack each other or call other team members by names
- Open team meetings
- Manage the timing of meetings and breaks
- Handle disruptions
- Assign responsibilities
- Assign resources to carry out group tasks
- Close out the meeting
- Clarify next steps and actions the group agreed to take

What OD Practitioners Do in OD Interventions

During OD interventions, OD practitioners should:

- Introduce themselves
- Explain their roles
- Review steps in the Action Research Model or the Appreciative Inquiry Model that they will use in working with the group to establish expectations about the practitioner's role
- Communicate how they will work with groups
- Comment on individual issues and group relationships of importance to the group working together effectively
- Facilitate discussions with group members about how they may improve group interaction or group dynamics

- Establish a psychological contract with participants about what they will do—and what they will not do
- Maintain claims of confidentiality and anonymity
- Pinpoint areas to improve
- Facilitate action planning
- Work with groups to monitor implementation of change efforts, tracking metrics and feeding them back to group members to encourage corrective action or celebrations as conditions warrant
- Help group members establish group charters and "rules of group engagement"
- Offer strategies to encourage adoption/institutionalization of ways to improve project results
- Separate from client groups effectively
- Facilitate celebrations
- Encourage managers and team members to improve their own sensitivity to group process and improve their own skills as process consultants

What the Team Members Should Do in OD Interventions

During OD interventions, team members should:

- Participate as they wish in group discussions
- Participate as they wish in group or team problem solving and decision making
- Encourage other group members to participate in decision making
- Take steps to encourage participation in group discussions by silent group members
- Observe any team charters or rule of group engagement that have been established
- Treat other group members with respect and dignity
- Respect the timing of meetings and breaks
- Avoid creating, or intensifying, disruptions
- Follow through on any responsibilities assigned
- Wisely use resources to carry out group tasks
- Participate in meetings
- Introduce themselves
- Explain their roles
- Communicate with others

- Take no steps to make it more difficult for the group to work together effectively
- Provide feedback to other group members about noteworthy behavior—particularly as it might affect the group's task achievement or group dynamics
- Observe any requests for confidentiality and anonymity
- Pose questions about group dynamics or about task achievement
- Facilitate action planning discussions
- Work with the group to measure improvements
- Participate in, and comply with, group charters and "rules of group engagement"
- Help transfer the change effort successfully
- Help to establish terms by which consultants will be called back to previous clients to help when needed
- Contribute to efforts to celebrate group successes
- Help to encourage managers to improve their mindfulness of group feelings

What Do OD Practitioners Devote Most of Their Time to Doing During Implementation?

OD interventions can be brief (a single meeting or even a brief interaction) or long (extending many years). But the OD practitioner's role is to provide information continuously to individuals and groups about the problems they identified, the solutions they pinpointed, the action plans they devised, and the metrics they chose to monitor. The practitioner does not play expert; rather, he or she facilitates continuing decision making among members of a client group. If the client is an entire organization, then efforts must be made to collect information about change implementation and feed it back to all key stakeholders. That must be done in many ways. Indeed, ensuring effective communication over time is an important role to be played by OD practitioners.

Discussion Questions

1. Define *OD intervention,* and distinguish it from other efforts to implement change.
2. How might values and assumptions influence OD interventions? Describe.

3. Why might OD interventions fail? Explain how management commitment might be lost, and what could OD practitioners do to sustain continuing management commitment even over long implementation efforts.

4. The model shown in Figure 1.3 illustrates the relationships between problems, OD interventions/solutions, and size of change efforts. Can you draw a comparable model that shows the relationships between strengths, OD interventions, and size of change efforts? Do so.

References

Bunker, Barbara, and Billie, Alban. 1996. *Large Group Interventions: Engaging the Whole System for Rapid Change.* San Francisco, CA: Jossey-Bass.

Bunker, Barbara, and Billie, Alban. (Eds.). 2006. *The Handbook of Large Group Methods: Creating Systemic Change in Organizations and Communities.* San Francisco, CA: Jossey-Bass.

Franz, Timothy. 2012. *Group Dynamics and Team Interventions: Understanding and Improving Team Performance.* New York: Wiley-Blackwell.

Margulies, Newton, and Anthony, Raia. 1975. *Organizational Development: Values, Process, and Technology.* New York: McGraw-Hill.

Michie, Susan, Lou, Atkins, and Robert, West. 2014. *The Behaviour Change Wheel: A Guide to Designing Interventions.* Bream, UK: Silverback Publishing.

Walton, Richard. 1969. *Interpersonal Peacemaking: Confrontations and Third-Party Consultation.* Reading, MA: Addison-Wesley.

/

Chapter 2

Understanding Different OD Intervention Models

Sohel M. Imroz

Contents

Overview

The previous chapter illustrated a few examples of small-scale (for groups) and large-scale (for organizations) organization development (OD) interventions. OD interventions can also be carried out for individuals, multiple groups, departments, an industry, or a community. This chapter discusses several popular OD intervention and change management models such as the following:

- Action Research Model
- Appreciative Inquiry Model
- Process Consultation
- Kotter's Change Management Model
- McKinsey's 7-S Change Management Model
- ADKAR Change Management Model
- Kubler-Ross' Five Stage Model
- Lewin's 3-Stage Change Management Model

We learned from Chapter 1 that Action Research Model (ARM) and Appreciative Inquiry Model (AIM) are OD intervention change efforts that are planned and participative. Process Consultation (PC) is also a participative change effort when the OD practitioners work alongside the clients to co-create solutions and help the clients help themselves. The rest of the models discussed in this chapter are change management models that generally place accomplishment of project tasks above stakeholder participation and shared decision making. However, these models could also be carried out in a participative manner if the practitioner does not play the role of an "expert"; rather, the practitioner facilitates client participation and decision making.

Any model that relies on participants making decisions can be OD. For instance, Kotter's model can be OD if a practitioner draws out information and decisions from the people in the change effort, but it is not OD if the managers make all the decisions and impose their will, or the practitioners do the diagnosis and then make recommendations. OD is about facilitated change. And this book is about OD change efforts as they are implemented.

Action Research Model (ARM)

ARM is a popular model for facilitating organizational change and interventions. ARM promotes organizational change by involving and collaborating with the client in identifying the problem, data gathering, diagnosis and assessment, action planning, and problem-solving steps (Cummings & Worley 2015). OD practitioners want to get a better understanding about the change effort in which they are involved in order to help the clients become more cognizant of their own environment and condition. Lewin (1946, 35) defined ARM as "a comparative research on the conditions and effects of various forms of social action and research leading to social action." ARM involves participants in social situations to improve their practices or to improve the situation in which their practices take place (Carr & Kemmis 1986; Meyer 2000).

Unlike traditional research, the type of situations or problems addressed in ARM are real-world, are practical, and may be experienced by the research practitioner directly or indirectly (Craig 2009). While ARM is "collaborative, participatory, and reciprocal," results of ARM are "tentative, critical, and less definite than traditional research" (Schmuck 2006, 30). Koshy et al. (2010) have listed several features of ARM worthy of consideration. First, ARM involves action, evaluation, and critical reflection based on evidence gathered to improve practice. Second, reflections are based on participants' interpretation of evidence. Third, ARM is participative, collaborative, situation based, and context specific. Finally, in ARM, findings are not absolute, but they emerge as the situation develops and more action, evaluation, and critical reflection take place based on new evidence.

To have a successful ARM process, OD practitioners must engage participants. The collaborative and participative nature of ARM makes this a natural choice for OD practitioners to guide OD change efforts. ARM is usually carried out in the following eight phases: Entry (problem identification), Start-Up (consultation with an expert), Assessment and Feedback (data collection, preliminary diagnosis, and feedback to key stakeholders), Action Planning (creation of action items to carry out the changes), Intervention (implement the action items), Evaluation, Adoption, and Separation (tracking results and taking over the OD practitioners' roles as they leave). Chapter 3 elaborates on these steps.

Appreciative Inquiry Model (AIM)

Founded by David Cooperrider and Suresh Srivastava in 1980, AIM is a positive, collaborative, and strength-based approach to organizational change (Moore 2020). AIM is a positive approach because it promotes organizational change by asking positive questions—questions that focus on *what is working*, rather than *what is not working*. AIM is collaborative because it supports full-voiced active participation and dialogue from the participants in order to "construct a more desirable future" (Cooperrider & Sekerka 2006, 225). AIM is strength based because it explores participants' strengths; encompasses the values, beliefs, and capabilities of an organization "at its best"; and embraces "collective understandings around what makes up the best of us" (Moore 2020, para. Key Concepts in AI).

The AIM process consists of four distinct steps: *Discovery, Dream, Design,* and *Destiny*. In the discovery step, participants identify and appreciate what works. A majority of the organization's members and stakeholders participate in interviews and identify the organization's strengths, best practices, and sources of excellence and peak performance (Cooperrider & Sekerka 2006). Discussing and exploring past successes can also be valuable in this step. Since the discovery step is focused on uncovering strengths, participants should stay away from the problem-focused or deficit-based mindset.

In the second step, dream, participants imagine "what might be" and envision a compelling, memorable, and ambitious picture of the future they really want—a future where the organization and its members are fully engaged and successful in accomplishing the strategic objectives. Since the AIM process encourages a wide range of participants to be engaged in the discussion, the "dream" may represent multiple perspectives, opinions, and understandings. Participants end up co-creating the ideal future by asking positive questions and using positive language and thinking.

In the design step, co-creation of the desired future continues but the goal is to reach a real, positive, and shared vision in an inclusive, safe, and supportive environment where everybody feels valued and heard (Moore 2020).

Once the shared vision for the future is clear, participants discuss what actions are needed today to reach that vision and bring the dream to life. According to the Center for Values-Driven Leadership (2017), participants should be as strategic and tactical as possible in the design step. New initiatives and projects needed to take the participants from their dream to destiny (the final step) are identified in the design step.

Finally, in the destiny step (sometimes also called the delivery step), participants construct the future by implementing the design, executing the actions, and revising the actions as needed. In this step, participants also embed the new design and actions into their groups, communities, and organizations. Implementing new designs and actions is likely to generate additional discoveries and keep the 4-D cycle moving forward.

Process Consultation (PC)

PC focuses on the relationships among team members to improve team effectiveness. It does not expect the OD practitioners to play the role of an expert who would arrive on the scene to prescribe solutions to the problems that the organization has identified. The PC approach encourages the clients and the OD practitioners to act as equals and assumes that identification and understanding of the problem(s) is also part of the process. In PC, the primary role of an OD practitioner is to serve like a mirror so that the client sees the reflection of how they interact with one another and perform as a team (McLean 2006).

"Process consultation is the creation of a relationship with the client that permits the client to perceive, understand and act on the process events that occur in the client's internal and external environment in order to improve the situation as defined by the client" (Schein 1999, 20). PC is a developmental approach that seeks to empower the clients to solve their own problems (Schein 1987). Mamlin (2017) described the following three tenets recognized by PC. First, the clients know more about their own situation and its complexity than the OD practitioners do. The clients also know best what works in their organizational environment and culture. Second, the clients have psychological ownership of the activities. Finally, the clients must be helped to remain proactive, and the OD practitioners should focus on developing the clients' capabilities to solve their own problem. The main emphasis of PC is on human processes and broader organizational issues (Mamlin 2017). Human processes may include relationships and communication among group members and intergroup processes. Broader organizational issues can be organizational culture, values, and norms.

An essential part of Schein's PC model is "active inquiry." Active inquiry involves building up the client's status and confidence, gathering as much information as possible about the situation, engaging the client in the process of diagnosis and action planning, and creating a safe environment for the client to share facts and feelings (Beitler 2005). In addition to active inquiry, Schein (1999, 242–245) presented the following 10 key principles of PC:

- Always try to be helpful.
- Always stay in touch with the current reality.
- Access your ignorance.
- Everything you do is an intervention.
- It is the client who owns the problem and the solution.
- Go with the flow.
- Timing is crucial.
- Be constructively opportunistic with confrontive interventions.
- Everything is a source of data; errors are inevitable—learn from them.
- When in doubt share the problem.

Kotter's Change Management Model

John Kotter's Change Management Model is one of the most popular and most adopted models in the world. Organizations often encounter many barriers (e.g., lack of leadership and teamwork, fear of the change, negative attitude) that can make it difficult to implement organizational changes. Kotter's model outlines how to implement changes systematically and effectively in an organization by overcoming these barriers. This model has eight steps with each step focusing on employees' responses to the change.

Increase Urgency

Creating a sense of urgency among managers and employees may be the best way to motivate and engage them during the change implementation process. No organizational change initiative can be successful without the support and motivation of the employees. To create a sense of urgency, a SWOT analysis can be conducted to identify and analyze the organization's internal and external factors in making a business decision. A sense of urgency can also be increased by openly discussing the problem with the employees, why the change is needed, possible solutions, and how the solutions can be implemented.

Build the Guiding Team

The purpose of this step is to assemble a coalition team with the right set of skills, personalities, qualifications, and authority that will be responsible for the driving change within the organization. An effective guiding team must have a common understanding of the need for change, the risks and challenges associated with the change, the mission and purpose of the team, and the roles and responsibilities of all the team members. The guiding team must also be aware of the communication channels as well as the critical success factors of the change along with the processes for measuring success, making decisions, and tracking issues.

Develop Vision and Strategies

The objectives of this step are (a) to create a clear and appealing vision to direct the change initiative and (b) to develop effective strategies to accomplish the vision. The vision should be aligned with the change initiative and core organizational values. The employees' ideas, emotions, and creativity must be taken into consideration when developing the vision and strategies. The vision and strategies should be communicated frequently and must be simple and easily understood by all.

Communicate the Vision and Strategies

In this step, the focus is to frequently communicate the vision and strategies about the changes being implemented with the employees and be transparent with the communication. To communicate effectively, the change leaders should demonstrate the desired behavior expected from the employees, encourage employee feedback, openly and honestly address their feelings (e.g., concerns, fears, anxieties, uncertainties), and avoid any doubt or confusion when communicating the message (Athuraliya 2020b).

Empower Action

The purpose of this step is to remove the roadblocks and collect feedback from the employees in a constructive way. Roadblocks are barriers to implementing the organizational change and may appear in the form of

inefficient processes, employees' resistance to change, ineffective management policies and practices, or organizational red tape. To overcome the
barriers, the change leaders must have a clear understanding of the barriers.
Open communication with the employees and other stakeholders is always
helpful in overcoming resistance to change. Organizational policies, processes, practices, and structure must be aligned with the vision and direction
of the change. Employees need to be empowered and recognized for their
positive efforts toward implementing the change.

Accomplish Short-Term Wins

The focus of this step is to accomplish short-term goals or quick wins to
encourage employees to rally behind the change initiative instead of just
waiting for the end result, which may take a long time to materialize. Short-
term goals should be feasible, nontrivial, unambiguous, and aligned with the
change initiative's ultimate goals or objectives. Breaking down the whole
change initiative into smaller sub-projects with milestones is a good way to
identify short-term goals and accomplish quick wins. Employees responsible
for accomplishing the quick wins should be properly recognized and rewarded in order to encourage other employees and boost employee morale.

Build on the Change

The purpose of this step is to reinforce the change and make continuous improvement. Accomplishing quick wins is a great start, but the real objective
should be achieving the ultimate change goals and objectives. After each quick
win, it is important to reflect on the lessons learned—what went right, what went
wrong, what could be done differently, and what needs to be improved.
Unnecessary organizational policies, processes, or practices should be eliminated
or redesigned to make them effective and ensure continuous improvement.
Employees who are practicing the new behaviors and facilitating the change
should be recognized and rewarded. Change leaders should also keep reminding
employees of the vision, updated strategies, and communicate success stories.

Make the Change Stick

The purpose of this step is to make the change stick by incorporating it with
the culture and "normal" way of doing things. The change must be reflected
in the new organizational norms, values, policies, and practices.

Organizational changes don't happen overnight, and challenges are unavoidable. It is important to be patient and persistent while the change management process is going on. To make changes stick and anchor the changes in the corporate culture, leaders must continue to communicate the benefits of the change, celebrate success stories, recognize employees' valuable contributions toward the change, provide training and development opportunities to the employees relevant to the change, and remove or reassign employees who are impeding progress.

McKinsey's 7-S Change Management Model

McKinsey's 7-S Change Model was developed by Robert Waterman and Tom Peters, two consultants at McKinsey and Company, in the late 1970s (MindTools 2020). Organizations use this model to assess and analyze internal elements and situations that affect organizational success. According to the 7-S Change Model, there are seven internal elements (Strategy, Structure, Systems, Shared Values, Style, Staff, and Skills) which are considered to be interlinked. These seven elements can be divided into two categories—hard and soft elements. Strategy, Structure, and Systems are hard elements, and the other four are soft elements. Hard elements are easier to identify. They can also be directly influenced by the management and decision makers (Athuraliya 2020a). Although the soft elements are less tangible and more difficult to identify, they are as important as the hard elements when affecting organizational success. All seven elements must be aligned and reinforced for organizational success, and companies should be aware of them when implementing change. The following sections provide a short description of these elements:

- **Strategy:** Strategy is the course of action the company can pursue to achieve and maintain strategic goals (Dessler 2017) and competitive advantage (Athuraliya 2020a). The course of action should consist of decisions and action steps that need to be taken to address the changes in the company's internal and external environments.
- **Structure:** Structure refers to the organizational structure or how the company is organized. The structure is often illustrated as an organizational chart which shows how departments and teams are structured and who reports to whom.

- **Systems:** Systems are the activities and procedures used by the staff to complete day-to-day jobs and responsibilities.
- **Shared values:** Shared values refer to the "superordinate goals" (Athuraliya 2020a) or the core values of an organization according to which it operates. Shared values of an organization are often manifested by its corporate culture and general work ethic (MindTools 2020). Shared values can also represent the company's standards, norms, attitudes, and beliefs (Athuraliya 2020a). Athuraliya (2020a, para. Shared Values) regarded shared values as "the organization's most fundamental building block that provides a foundation for the other six elements."
- **Style:** Style refers to the management style of the company's leaders and executives. It includes their actions, interactions, and behaviors that can influence strategic decisions, employee motivation, and organizational performance (Athuraliya 2020a).
- **Staff:** This element refers to the number of employees in the organization, recruitment practices, employee development opportunities, remuneration policies and procedures, and other motivational considerations (Athuraliya 2020a). Staff or human resources are the organization's most valuable strategic assets.
- **Skills:** Skills are the capabilities and competencies possessed by the employees working in the organization. Core competencies or skills of employees are intangible (Athuraliya 2020a) but they play a vital role in achieving organizational success.

ADKAR Change Management Model

The Prosci (Professional Science) ADKAR model focuses on the people side of the change and believes that "organizational change only happens when individuals change" (Prosci, n.d.). One of the major reasons of failure when implementing organizational change lies on the people side: Employees do not understand the benefits of implementing the change; they are not prepared to be successful after the change is implemented; or leaders cannot successfully manage the employees' resistance to change (Prosci, n.d.). By using the ADKAR model, change leaders can focus on "the identification and evaluation of the reasons why change is working or not, and why desired results are not being obtained" (Jouany & Martic 2020, para. ADKAR Change Management Model). ADKAR Model stands for Awareness, Desire, Knowledge, Ability, and Reinforcement. The following section elaborates these acronyms:

- **Awareness** clarifies why the change is needed and the requirements of the change. Prosci (n.d.) presented seven factors to build awareness of the need for change: communications from others, access to information, an event, an observable condition, readily available business information, catastrophic disaster, and gradually weakening financial performance. Activities such as messages from senior leaders and change sponsors, managers' conversations, and regular communication to general employees are critical in building the awareness. According to Athuraliya (2019), awareness can be achieved by addressing the following:
  - Understand what is working in the organization and what isn't.
  - Be aware of all the options—why the change is needed now and the risk or cost of not implementing the change.
  - Explain the business drivers, opportunities, or problems that warrant the change.
  - Focus on the most critical reason(s) for change.

Prosci (n.d.) also listed several resisting factors that can make awareness difficult to achieve: comfort with the status quo, credibility of the change leaders, sponsors, or sources sending the message, denial of the factors calling for the change, debate and disagreement over the reasons for change, and rumors of misinformation. These limiting factors must be properly dealt with to successfully raise awareness of the change's necessity.

- **Desire** means to support the change and be part of implementing it. Simply being aware of the change does not automatically guarantee having the desire to implement it. The needs and reasons for the change must become "personal and organizational motivating factors" (Prosci, n.d.) to move forward from awareness to the desire state to support and implement the change. Table 2.1 provides a list of common motivators for participating in a change, tactics for building desire, and potential resisting factors when moving from awareness to desire.

Table 2.1   Moving from Awareness to Desire

Motivators for Participating in a Change	Tactics for Building Desire	Potential Resisting Factors
■ Likelihood of gain or achievement (incentive). ■ Fear of consequence (risk or penalty). ■ Desire to be part of something (to belong). ■ Willingness to follow a leader you trust. ■ Alternative is worse.	■ Active and visible primary sponsor. ■ Strong sponsorship coalition. ■ Personal engagement by coaches. ■ Proactive management of resistance. ■ Strong employee involvement in creating the needed solution. ■ Incentive programs aligned with the change.	■ Comfort or security with how things are now. ■ Fear of the unknown. ■ Change not aligned with a person's self-interest or values. ■ No answer to *What's in it for me?* ■ Negative history with change on a personal level (low confidence of success). ■ An individual's personal situation—financial, career, family, or health. ■ An organization's track record with change.

Note. Adapted from Prosci (n.d., para. Making the Transition from Awareness to Desire).

- **Knowledge** provides the know-how to drive change. Simply having the awareness and desire to implement the change will not be successful without the knowledge of implementing the change. According to Prosci (n.d.), two types of knowledge are needed to implement the change:
  - Knowledge of how to change (what to do during the transition)
  - Knowledge of how to perform effectively after the change is implemented (skills and behaviors needed to support the change)

Table 2.2 provides a list of critical success factors, tactics, and potential resisting factors when building knowledge.

- **Ability** refers to OD practitioners' skill and capability to incorporate the change on a regular basis. The change leaders must demonstrate skills and behaviors to translate the knowledge into performance and produce desired results. Table 2.3 provides a list of critical success factors, tactics, and potential resisting factors when fostering ability.
- **Reinforcement** means strengthening of the skills and behaviors. The leaders must reinforce skills and behaviors to make the change

Table 2.2 Building Knowledge

Critical Success Factors	Tactics for Building Knowledge	Potential Resisting Factors
■ Training and education. ■ Experience. ■ Access to information. ■ Mentoring.	■ Formal training programs. ■ Job aides. ■ One-on-one coaching. ■ User groups and forums. ■ Troubleshooting guidance.	■ Gap between current knowledge levels and desired knowledge levels. ■ Insufficient time (conflicting demands). ■ Inadequate resources available for training. ■ Lack of access to the necessary information. ■ Capacity to learn.

Note. Adapted from Prosci (n.d., para. Building Knowledge).

Table 2.3 Fostering Ability

Critical Success Factors	Tactics for Fostering Ability	Potential Resisting Factors
■ Practice. ■ Time. ■ Coaching or role-modeling behavior. ■ Access to right tools. ■ Feedback.	■ Direct involvement of coaches. ■ Access to subject matter experts. ■ Performance monitoring. ■ Hands-on practice during training. ■ Availability of expert resources to help employees.	■ Inadequate time available to develop skills. ■ Lack of support. ■ Existing habits contrary to the desired behavior. ■ Psychological blocks. ■ Limitations in physical abilities. ■ Individual capabilities (personal limitations).

Note. Adapted from Prosci (n.d., para. Fostering Ability).

stick. Successful reinforcement of a change prevents employees from going back to their old ways of doing things prior to implementing the change. Table 2.4 provides a list of critical success factors, tactics, and potential resisting factors when building reinforcement.

Table 2.4 Building Reinforcement

Critical Success Factors	Tactics for Fostering Reinforcement	Potential Resisting Factors
■ Celebrations. ■ Rewards and recognition. ■ Feedback. ■ Corrective actions. ■ Visible performance measurement. ■ Accountability mechanisms.	■ Publicly visible performance scoreboards that positively show compliance to a new process. ■ Feedback from supervisors directly to employees, including saying "Thank you." ■ Visible recognition by senior-level sponsors. ■ Project-sponsored celebrations for employees. ■ Compensation and appraisal systems designed to support the change.	■ Rewards not meaningful or not associated with achievement. ■ Absence of reinforcement for accomplishments. ■ Negative consequences, including peer pressure for desired behavior. ■ Incentives that directly oppose the change.

Note. Adapted from Prosci (n.d., para. Building Reinforcement).

Kubler-Ross' Five Stage Model

This model is also known as the "Grief Model" developed by Elisabeth Kubler-Ross based on her research on dying and death (Belyh 2019). It was originally developed to describe the various emotional states and stages people go through when they are nearing end of life. However, it has been applied to other life situations such as people suffering from changes in work, loss of job, personal trauma, and other tragic incidents (Jouany & Martic 2020). According to Jouany and Martic (2020), this model is employee-oriented and focuses on their feelings, concerns, and needs. Therefore, this change model can help employers better understand their employees and empathize with them. These employers are more likely to overcome the most challenging barriers of successful change management such as employees' resistance to change, lack of communication, etc. (Jouany & Martic 2020). Following are the five stages associated with the Kubler-Ross Model that employees may be going through during organizational change.

Shock or Denial

In this stage, employees often are unable to accept the change or are not willing to recognize that the change is happening (Jouany & Martic 2020). Depending on the severity of the change, employees may experience varying degrees of shock or numbness (Belyh 2019) and may think "if we can pretend that the change is not happening, if we keep it at a distance, then maybe it will all go away" (Connelly 2018, para. Shock or Denial).

Anger

When employees finally realize that the change is for real and affecting them, their initial shock and denial converts into anger (Jouany & Martic 2020). In this stage, employees may become more irritable; vent their anger in different ways; and start blaming themselves, their friends and families, their coworkers, their bosses, the economy, the government, or even God (Connelly 2018).

Bargaining

During the bargaining stage, employees want to avoid the change's worst possible outcome and get the best possible solution or the most favorable result (Jouany & Martic 2020). Belyh (2019, para. Bargaining) has described this stage as "a way for people to avoid ending up with the worst case scenario and is a natural reaction to avoid the extreme change." Connelly (2018) has offered few examples of what people might do in this stage: attempt to postpone what is inevitable, put off the change as long as possible, or find a way out of the situation. In workplace settings, employees might work harder and extra hours in this stage to avoid an upcoming layoff or downsizing (Connelly 2018).

Depression

When employees realize that bargaining is not working and that achieving the desired outcome is unlikely, they may get depressed and become hopeless (Jouany & Martic 2020) and uncertain about the future (Belyh 2019). In this stage, employees may exhibit common symptoms of depression such as low level of energy, lack of commitment, disengagement from work, lack of motivation or excitement, etc. (Belyh 2019). These behaviors can lead to increased absenteeism as employees take days off and more sick leave (Connelly 2018).

Acceptance

In this stage, employees realize that there is no point being depressed or fighting the change anymore. They either quit or get on board with the change by finally accepting what is happening (Belyh 2019; Jouany & Martic 2020). Connelly (2018) has described this stage as a "creative space" because it "forces people to explore and look for new possibilities" (para. Acceptance). It is also very common to see employees being brave in accepting the change, learning a lot about themselves, and ultimately using the change positively to further enhance their career.

According to Connelly (2018), it is normal for human beings to move between these stages, but what is concerning is if they get stuck in one of these stages. People can very easily get stuck in the anger and depression stages, and it may be advisable for them to seek professional help if necessary (Connelly 2018).

Lewin's 3-Stage Change Management Model

Kurt Lewin's 3-Stage Model is one of the most popular, accepted, and effective change management models. This model is the base of many other models, including ARM. The 3-Stage Model is very helpful for companies to "better understand organizational and structured change" (Jouany & Martic 2020, para. Lewin's Change Management Model). Lewin's change management model describes the three main stages that every change management process must go through: pre-change, during change, and post-change. Lewin referred to these three stages as unfreezing, moving or changing, and refreezing.

Unfreezing

The first stage of Lewin's change management model involves preparation for the change. The crucial steps of this stage are to recognize that the change is essential and to openly and honestly communicate with employees explaining why the change is necessary. The main goal is to overcome employees' resistance to change. Edgar Schein identified three processes to achieve unfreezing: "disconfirmation of the validity of the status quo, the induction of guilt or survival anxiety, and creating psychological safety" (Burnes 2006, 142). In other words, those impacted by the change must feel safe from negative consequences before rejecting the old behaviors in favor of the new ones.

Moving or Changing

When the unfreezing stage is complete and the impacted employees are open to change, the next stage, also known as the *transitioning* stage, begins. This is the stage where the changes are implemented. Changes may result in adopting new behaviors, processes, or ways of doing things. Uncertainty and fear are common when transitioning to the new reality, so most people struggle in this stage. Just like the first stage, effective leadership, open employee communications, education, and support are crucial to successfully carry out the transitioning stage (Jouany & Martic 2020).

Refreezing

This is the stage in which the change (new state) is reinforced, stabilized, solidified, and accepted. The new routine becomes normal. Lewin found the refreezing stage to be especially important so that people do not revert back to their old ways of thinking or doing things (i.e., prior to the implementation of the change). Leaders should make sure that changes are continuously reinforced even after they have been implemented. Positive rewards and acknowledgment of efforts are often used to reinforce the changes.

Key Lessons Learned

This chapter provided a brief description of a few common OD intervention and change management models. The rest of the book is based on one of the most popular OD intervention models—the ARM. Chapter 3 discusses all the steps of the ARM. Chapters 4, 5, and 6 focus on OD interventions at the individual level. Chapters 7 and 8 talk about OD interventions for small groups. The focus of the rest of the chapters is intermediate-size (Chapter 9), large-scale (Chapter 10), industry-wide (Chapter 11), and community-wide (Chapter 12) OD interventions. Each chapter illustrates a case study, elaborates on how to carry out the intervention, and provides at least one useful tool for OD practitioners. The last two chapters of the book discuss the future of OD interventions (Chapter 13) and the unique issues found when implementing OD interventions (Chapter 14).

Discussion Questions

1. There are several definitions of OD provided in this chapter. Which one do you most relate to? Why?
2. Which OD intervention model do you prefer? Explain.
3. Describe advantages and disadvantages of all the OD intervention models in this chapter.
4. Do you think a certain OD intervention model is more appropriate for a certain type of OD intervention? Explain.
5. What competencies do you think are most valuable for an OD practitioner?

References

Athuraliya, Amanda. 2019. "The Ultimate List of Change Management Tools to Drive Change Like a Pro." *Creately* (blog). January 29, 2019. https://creately.com/blog/diagrams/change-management-tools-list/

Athuraliya, Amanda. 2020a. "The Easy Guide to the McKinsey 7S Model." *Creately* (blog). November 10, 2020. https://creately.com/blog/diagrams/mckinsey-7s-model-guide/

Athuraliya, Amanda. 2020b. "The Easy Guide to Kotter's 8 Step Change Model." *Creately* (blog). November 11, 2020. https://creately.com/blog/diagrams/kotters-8-step-change-model/

Beitler, Michael. 2005. "Active Inquiry in Organizational Change." November 19, 2020. https://ezinearticles.com/?Active-Inquiry-in-Organizational-Change&id=80877

Belyh, Anastasia. 2019. "Major Approaches & Models of Change Management." *Cleverism* (blog). September 20, 2019. https://www.cleverism.com/major-approaches-models-of-change-management/

Burnes, Bernard. 2006. "Kurt Lewin and the Planned Approach to Change: A Re-Appraisal." In *Organization Development*, edited by Joan V. Gallos, 133–157. San Francisco, CA: Jossey-Bass.

Carr, Wilfred, and Stephen, Kemmis. 1986. *Becoming Critical: Education, Knowledge and Action Research*. London, UK: Falmer Press.

Center for Values-Driven Leadership. 2017. "What Is Appreciative Inquiry? A Short Guide to the Appreciative Inquiry Model & Process." May 9, 2017. https://cvdl.ben.edu/blog/what-is-appreciative-inquiry/

Connelly, Mark. 2018. "Kubler-Ross Five Stage Model." *Change Management Coach* (blog). August 30, 2018. https://www.change-management-coach.com/kubler-ross.html

Cooperrider, David L., and Leslie E., Sekerka. 2006. "Toward a Theory of Positive Organizational Change." In *Organization Development*, edited by Joan V. Gallos, 223–238. San Francisco, CA: Jossey-Bass.

Craig, Dorothy Valcarcel. 2009. *Action Research Essentials*. San Francisco, CA: Jossey-Bass.

Cummings, Thomas, and Christopher, Worley. 2015. *Organization Development & Change*. Stamford, CT: Cengage Learning.

Dessler, Gary. 2017. *Human Resource Management*. Boston: Pearson Higher Education.

Jouany, Valene, and Kristina, Martic. 2020. "5 Change Management Models to Take a Look at." *Smarp* (blog). July 23, 2020. https://blog.smarp.com/5-change-management-models-to-take-a-look-at

Koshy, Elizabeth, Valsa, Koshy, and Heather, Waterman. (2010). *Action Research in Healthcare*. Los Angeles, CA: Sage Publications.

Lewin, Kurt. 1946. "Action Research and Minority Problems." *Journal of Social Issues* 2(4): 34–46. https://doi.org/10.1111/j.1540-4560.1946.tb02295.x.

Mamlin, Joe. 2017. "Teach a Man to Fish: Understanding Process Consultation." November 19, 2020. https://www.grayspeakstrategies.com/articles-archive/2017/11/12/teach-a-man-to-fish-understanding-process-consultation.

McLean, Gary. 2006. *Organization Development: Principles, Processes, Performance*. Oakland, CA: Berrett-Koehler Publishers.

Meyer, Julienne. 2000. "Using Qualitative Methods in Health-Related Action Research." *British Medical Journal* 320: 178–181. https://doi.org/10.1136/bmj.320.7228.178

MindTools. 2020. "McKinsey 7-S Framework: Making Every Part of Your Organization Work in Harmony." MindTools (blog). November 17, 2020. https://www.mindtools.com/pages/article/newSTR_91.htm#:~:text=The%20model%20was%20developed%20in,for%20it%20to%20be%20successful

Moore, Catherine. 2020. "What is Appreciative Inquiry? A Brief History & Real Life Examples." PositivePsychology (blog). November 20, 2020. https://positivepsychology.com/appreciative-inquiry/

Prosci. n.d. "The Prosci ADKAR Model: A Simple but Powerful Model for Driving Successful Change in Individuals and Organizations." *Professional Science.* Accessed August 28, 2020. https://www.prosci.com/adkar

Schein, Edgar. 1987. *Process Consultation: Lessons for Managers and Consultants.* Reading, MA: Addison-Wesley.

Schein, Edgar. 1999. *Process Consultation Revisited: Building the Helping Relationship.* Reading, MA: Addison-Wesley.

Schmuck, Richard. 2006. *Practical Action Research for Change.* Thousand Oaks, CA: Corwin Press.

Chapter 3

Steps for Implementing the OD Intervention Model: From Entry to Separation

Sohel M. Imroz

Contents

Overview

In Chapter 2, we learned about few popular organization development (OD) intervention models. Chapter 3 discusses the steps for implementing one of the models—the Action Research Model (ARM). While the ARM has been described in various ways, most people would agree it includes eight steps (Rothwell 2015; Rothwell et al. 2015). The rest of this chapter elaborates these steps:

- Entry (problem identification)
- Start-Up (consultation with an expert)
- Assessment and Feedback (data collection, preliminary diagnosis, and feedback to key stakeholders)
- Action Planning (creation of action items to carry out the changes)
- Intervention (implement the action items)
- Evaluation, Adoption, and Separation (tracking results and taking over the OD practitioners' roles as they leave)

Step 1: Entry

The Entry step is the beginning of an OD process. According to McLean (2006), three major focuses of this step are marketing (how the OD practitioners obtain work), the first meeting or the initial dialogue between the clients and the practitioners, and the contracting process (e.g., finalizing a written contract, a letter of agreement, or a memorandum of understanding between the client and the practitioner). The contracting process may also include a signed non-disclosure agreement.

Marketing

Marketing involves promoting the practitioners' skills, competencies, and expertise to obtain OD-related work, assignments, or projects. McLean (2006) listed many approaches practitioners can use for marketing: word of mouth, networking, websites, printed materials, request for proposals (RFPs), visibility, contract agencies, and doing *pro bono* work. Word of mouth is referrals and recommendations from previous employers or clients, colleagues, and professional friends, and can be the most effective approach in getting new clients. Networking can be developed through participating in professional or community organizations, current or former associates and coworkers, friends and family, and former classmates, instructors, or professors (2006; McKay 2019). It is strongly recommended for practitioners to have a high-quality and professional website that includes their personal information (i.e., name, photo, contact information, education, and qualification), areas of expertise, list of past clients, client testimonies, brief description of completed projects, and publications (e.g., books, journal articles, whitepapers). Printed materials can be the practitioner's business card, stationery supplies, or brochures. A request for proposal (RFP) is an official document that announces and provides details about a project and solicits bids from practitioners to help complete the project (Kenton 2020). Many practitioners gain increased visibility and prominence by writing (e.g., books, journal articles, and whitepapers), presenting in conferences and seminars, and teaching. OD practitioners can register with contract or staffing agencies to make a connection with multiple hiring managers looking to find the right person to do their work. Sometimes practitioners undertake professional work voluntarily and without (or reduced) payment. This type of pro bono (meaning *for the public good*) work is an excellent way to give back to the community and shows the practitioners' social responsibilities and moral and ethical values. McLean (2006, 36–39) provided an excellent list of possible advantages and disadvantages of these marketing approaches.

The First Meeting

Two main purposes of the first meeting or the initial dialogue between the client and the OD practitioner are (a) to discuss the work that needs to be done, and (b) to determine whether the practitioner is the right person for the work. McLean (2006, 47–51) listed the following tasks to be completed during the initial dialogue between both the parties.

- Determine whether the parties can work together.
- Present the problem.
- Conduct preliminary assessment.
- Determine the client's readiness to change.
- Establish the OD practitioner's credibility.

When determining if the parties can work together, McLean (2006) advised that caution should be taken and rash decisions should be avoided by all the participants. Oftentimes the client knows not only what the problem is, but also what needs to be done to fix the problem (2006). However, it is also very common when the client fails to distinguish the problem (the root cause) from the symptoms (indicators that a problem exists). When the problem has been presented, the practitioner should ask meaningful probing questions and conduct preliminary assessments to better understand the root cause and the symptoms. At the end of the preliminary assessment, both the parties should agree on the root cause(s) of the problem, and not the symptoms, that need fixing. In the next step, the practitioner should determine the client's readiness to change. It is not advisable for practitioners to commit to a project and put their reputation on the line when the client is not ready for change and unwilling to provide the resources to complete the project. Before a contract is signed, OD practitioners should continue to build credibility and trust by being professional, sincere, respectful, and accountable during the initial dialogue with the client. And once the contract is signed, the practitioner's credibility should remain intact throughout the project. It is not necessary to complete all these tasks in one meeting session, and the initial dialogue may take place over several days or even weeks.

The Contracting Process

At the end of the initial dialogue, if both the clients and the practitioners agree to work together and decide to move forward with the project, the next step is preparing and finalizing a contract, a letter of agreement, a memorandum of understanding, or a non-disclosure agreement. As a general rule, a contract or a letter of agreement is legally binding and simply requires "a meeting of the minds (agreement) with specific terms (price, dates, promise of performance, in return for, etc.) between two (or more) individuals where a benefit (consideration) is exchanged" (Rafter & Charles, 2013). A memorandum of understanding (MOU) between two or more parties may outline the responsibilities of each of the parties, but is not legally binding (Content Team 2017). An MOU is usually the first step toward creating a legally binding letter of agreement or contract. A non-disclosure agreement (NDA) establishes a legally binding relationship between the clients and practitioners to protect the client's confidential information from being shared with outsiders (Twin 2020). Table 3.1 provides a list of useful websites with examples of each of these . McLean (2006) suggested the following items to be included and thoroughly explained in a contract:

- Roles and responsibilities of all parties—who will do what
- Project scope and desired outcomes
- Project duration and timeline
- Project confidentiality
- Required resources
- Billing, reimbursement, and fees

Table 3.1 Useful Websites

Topic	Website
Contract or Letter of Agreement (LOA)	https://www.shrm.org/resourcesandtools/tools-and-samples/hr-forms/pages/cms_006670.aspx
Memorandum of Understanding (MOU)	https://templatelab.com/memorandum-of-understanding/
	https://formswift.com/downloads/memorandum-of-understanding/memorandum-of-understanding.pdf
Request for Proposal (RFP)	https://blog.hubspot.com/marketing/rfp-template
	https://www.indeed.com/hire/c/info/rfp-request-for-proposal
	https://www.business-in-a-box.com/template/request-for-proposal-D1270/
Non-disclosure Agreement	https://www.shrm.org/resourcesandtools/tools-and-samples/hr-forms/pages/cms_002097.aspx

- Project deliverables
- Recourse for nonperformance and noncompliance

Step 2: Start-Up

When an agreement or a contract is signed, the OD practitioners start stepping into the organizational environment. The start-up step is very important in an OD intervention project as the practitioners try to understand issues surrounding the problem and secure commitment from the project sponsor and stakeholders. McLean (2006) suggested three primary objectives for this step: the infrastructure needs to be established, the project management policies and practices should be formalized, and the team with which the practitioners will be working should be formed.

To successfully establish the infrastructure, the practitioners must have at least a workplace, necessary technological equipment (e.g., computer or laptop, office phone, mobile devices), and access to internet and shared drives. These tasks are often taken care of during the onboarding process when organizations hire a new employee or a practitioner. An onboarding checklist helps the new hire, HR, and hiring manager make sure they are completing all the necessary tasks to prepare for onboarding new hires and guide them in becoming part of a successful team.

The OD practitioners should formalize project management policies and practices to track "what is to be done, by whom, and when" (61). These policies and practices can be for managing tasks (sub-tasks, task dependencies), requirements (business rules, functional, technical), users and roles, workflows, reporting (dashboards, custom reports, status reporting), budgeting (forecasting, risk management), and time tracking (billable hours, non-billable hours). It may not be possible to make explicit decisions on all these matters during the start-up step, but the more decisions are made up-front, the less chances of misunderstanding during the subsequent steps.

To carry out the OD intervention, if the practitioners need to form a team, McLean (2006) offered three recommendations. First, the practitioners should identify a "point person within the client organization" (62)—a person who can be approached for information or assistance on any general or specific topic. Second, the practitioners should create a *project steering committee*—a decision-making body within the OD intervention scope that consists of top managers and other stakeholders. In general, the project steering committee's role is to "provide advice, ensure delivery of the project outputs, and the achievement of project outcomes" (Law and Justice Foundation n.d., 1). Third, the practitioners should have access to the senior management within the client organization or the project sponsor. No OD intervention can be successful without their meaningful support throughout the project.

Before proceeding to the next step (Assessment and Feedback) of the OD intervention process, the practitioners should collaborate and consult with the project sponsor and steering committee, and jointly decide which assessment approach to use. Common assessment approaches are observation, secondary data, one-on-one interview, group interview, and questionnaire/survey (McLean 2006). The practitioners should advise on the potential advantages, disadvantages, and cost of the assessment approaches and help the team make an informed decision. A decision should also be made in the start-up step about who to involve in the assessment. There are several ways to select samples from a population: random sampling, systematic, stratified, clustered, convenience, quota, judgment or purposive, and snowball (Health Knowledge 2020). When the team is formed with which the practitioners will be working, the practitioners should also develop a timeline and feedback process for the assessment (McLean 2006). They must understand "who is to receive the feedback, who will deliver it, and how it will be delivered" (65) before moving on to the Assessment and Feedback step.

Step 3: Assessment and Feedback

The important goals of assessment and feedback step are to pinpoint challenges (problems), prioritize the relative importance of the challenges, determine strategies or approaches (solutions) to address the challenges, prioritize the relative importance of the solutions, and finally, elaborate how the participants work together and achieve results. This step consists of assessment (also known as *diagnostic*) and feedback.

The primary aim of the assessment step is to provide the OD practitioners and other stakeholders with data and a clear basis for decisions about what OD interventions are appropriate going forward. As mentioned in the previous section, common assessment approaches are observation, secondary data, one-on-one interview, group interview, and questionnaire/survey. Based on the approaches used, the data collected may be qualitative or quantitative in nature. Data must be reliable and valid before being analyzed. Quantitative data analysis methods can be descriptive (e.g., mean, median, mode, percentage, frequency, range) or inferential (e.g., correlation, regression, analysis of variance). Popular qualitative data analysis methods are content analysis, narrative analysis, discourse analysis, and grounded theory.

After collecting and analyzing data, the practitioners usually prepare a report and share the findings. Feeding back the diagnostic results to appropriate stakeholders is perhaps the most important task in this step. McLean (2006, 97–99) raised a few questions OD practitioners should answer when feeding back the results:

- Who should provide and receive the feedback?
- What should be the feedback format?
- What should be included in the feedback?

To establish an effective feedback process, practitioners should be familiar with different types of workplace feedback and their properties or characteristics. Inamdar (2019) classified workplace feedback into four categories: negative, positive, negative feedforward, and positive feedforward. Feedback about past behaviors that did not produce desired results is negative feedback. Positive feedback is about past behaviors that produced desired outcomes. Negative feedforward and positive feedforward messages are usually prescriptive in nature. Negative feedforward messages help recipients avoid unwanted future behaviors, while positive feedforward messages are affirming comments about future behaviors.

Cummings and Worley (2015, 142–143) mentioned nine properties of effective feedback data. Effective feedback data should be relevant, understandable, descriptive, verifiable, timely, limited, significant, comparative, and unfinalized. OD practitioners should be aware of these properties when creating the content of feedback. They typically share feedback to organizational stakeholders in a meeting or series of meetings. Feedback sharing meetings might cause anxiety in some participants and could result in defensive behaviors from them. Therefore, practitioners should manage these meetings in such a way that constructive discussion can take place and problem solving can occur (2015). According to Cummings and Worley (2015), the most important objective of the feedback step is to make sure that the organization members own the feedback data.

Step 4: Action Planning

In the action planning step, the OD practitioners and participants work together to create action plans to implement the agreed-upon strategies or approaches (solutions) and address the challenges (problems). Having a well-thought-out action plan reduces the possibility of missing out on a critical task and saves time, energy, and resources in the long run. Thus, an action plan can increase efficiency, accountability, and credibility in the OD process. An action plan consists of a number of tasks, and each task should provide the following information:

- **What** are the tasks?
- **Who** will carry out each task?
- **By when** will each task be completed?
- **What resources** (e.g., financial, staff) are needed to complete each task?
- **Communication** (who should know what?)

Completeness, clarity, and recency are three basic characteristics of a well-rounded action plan. The action plan should contain all the necessary tasks to complete the project successfully. To ensure clarity, each task should contain the *what, who, by when, what resources*, and *communication* information. The action plan is always a "work in progress." The tasks should reflect the most recent work conditions and anticipate newly emerging barriers or challenges. Table 3.2 illustrates an action plan example used by the author in the past.

Table 3.2 Action Planning

Project name: _____

Goal: _____

Strategy: _____

Outcome: _____

Team Leader: _____ OD Practitioner: _____

TASKS

Task	Who	By When	Resources (Financial, Staff, etc.)		Emerging Barriers or Challenges	Communication
What needs to be done?	Who will complete the task?	By what date will the task be done?	Resources available	Resources needed	What are the newly emerging barriers or challenges? How should they be addressed?	Who should be informed or involved with these tasks?
1.						
2.						
3.						
4.						

Note: Author's original creation.

The importance of creating a well-rounded action plan cannot be over-emphasized. The next OD process step (Intervention) should not commence until the action plan is created and agreed on. Athuraliya (2020) outlined six easy steps explaining how to write an action plan. These steps are as follows:

- Define the end goal using SMART criteria (Specific, Measurable, Attainable, Relevant, and Timely).
- List all the tasks to be completed to achieve the end goal.
- Prioritize the tasks, and set a deadline for each task.
- Set milestones—intermediary goals leading up to the end goal.
- Identify the resources available and needed to complete each task.
- Visualize the action plan as a table, flowchart, or Gantt chart. This document should be shared with the project sponsor, stakeholders, and other participants as needed.
- Monitor, evaluate, and update the action plan as needed.

Step 5: Intervention

The intervention step is about implementing the changes that have been planned and agreed upon during action planning. Cummings and Worley (2015, 157) defined an intervention as "a sequence of activities, actions, and events intended to help an organization improve its performance and effectiveness." To successfully complete this step, OD practitioners should understand what effective interventions are and how to design effective interventions.

According to Cummings and Worley (2015), there are three criteria of effective interventions. First, the extent to which the intervention is relevant to the organization. Second, the degree to which the intervention is based on valid knowledge of outcomes. Third, the extent to which the intervention increases the organization's change management ability. Cummings and Worley (2015, 164–173) also mentioned two sets of contingencies that can affect design of effective interventions—"contingencies related to the change situation" and "contingencies related to the target of change." Contingencies related to the change situation are individual differences among organization members, organizational factors, dimensions of the change process itself, national culture, and economic development. Contingencies related to the target of change are about organizational issues (e.g., strategic issues, human resource issues) and organizational function at different levels (e.g., individual, group, organization, and transorganization). Success of interventions depends on these two contingencies.

OD interventions can be aimed at different levels: individual, small group, intermediate-sized, large scale, industry-wide, and community. There are many examples of individual interventions (McLean 2006): T-groups, coaching, mentoring, self-awareness, training and development, leadership development, multirater (360-degree) feedback, job description and design, conflict management, action learning, etc. Intervention with small groups usually consist of less than 15 members (French & Bell 1999). Commonly used interventions for small groups are about improving team building, communication and trust, group collaboration, and diversity awareness. The intermediate-sized interventions are for the people assigned in a group which is larger than a team but smaller than an organization or a department. Interventions between two or more groups may be considered as intermediate-sized interventions. Large-scale intervention is an approach for "organising [sic] sustainable changes with active involvement of stakeholders throughout the whole system" ("Large Scale Interventions English" n.d.). Industry and community-level OD interventions can respectively impact an entire industry or a particular geographic area. The rest of the book will elaborate on each of these interventions at greater length.

We learned from the previous section that action planning process includes involving key stakeholders, evaluating and prioritizing relevant data, agreeing on the changes to be made, developing a change strategy, and clarifying roles and responsibilities (Warrick 2016). The following section illustrates six recommendations, also offered by Warrick (2016, 189), that OD practitioners can practice for a successful intervention step.

- Keep the big picture in mind.
  - Focus on the change goals.
  - Take a system approach to change.
- Use a sound change management plan.
  - Use an action-planning change model.
  - Build a good feedback mechanism to detect unsolved issues, discouragement, or lack of trust.
- Adapt action plan and interventions to changing conditions.
  - Be knowledgeable of the changing conditions.
  - Use feedback mechanism.

- Keep people engaged.
  - Involve senior leaders in the change process.
  - Communicate and celebrate progress.
  - Recognize and value group members' efforts.
- Identify and manage resistance to change.
  - Communicate persuasive reasons for change.
  - Use assessment data to encourage change.
  - Involve key stakeholders.
- Follow through and learn from the implementation process.
  - Assess what has been accomplished.
  - Evaluate what is yet to be accomplished.
  - Acknowledge when there is a failure.
  - Document lessons learned.

Steps 6, 7, and 8: Evaluation, Adoption, and Separation

Evaluation tracks results against objectives or intentions (Rothwell & Jones 2017). The evaluation step may take place on an ongoing basis throughout the intervention (formative evaluation), at the end of the intervention (summative evaluation), or periodically over time after the completion of the intervention (longitudinal).

Formative evaluation is typically done by observation, discussion, questioning, process evaluation, self-evaluation, and peer evaluation. McLean (2006, 307–315) listed several approaches to summative evaluation: repeating the same assessment that was used during the assessment step, return-on-investment model, Kirkpatrick's four levels of training evaluation (reaction, learning, behavior, and result), balanced scorecard, control group experiment, and systems perspective evaluation. The following are a few benefits of evaluation:

- Evaluation shows the progress made toward intervention goals and objectives. Evaluation also provides the ability to determine what intervention approaches are most effective.
- It provides ongoing assessment of intervention design and implementation to identify areas of improvement.
- It demonstrates economic or human impact.

- It provides the foundation for interpreting an organization or intervention's worth to its stakeholders.
- It informs project sponsors and other stakeholders about intervention successes.
- It gives managers the performance information to make better operational decisions.
- It identifies needs not fulfilled and allows for the development of new interventions to serve those needs.

Adoption means that the changes are institutionalized (McLean 2006) and changes become part of the organization's normal operation (Cummings & Worley 2015). Successful adoption also means that team members are gradually taking over the roles of the practitioners. There is more than one way to do that. For instance, the team leader may take over the role and facilitate a discussion at the end of each meeting to draw attention to how well the team worked together during the meeting to achieve results and how the team might improve in the future. As another example, one team member might be assigned to play the practitioner's role by the team leader and then, at meeting's end, to facilitate a team conversation on how well the team performed.

The adoption step is usually carried out only if the evaluation step finds that the OD intervention was successful. McLean (2006) mentioned two factors influencing the adoption process: the degree of joint efforts of the practitioners and the clients in carrying out the OD intervention, and the degree of the client organization's involvement throughout the intervention process. Cummings and Worley (2015, 222) presented a framework that identified three factors affecting adoption and institutionalization of OD changes: organization characteristics, intervention characteristics, and institutionalization processes. Organization characteristics include congruence, stability of environment and technology, and unionization. Intervention characteristics are goal specificity, programmability, level of change target, internal support, and sponsorship. Examples of institutionalization processes are socialization, commitment, reward allocation, diffusion, and sensing and calibration. Cummings and Worley (2015) also offered five indicators of institutionalization of changes: knowledge, performance, preferences, normative consensus, and value consensus. Finally, adaptability, flexibility, and ongoing feedback are essential for the adoption step to be successful,

Quite often the ultimate test of adoption centers around separation. Will the changes persist once the OD practitioners leave? If the answer is "yes," then a change in group norms occurred; if the answer is "no," then the change was not effective. Separation is the final step of the action research model. In this step, the practitioners leave the OD change initiative.

There are many reasons an OD practitioner might leave a project: successful completion of the project, a better job offer, budget cuts, downsizing, a merger and acquisition, dissatisfaction with the project, or dissatisfaction with the practitioner's performance (McLean 2006). Whatever may be the reason, it is important that the separation step is carried out amicably, ethically, and in a professional manner by all the parties involved. One of the most important goals when separating from a project is not to "burn any bridges." In this light, depending on circumstances, the practitioner should try to address the following questions before the separation step completes:

- What is in your contract with your client? Are there legal ramifications for ending the contract?
- What will be the impact on your client? Can the client be successful and work independently after you leave?
- How would you transfer knowledge and skills to your client?
- What documentation, guidelines, or advice have you prepared for the client before leaving?
- What are the alternatives for your client?
- How might this affect your reputation?
- What can you learn from this situation?

Key Lessons Learned

This chapter elaborated on the steps of the OD change process using the ARM. The need for a change becomes apparent in the entry step. A need is identified and someone (usually the sponsor) searches for a person who is skilled enough to examine the problem or facilitate change (the OD practitioner). In the start-up step, the OD practitioner gets into the scene, works to describe issues surrounding the problem, and tries to secure commitment to an intervention or change effort. The practitioner conducts assessments, collects details about the problem, and feeds the results back to the client in the assessment and feedback step. The practitioner then works jointly with management and other stakeholders to formulate an action plan. During the intervention step, the practitioner helps to implement the action plan, and the change process is carried out. In the evaluation step, the practitioner assists the client to evaluate the intervention's progress and success. If adopted successfully, the changes are institutionalized and become part of the client's normal operation. Finally, the practitioner leaves the change process when the separation step concludes.

Discussion Questions

1. What specific questions should an OD practitioner ask in each step of the ARM?
2. Explain what an open and closed client system is. What interventions should OD practitioners use to test for their client's degree of openness to learning?
3. What roles should OD practitioners play to successfully complete the action planning step? Do you think OD practitioners require different roles in different steps of implementing a change project? Explain.
4. What are the biggest challenges of OD practitioners in carrying out an OD change project? How can they overcome these challenges?
5. What are the benefits and challenges of formative, summative, and longitudinal evaluation?
6. What other advice would you offer to the OD practitioner and the client to better adopt and institutionalize an OD change effort?
7. This chapter listed several questions OD practitioners should address before the separation step ends. What considerations should the clients address in the separation step?

References

Athuraliya, Amanda. 2020. "The Easy Guide to Developing an Effective Action Plan." *Creately* (blog). July 13, 2020. https://creately.com/blog/diagrams/how-to-write-an-action-plan/

Content Team. 2017. "Memorandum of Understanding." Legal Dictionary. Updated January 7, 2017. https://legaldictionary.net/memorandum-of-understanding/

Cummings, Thomas G., and Christopher G. Worley 2015. *Organization Development & Change*. Stamford, CT: Cengage Learning.

French, Wendell, and Cecil, Bell. 1999. *Organization Development: Behavioral Science Interventions for Organization Improvement*. Upper Saddle River, NJ: Prentice-Hall.

Health Knowledge. 2020. "Methods of Sampling from a Population." Health Knowledge Education, CPD, and Revalidation from PHAST. https://

www.healthknowledge.org.uk/public-health-textbook/research-methods/1a-epidemiology/methods-of-sampling-population

Inamdar, Anand. 2019. "Types of Feedback: Everything You Need to Know." Upraise Together. https://upraise.io/blog/types-of-feedback/

Kenton, Will. 2020. "Request for Proposal (RFP)." Investopedia. https://www.investopedia.com/terms/r/request-for-proposal.asp

"Large Scale Interventions English." n.d. Accessed August 11, 2020. http://www.largescaleinterventions.com/english%20version/index_English2.htm

Law and Justice Foundation. n.d. "Implementing a Project: The Role of a Steering Committee." Law and Justice Foundation of New South Wales. http://www.lawfoundation.net.au/ljf/site/templates/resources/$file/SteeringCommittee.pdf

McKay, Dawn Rosenberg. 2019. "How to Build and Maintain a Professional Network." https://www.thebalancecareers.com/building-growing-and-maintaining-a-professional-network-525834

McLean, Gary. 2006. *Organization Development: Principles, Processes, Performance*. Oakland, CA: Berrett-Koehler Publishers.

Rafter III, Rixon, Charles. 2013. "What's the Difference Between a "Contract" and a "Letter of Agreement"?" *Avvo* (blog). February 26, 2013. https://www.avvo.com/legal-answers/what-s-the-difference-between-a--contract--and-a---1133570.html.

Rothwell, William J. (Ed.). 2015. *Organization Development Fundamentals: Managing Strategic Change*. Alexandria, VA: ATD Press.

Rothwell, William J., and Maureen C. Jones (Eds.). 2017. *Evaluating Organization Development: How to Ensure and Sustain the Successful Transformation*. London: CRC Press.

Rothwell, William J., Jaqueline M. Stavros, and Ronald L. Sullivan (Eds.). 2015. *Practicing Organization Development: Leading Transformation and Change*. New York: Wiley.

Twin, A. 2020. "Non-Disclosure Agreement (NDA)." Accessed November 10, 2020. https://www.investopedia.com/terms/n/nda.asp

Warrick, D. D. 2016. "Launch: Assessment, Action Planning, and Implementation." In *Practicing Organization Development: Leading Transformation and Change*, edited by William Rothwell, Jacqueline Stavros, and Ronald Sullivan, 173–194. Hoboken, NJ: Wiley.

INDIVIDUAL AND SMALL-GROUP INTERVENTIONS

## Chapter 4

Individual Interventions: Instrument-Guided Development

Marie Carasco

Contents

Overview

This chapter discusses assessment instruments typically used for individual-focused organization development (OD) interventions and will cover the following areas:

- Individual differences: Personality, temperament, and traits
- Use of individual-focused assessment in OD interventions
- Common personality assessments and inventories
- Choosing assessment instruments
- Assessment reliability and validity
- Ethical considerations

The landscape of assessment instruments, personality tests, and inventories is extensive. "The $500-million-a-year industry has grown by about 10% annually in recent years" (Meinert 2015). In the field of OD, assessment instruments and inventories are one of many tools that can serve as a foundational source of information used to support a client in achieving an expressed goal or to increase awareness. Instrument-guided development in individual interventions allow the OD practitioner to tailor the client engagement based on an individual's personality, strengths, and development areas.

Individual Differences: Personality, Temperament, and Traits

OD interventions typically include some form of data collection. "Most of the data collection methods used in OD aim to elicit two things: the correct kind of data, and data that will increase the commitment of the people in the organization" (Cheung-Judge & Holbeche 2015, 82). For individual-based OD interventions assessment instruments are often the primary source of data. An *individual intervention* is an OD method for change that is person-focused.

Examples include counseling/coaching, training, individual goal setting, performance appraisal systems, statistical process control, job descriptions, values clarification, life and career planning, people-policy development, procedure manuals, and process improvement (Rothwell et al. 1995). Individual interventions can also include work redesign, Gestalt OSD, and behavior modeling (French & Bell 1999).

The foundation to individual interventions in OD is a basic understanding of individual differences grounded in the concepts of personality, temperament, and traits. The human personality has a number of facets. In fact, "[t]he Big Five personality traits are the most basic dimensions that shape the structure of human personality and underlie the regularities in people's thinking, feeling, and behavior" (Löckenhoff & Costa 2007, 115). The *Big Five Personality Traits* are the "dimensions that shape the structure of human personality and underlie the regularities in people's thinking, feeling, and behavior ... [on a] continuum between two extreme poles: *Neuroticism* (vs. Emotional Stability), *Extraversion* (or Surgency), *Openness to Experience* (also called Culture or Intellect), *Agreeableness* (vs. Antagonism), and *Conscientiousness*" (Löckenhoff & Costa 2007, 115). Moreover, "[p]ersonality is structured hierarchically; at the broadest or *domain* level are the Big Five, and below them, at a lower level of generality, are narrower traits or *facets*" (Löckenhoff & Costa 2007, 115), and "[a]ll people, regardless of gender, age, or culture, share the same basic personality traits, but people differ in their relative standing on each of the traits" (Löckenhoff & Costa 2007, 115).

Personality traits "describe individual differences in human beings' typical ways of perceiving, thinking, feeling, and behaving that are generally consistent over time and across situations" ("Trait Theory" 2008, 425). They are also "the primary unit of personality description, [and] are relatively enduring ways in which individuals differ" (Lanning 2008, 722). There is a distinction between personality traits and an individual's *temperament,* which "refers to a set of stable, biologically based individual differences in reactivity and regulation, often present during infancy but malleable to internal and external changes across the life span. It reflects the foundational components of personality in humans and other primates and social animals" (Swanson & Putnam, 2019, 872).

More often than not *personality assessments* are the diagnostic instruments of choice in individual interventions. "Personality assessment, in its broadest sense, includes any technique that is used to describe or make inferences about the characteristic traits, attitudes, beliefs, values, needs, motives, emotional states, coping styles, or aspirations of an individual" (Lanning 2008, 721).

These assessments also employ the use of *personality inventories,* which "are questionnaires that provide scores on a number of traits or characteristics. These measures typically take 30 to 75 minutes to complete and are intended for administration to adults" (Lanning 2008, 724).

Use of Individual-Focused Assessment in OD Interventions

The field of OD has foundational approaches that can be applied across interventions. "All OD programs have three basic components: diagnosis, action and program management. The diagnostic component represents a continuous collection of data about the total system, its subunits, its processes, and its culture" (French & Bell 1999, 105). In fact, diagnosis begins with a focus on what has been expressed as an area of concern. OD practitioners need to determine an individual's/system's strengths, problem areas, unrealized opportunities as well as any discrepancy between a desired future state with the current state (French & Bell 1999). When applied to individual-focused interventions such as coaching, counseling, life and career planning, education and trainings for knowledge and skill development, work redesign, behavior modeling, or Gestalt OSD, assessment instruments are often the first and primary diagnostic tool used to provide insight into a client's personality and preferences, as well as an individual's or organization's strengths and development areas. In fact, "[a]ssessment data are vital to human resource management and thus have to be valid, reliable, and objective in the first place to sustain all personnel decisions that are taken" (Hornke 2003, 89). We will discuss assessment validity and reliability later in this chapter. It's worth mentioning that "[o]ne approach to systematize assessment in applied fields in general, and of work and organization in particular, is to take an Individual, Group, or Organizational perspective" (Hornke 2003, 88). This chapter will focus on the individual perspective, namely personality-based tests (instruments) used to provide an understanding of an individual's strengths and development areas.

Instrument-guided development in individual-based OD interventions are used by a number of stakeholders that have particular terminology when referring to the tools used. "Human resources personnel, coaches, psychologists, and instructional designers call corporate personality tests 'assessments.'" Moreover, "[t]ests of honesty or integrity usually are referred to as 'personality surveys.' These types of assessments also can be labeled questionnaires, indicators, classifiers, sorters, or profilers" (Hart & Sheldon 2007, 16). These assessment instruments are unified in purpose: "to provide self-insight, explore values, and reveal habits of how people take in information, process data, and make decisions" (16). It's also important to mention that many of these assessments are what are referred to as self-report instruments or self-report tests. "[S]elf-report tests … rely on information that you are willing to provide … [and] because they are self-report tests, you are unlikely to learn anything about yourself that you didn't already know" (Janda 2001, 5). This is significant and should be kept in mind when sharing results with assessment takers who might disagree with results.

Hart and Sheldon (2007) inform us that personality tests are given for three reasons. First, to reduce financial risks when selecting new hires. Second, as a way of identifying areas for improving team-building and decision-making skills of time-pressed executives. Third, to leverage it for screening out individuals that may be prone to violence in the workplace. Hornke (2003) highlights "assessment of an individual does not stop at job entry. Any job confronts incumbents with a variety of minor and major challenges. One of these is to learn to function well at a certain position. Thus learning gains or developing several competencies are of interest to assessors" (89). In fact, employers rely on assessments "to reduce risk, wasted time, and fiscal insecurities related to human resources. Abilities tests, often given along with personality profiles, measure abstract reasoning measures and cognitive intelligence. Abilities tests measure job skills and/or intellectual reasoning abilities or "critical thinking" (Hart & Sheldon 2007, 83).

While many organizations find value in the use of assessments "[m]ost organizational psychologists agree that the majority of corporations are not consistent in the types of tests they administer" (Hart & Sheldon 2007, 97). As noted earlier, organizations use assessment tests for a number of reasons. When it comes to the administration of those tests, "[m]ost personality tests in corporate settings are used for team-building, and the tests may be given by coaches, instructional designers, or members of the HR department" (Hart & Sheldon 2007, 17). It's worth noting that in the field of OD "[s]elf-diagnostic surveys are widely used in human relations training and in laboratory training settings … For successful intervention, the consultant must have expertise in the use of a particular instrument" (French & Bell 1999, 249). Therefore, having an unqualified person interpret assessment results can be highly detrimental to the assessment taker. It is recommended that each group member or group leader have his or her individual assessment results reviewed on a one-on-one basis with someone qualified to administer and review the assessment outcomes. Moreover, it's also important to inform the assessment taker how his or her results will be used or shared based on organization expectations. Another important area to highlight by way of caution is what French and Bell refer to as a "dysfunctional aspects of using instrumented training techniques in OD [which] happens when an OD consultant lets his or her 'kit bag' of diagnostic surveys drive the selection of interventions" (French & Bell 1999, 249). Given this tendency to lean on the familiar, it is imperative the practitioner and organization sponsors exercise flexibility in selecting assessments that are appropriate for the situation/data points of interest rather than using what is comfortable or readily available.

The use of assessment instruments in grounded in the hope for different outcomes. In fact, results of the assessment can lead to "improvement of the interaction with the individual and the work place by considering human factors for improved functioning, by motivating the individual, by designing up to date remuneration schedules, by considering aptitude treatment interactions in designing effective training programs" (Hornke 2003, 89). At the end of the day, "psychological assessment is a work-life-long companion activity which serves the individual and the organization in order to fruitfully monitor the interaction between both of them" (Hornke 2003, 89).

Many OD professionals have retained certifications in any number of assessment instruments and present the use of those assessments as a potential individual-intervention. You'll find more on ethical considerations with assessment instruments later in this chapter, which highlight the importance of certification/qualification in the use of an instrument. It is worth mentioning that practitioners presenting the use of assessment instruments should also determine how and with whom results will be shared.

Instruments Used for Individual-Based OD Interventions: Common Personality Assessments and Inventories

Assessment instruments used in corporate settings typically measure the following: "honesty (integrity), anger management, entrepreneurial aptitude, stress tolerance, leadership, cognitive intelligence abilities (IQ), emotional maturity, personality preference and profiling, extroversion, aptitudes, attitudes (race relations or beliefs), blind spots … decision-making ability, neuroticism, performance, speed recognizing individual differences, openness, reliability, conscientiousness, and agreeableness" (Hart & Sheldon 2007, 25). When it comes to roles based on organization hierarchy "[e]xecutives are given more personality assessments than entry-level applicants, but entry-level applicants take more tests of integrity/honesty and job-skill performance ... [In fact,] measuring decision-making ability and personality profile stand out in personality assessments when testing potential leaders, managers, and executives. Corporate testing for a particular trait is widely used to improve pre-hiring decisions" (Hart & Sheldon 2007, 25).

If one were to perform an online search for assessment instruments, the results would be quite extensive. When it comes to assessment instruments that are commonly used for individual-based interventions, it depends on the practitioner. See Table 4.1 for a list of five assessments that cover personality preferences, talent identification, career exploration, interpersonal needs, and conflict. It may be helpful for OD practitioners to explore the *Mental Measurements Yearbooks* published by Buros Center for Testing. These books help practitioners to choose among a vast array of standardized tests as well as the latest assessments and instruments in a number of social science fields.

Choosing Assessment Instruments

To choose an assessment instrument, ask and answer questions based on the categories noted in Figure 4.1.

History and Reliability

- What is the history of this instrument? What was it designed to do?
- What research (if any) has been done to see if the assessment is reliable and valid? (more on this in the next section)

Training, Resources and Cost

- Is there training required? If so, how long is the training, and much would it cost?
- Are resources available for you and your clients?
- Are resources available in print and online?
- How much will it cost you to administer the assessment?

Table 4.1 Common Assessment Instruments

Instrument Name	Description of Instrument	Empirically Validated?
Myers-Briggs Type Indicator (MBTI ®)	■ A preference-based self-report instrument influenced by Carl Jung's theory of psychological type. There are 16 personality types based on combinations of preferences regarding an inner or outer world, how information is taken in, how decisions are made, and openness to new information. ■ *Uses include:* personality preferences, career choice, learning, and personal growth	No
16PF Questionnaire (16 Personality Factors)	■ An empirically validated personality instrument designed for use in business to identify potential, suitability, and development areas. ■ *Uses include:* talent identification, defining competencies, leader development, hiring decisions, and culture fit	Yes
Strong Interest Inventory® (Strong)	■ A career and leisure interests-focused assessment to identify a work personality in 30 areas of interest, and ranks 5 or 10 occupations from a list of 260 roles. The assessment measures interests in four categories: General Occupational Themes, Basic Interest Scales, Personal Style Scales, and Occupational Scales ■ *Uses include:* selecting a college major, career choice, career development, employee engagement, re-entering the workforce.	Yes
The Fundamental Interpersonal Relations Orientation-Behavior (FIRO-B®)	■ A self-report instrument that helps with relationships in the workplace, specifically identifying the behaviors and needs that shape interactions.	Yes
	■ *Uses include:* measuring interpersonal behavior needs, personal development, communication workshops, career development, team building, management development, building trust, conflict management.	

(Continued)

TABLE 4.1   Common Assessment Instruments (Con't.)

Instrument Name	Description of Instrument	Empirically Validated?
Thomas-Kilmann Conflict Mode Instrument (TKI®)	■ A preference-based self-report instrument that measures preferred responses to conflict and associated outcomes. There are five conflict styles along two dimensions: assertiveness and cooperativeness.	Yes
	■ *Uses **include:*** conflict management, communication workshops, personal development.	

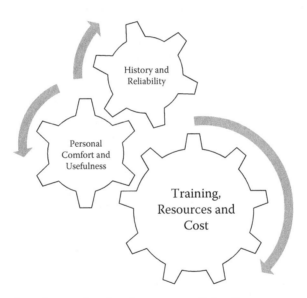

Figure 4.1   Evaluation Categories for Assessment Selection.

Personal Comfort and Usefulness

- Do you like the instrument?
- Are you comfortable with the assessment, and can you easily explain it to clients?
- How will using this instrument support your clients' needs?
- Will this assessment instrument help to support the work you do?

Assessment Reliability and Validity

The issue of reliability and validity can have more or less significance to an OD practitioner depending on his or her training and client interests. "To yield useable data, surveys, assessment tools, and other data collection instruments need to be both reliable and valid. Reliability is a measure of the degree to which such instruments consistently measure a characteristic or attribute" (Wienclaw 2014, 32). "Reliability can be estimated through the use of parallel forms of the instrument, repeated administration of the same form of the instrument, subdivision of the instrument into two presumably parallel groups of items, and analysis of the covariance among the individual items" (35). Validity, on the other hand, is "the degree to which a survey or other data collection instrument measures what it purports to measure. A data collection instrument cannot be valid unless it is reliable" (Wienclaw 2014, 35). In other words, the best assessment instruments not only measure what they say they measure, but do so every time the instrument is used.

The question then becomes, do OD practitioners need to limit their selection and only use instruments that are both reliable and valid? The answer will be rooted in your client's expectations, your trust in the results of an instrument, and your level of comfort using an instrument. If you choose to use an instrument that has no documented empirical research to support its validity or reliability, it's also important to set the expectations with the client by explaining what the results will mean and why you use the instrument.

Ethical Considerations

Ethical issues are pervasive in every discipline. For OD practitioners choosing to use assessments to support their work, it is important that the practitioner only administer assessments that he or she is qualified to do so. Qualifications can be attained by earning a specific degree, attending a training workshop from the assessment provider, or simply following the directions outlined. Tremendous harm can be done to a client and the field of OD when a practitioner provides erroneous assessment results and/or conveys the results in ways that are insensitive. To help mitigate these risks, it is highly advisable that the OD practitioner not only obtain training for each instrument that he or she plans to use, but also "take" the instrument and have a debrief conversation with a qualified assessment provider. Doing so will bridge the theoretical understanding of the assessment instrument with the practical use of it.

Business Case

As the newest member of the c-suite, Robert, a senior executive in the media and advertising industry, struggled to bring his voice into the room and was reluctant to challenge his colleagues. After only 1-year in his role, the CEO informed him of his need to get it together before the end of the year and asked the VP of Human Resources to intervene.

The following describes some of the steps taken as part of Robert's individual intervention:

Step 1: Entry

Robert's issues with communication were observed by the CEO of the organization during executive meetings. Those observations were discussed with the VP of Human Resources, who was tasked with identifying ways to help Robert improve his communication skills and credibility with his peers. The VP of Human Resources determined that executive coaching was the best approach since it would provide Robert with external objective support, the opportunity to be open in ways that he might not otherwise be able to within the organization, and the accountability needed to improve.

Step 2: Start-Up

After identifying a short-list of International Coach Federation (ICF) credentialed executive coaches, the VP of Human Resources scheduled meetings with Robert and each coach so that he could select the individual he was most comfortable with. In his initial meeting with his chosen coach, they discussed his understanding of why coaching was requested, his expectations, initial goals, a potential timeline, and the coach's approach. There were also separate meetings with the VP of Human Resources to confirm any additional expectations and to define parameters around communication and confidentiality, which were outlined in the consulting contract.

Step 3: Assessment and Feedback

The executive coach gained insight about Robert's challenges from four key stakeholder groups: Robert, the VP of Human Resources, the CEO, and his peers. Additional information was gathered through emails, calls, assessment reports, and observation. A series of several meetings were scheduled between the stakeholders and the coach, as well as assessment debrief meetings with Robert to gain a robust picture of the current state Robert's impact and influence in the organization.

Step 4: Action Planning

Robert identified short- and long-term goals for his coaching sessions based on feedback provided from stakeholders and his assessments. Those goals were integrated into his development plan. The timelines were negotiated between Robert and the CEO based on other objectives and performance expectations outlined for Robert that year. Final timeline agreements were shared with the executive coach.

Step 5: Intervention

While there were several assessment interventions used to support Robert's coaching engagement, a 360-degree feedback/multi-rater assessment will be highlighted in this case. Using a 360-degree feedback process can create a bit of anxiety for the leader because they will be evaluated by people they work with, including their manager, peers, employees, and sometimes clients. However, when leveraged correctly, a 360-degree feedback process will help to identify an individual's blind spots, as well as specific and actionable areas to improve effectiveness.

This instrument-guided assessment will provide Robert anonymous feedback from multiple stakeholders across and, if appropriate, external to his organization. The description shared in Table 4.2 is *by no means prescriptive*, but only lists the general steps taken in administering a 360-degree/multi-rater assessment. OD practitioners are admonished to obtain the appropriate credentials within the parameters of their places of residence and practice to provide accurate assessment and interpretations of a 360-degree/multi-rater inventory to clients and maintain a positive reputation for themselves and the field at large. Bear in mind that the OD practitioner should be prepared to

Table 4.2   Typical Steps Taken When Using a 360-Degree/Multi-Rater Assessment Tool

Step	Action	Responsibility
1	**Determine the stakeholder scope:** ■ Identify who in the organization and external to the organization will complete the 360-degree/multi-rater assessment. ■ Ensure there is a broad representation across the hierarchy of the company and the relationships (e.g., peers, manager, clients/customers, external contacts).	Sponsor and OD Practitioner
2	**Outline communication expectations and answer:** ■ How will the 360-degree/multi-rater assessment be shared with stakeholders? ■ When will the assessment period begin and close? ■ Who will receive the final reports? ■ What are the expectations around confidentiality? ■ Who will draft the communication email(s) (if needed) to the stakeholders participating in the 360-degree/multi-rater assessment?	Sponsor and OD Practitioner
3	**Select a 360-degree/multi-rater assessment:** ■ Identify an assessment that meets the scope of what is requested by the sponsor, and obtain qualifications to administer it, or ■ Make the case for the use of a 360-degree/multi-rater assessment that the OD practitioner is currently qualified to administer.	OD Practitioner
4	**Discuss the assessment process with the client:** ■ Schedule a meeting with the client to review the assessment process, general expectations, and timelines, and provide an opportunity to address any client concerns. ■ Share sample questions or a sample report of what the client can expect when the process has ended, including who else would be receiving the report.	OD Practitioner
5	**Draft the communication messages:** ■ *A Message that It's Coming:* Write an email informing the stakeholders about the 360-degree/multi-rater assessment that will be coming in (x-days/weeks) and whom they can contact with questions.	Sponsor and OD Practitioner

(Continued)

TABLE 4.2   Typical Steps Taken When Using a 360-Degree/Multi-Rater Assessment Tool (Con't.)

Step	Action	Responsibility
	■ *A Message that It's Here:* Write an email that will be sent with the distribution of the 360-degree/multi-rater assessment, including the timeline for completion. ■ *A Reminder:* Write an email that will be sent as a reminder when there are stakeholders who haven't completed the assessment (note: sometimes the 360-degree/multi-rater assessment will do this automatically after a certain time frame). ■ *A Thank You.* Draft an email to thank the participants once the process has ended.	
6	**Coordinate the distribution of the assessment:** ■ Typically, the Human Resources department might either provide the email addresses of the stakeholders participating in the 360-degree/multi-rater assessment that the OD practitioner can enter on the administrator side of the assessment site, or ■ In other instances, the Human Resources department will receive a link from the OD practitioner that was generated by the 360-degree/multi-rater assessment provider that can be distributed on behalf of the OD Practitioner.	Sponsor and OD Practitioner
7	**Evaluate the results:** ■ Based on your training and familiarity with the selected 360-degree/multi-rater assessment, read all the responses generated in the report. ■ Identify positive trends and development areas.	OD Practitioner
8	**Prepare to share the results:** ■ Generate the report for distribution as agreed. ■ Consider how you will share the results such as what questions you will ask the client (e.g., What surprised you? What do you agree with? What stood out the most? Where do you see the most alignment?). ■ Consider how you will share the results with non-client stakeholders (if applicable), and be prepared to talk about what next steps will be with you and the client, and to receive feedback on actions desired by the sponsor.	OD Practitioner

(Continued)

TABLE 4.2 Typical Steps Taken When Using a 360-Degree/Multi-Rater Assessment Tool (Con't.)

Step	Action	Responsibility
9	**Develop an action plan:**	Client and OD Practitioner
	▪ Schedule a meeting with the client to focus on actions and next steps for the short and long term. ▪ Based on communication expectations, share/reiterate sponsor-determined actions. ▪ Identify timelines and deadlines for each action. ▪ Agree on timelines and methods for check-ins/status checks.	
10	**Check in:**	Sponsor, Client, and OD Practitioner
	▪ Based on an agreed timeline, check in with the client and/or sponsor on progress towards the action plan. ▪ Agree to repeat the assessment in 12 to 18 months.	

share best practices in each step outlined in Table 4.2 to support the sponsor/decision-maker in making the most informed decisions.

Step 6: Evaluation

To ensure that the decision-makers are able to adequately assess the effectiveness of the 360-degree/multi-rater assessment as an intervention, it was important to provide detailed information on the process involved, what the assessment would provide, and the limitations in scope. Sharing sample reports was also helpful for the sponsor to anticipate the outcomes, which also served as a benchmark for evaluation. Finally, the action steps outlined from the 360-degree/multi-rater assessment and the integration of those actions into a development plan and current performance management expectations helped the decision-makers determine the usefulness of the process.

Step 7: Adoption

Since this was an individual intervention that involved a limited number of stakeholders across the organization who provided feedback to Robert, the responsibility for the change rested with Robert. Through a series of meetings with the executive coach, the CEO, and the VP of Human Resources, he outlined actions to be taken in the short and long term such as: experimenting with new behaviors, building relationships with his peers outside of the periodic meetings that included the CEO, as well as taking the initiative to ask for feedback on his new behaviors. In between his experiments, he would continue coaching sessions to work through challenges that would arise and adapt actions accordingly.

Step 8: Separation

After a six-month engagement, Robert's confidence increased as he began to receive positive feedback from the CEO and peers. He built relationships across the organization that made it easier to bring his voice into every space he entered, and he gained the courage to appropriately and assertively challenge his peers in the presence of the CEO. The VP of Human Resources and the coach had met periodically during the course of the coaching engagement to discuss Robert's progress, and when the sponsor felt that Robert had made sufficient improvement based on the feedback from the CEO, the coaching engagement ended based on the agreed contract. In a final session with Robert, the coach inquired about his plans to sustain his growth, at which time Robert simply reiterated his commitment to continue to do what is working for the next 6-months. The coach scheduled a final meeting with the CEO and VP of Human Resources to discuss Robert's progress and to inquire of their commitments (time, resources, training, additional coaching etc.) to support his development over the next 18 months. Based on the agreed communication approach, those commitments were shared with Robert, and the executive coach ended the consulting engagement.

Key Lessons Learned

- OD interventions typically include some form of data collection.
- The foundation to individual interventions in OD is a basic understanding individual differences grounded in the concepts of personality, temperament, and traits.

- Assessment instruments used in corporate settings typically measure the following: "honesty (integrity), anger management, entrepreneurial aptitude, stress tolerance, leadership, cognitive intelligence abilities (IQ), emotional maturity, personality preference and profiling, extroversion, aptitudes, attitudes (race relations or beliefs), blind spots … decision-making ability, neuroticism, performance, speed recognizing individual differences, openness, reliability, conscientiousness, and agreeableness" (Hart & Sheldon 2007, 25).
- While many organizations find value in the use of assessments "[m]ost organizational psychologists agree that the majority of corporations are not consistent in the types of tests they administer" (Hart & Sheldon 2007, 97).
- Having an unqualified person interpret assessment results can be highly detrimental to the assessment taker.

Discussion Questions

1. How has your personality and temperament changed over time? What has remained the same? To what do you attribute these changes? To what do you attribute the stability?
2. What is your experience with assessment instruments? Do you believe the instruments you took were valid and reliable? What gives you that impression?
3. Discuss advantages and disadvantages of using an assessment instrument that is both reliable and valid in lieu of one that is not?
4. How important might it be for an OD practitioner to "take" the assessment that he or she will administer to others? Explain.
5. Given the impact of COVID-19 on social interactions, what changes if any might OD practitioners anticipate seeing in the results of interpersonal assessments? (Table 4.3).

Tools

Table 4.3 Checklist for Using a 360-Degree/Multi-Rater Assessment Tool

Directions: Read this checklist to increase your awareness of areas to give attention when engaging in the use of a 360-degree/Multi-Rater Assessment Tool.

Have you...			Yes ☒	No ☒
1	Determined the Stakeholder Scope	■ Identified who in the organization and external to the organization will complete the 360-degree/multi-rater assessment? ■ Ensured there is a broad representation across the hierarchy of the company and the relationships (e.g., peers, manager, clients/customers, external contacts)?	☐	☐
2	Outlined Communication Expectations	■ Determined how the 360-degree/multi-rater assessment will be shared with stakeholders? ■ Determined when will the assessment period begin and close? ■ Agreed on who will receive the final reports? ■ Outlined what the expectations are around confidentiality? ■ Agreed who will draft the communication email(s) (if needed) to the stakeholders participating in the 360-degree/ multi-rater assessment?	☐	☐
3	Selected a 360-degree/Multi-rater Assessment	■ Identified an assessment that meets the scope of what is requested by the sponsor and obtained the qualifications to administer it? ■ Made the case for the use of a 360-degree/multi-rater assessment that the OD practitioner is currently qualified to administer?	☐	☐

(Continued)

TABLE 4.3   Checklist for Using a 360-Degree/Multi-Rater Assessment Tool (Con't.)

4	Discussed the Assessment Process with the Client	▪ Scheduled a meeting with the client to review the assessment process, general expectations, and timelines, and provide an opportunity to address any client concerns? ▪ Shared sample questions or a sample report of what the client can expect when the process has ended, including who else would be receiving the report?	☐	☐
5	Drafted the Communication Messages	▪ *Created A Message that It's Coming:* Wrote an email informing the stakeholders about the 360-degree/multi-rater assessment that will be coming in (x-days/weeks) and whom they can contact with questions? ▪ *Created A Message that It's Here:* Wrote an email that will be sent with the distribution of the 360-degree/multi-rater assessment, including the timeline for completion? ▪ *Created A Reminder:* Wrote an email that will be sent as a reminder when there are stakeholders that haven't completed the assessment (note: sometimes the 360-degree/multi-rater assessment will do this automatically after a certain time frame)? ▪ *Created A Thank You.* Drafted an email to thank the participants once the process has ended?	☐	☐
6	Coordinated the Distribution of the Assessment	▪ Checked in with the Human Resources department to confirm if they will provide the email addresses of the stakeholders participating in the 360-degree/multi-rater assessment that the OD practitioner can enter on the administrator side of the assessment site? ▪ Checked in with the Human Resources department to	☐	☐

(Continued)

TABLE 4.3 Checklist for Using a 360-Degree/Multi-Rater Assessment Tool (Con't.)

		confirm if they will receive a link from the OD practitioner that was generated by the 360-degree/multi-rater assessment provider that can distributed on behalf of the OD practitioner?		
7	Evaluated the Results	■ Read all the responses generated in the report? ■ Identified positive trends and development areas?	☐	☐
8	Prepared to Share the Results	■ Generated the report for distribution as agreed? ■ Considered how you will share the results such as what questions you will ask the client (e.g., What surprised you? What do you agree with? What stood out the most? Where do you see the most alignment?)? ■ Considered how you will share the results with non-client stakeholders (if applicable) and prepared yourself to talk about what next steps will be with you and the client, and to receive feedback on actions desired by the sponsor?	☐	☐
9	Developed an Action Plan	■ Scheduled a meeting with the client to focus on actions and next steps for the short and long term? ■ Shared/reiterated sponsor-determined actions? ■ Identified timelines and deadlines for each action? ■ Agreed on timelines and methods for check-ins/status checks?	☐	☐
10	Checked In	■ Based on an agreed timeline, checked in with the client and/or sponsor on progress towards the action plan? ■ Agreed to repeat the assessment in 12 to 18 months?	☐	☐

References

Cheung-Judge, Mee-Yan, and Linda, Holbeche. 2015. *Organization Development: A Practitioner's Guide for OD and HR*. London: Kogan Page. Kindle Edition.

French, Wendell, and Cecil, Bell. 1999. *Organization Development: Behavioral Science Interventions for Organization Improvement*. Upper Saddle River, NJ: Prentice-Hall.

Hart, Anne, and George, Sheldon. 2007. *Employment Personality Tests Decoded: Includes Sample and Practice Tests for Self-Assessment*. Franklin Lakes, NJ: Career Press.

Hornke, Lutz F. 2003. "Applied Fields: Work and Industry." In *Encyclopedia of Psychological Assessment*, edited by Rocío Fernández Ballesteros, 88–93. London: SAGE Publications Ltd.

Janda, Louis H. 2001. *The Psychologist's Book of Personality Tests: 24 Revealing Tests to Identify and Overcome Your Personal Barriers to a Better Life*. New York: Wiley.

Lanning, Kevin. 2008. "Personality Assessment." In *Personal and Emotional Counseling*, edited by Frederick T. L. Leong, Elizabeth M. Altmaier, and Brian D. Johnson, 721–729. Vol. 2 of *Encyclopedia of Counseling*. Thousand Oaks, CA: SAGE Publications. Gale eBooks.

Löckenhoff, Corinna E., and Paul T. Costa, Jr. 2007. "Big Five Personality Traits." In *Encyclopedia of Social Psychology*, edited by Roy F. Baumeister and Kathleen D. Vohs, 115–117. Vol. 1. Thousand Oaks, CA: SAGE Publications. Gale eBooks.

Meinert, Dori. 2015. "What Do Personality Tests Really Reveal?" *HR Magazine*, June 25. https://www.shrm.org/hr-today/news/hr-magazine/pages/0615-personality-tests.aspx

Rothwell, William. J., Roland, Sullivan, and Gary N. McLean. 1995. *Practicing Organization Development*. San Francisco, CA: Jossey-Bass/Pfeiffer Publishers.

Swanson, Jodi, and Samuel P. Putnam. 2019. "Temperament." In *Macmillan Encyclopedia of Families, Marriages, and Intimate Relationships*, edited by James J. Ponzetti, Jr., 872–879. Vol. 2. Farmington Hills, MI: Macmillan Reference USA. Gale eBooks.

Aaron, L. Pincus and Mark R. Lukowitsky, 2008. "Trait Theory." In *International Encyclopedia of the Social Sciences* (2nd ed.), edited by William A. Darity, Jr., 425–426. Vol. 8. Detroit, MI: Macmillan Reference USA. Gale eBooks.

Wienclaw, Ruth A. 2014. "Reliability." In *Research & Evaluation Methods*, 32–36. Sociology Reference Guide. Ipswich, MA: Salem Press. Gale eBooks.

Chapter 5

Individual Intervention: Executive and Management Coaching

Behnam Bakhshandeh

Contents

Overview

This chapter offers readers the elements of individual change intervention in organizations in the form of executive and management coaching as the first level of intervention. In this chapter, the readers will become familiar with definitions, distinctions, and processes of individual intervention, with some beneficial information about how executives or managers relate to employees and their productivity. Furthermore, this chapter covers some elements of self-realization and understanding of one's behavior and thought processes while working as an individual managing an organization. Chapter 5 covers the following areas:

- Definitions related to individual change intervention
- Executives and managers understanding their behaviors and mindsets
- Strategies or tactics needed for successful coaching intervention
- Emotional intelligence at work
- Appreciative inquiry and appreciative coaching as coaching instruments
- Step-by-step approach to conduct a coaching intervention as a form of individual OD intervention

It is fascinating when we notice our capacity to shift our thinking. Thinking is one of the key elements that distinguishes us from other species; it is our ability to envision and to redirect our minds to our interests. Human history is full of brilliant minds who focused their thinking in a specific area and produced unprecedented results and incredible inventions, of which all of us are taking advantage (Bakhshandeh 2009). Is it possible that these people are different from us? Do they have more brain cells, different genes, or possess something significantly unique? We all know, there is nothing that genetically, biologically, or physically differentiates them from others, including us, not even in their abilities, or in their life or professional circumstances! In most scenarios, they did not even have access to the internet, cell phones, or most up-to-date computers; in most cases, they did not have a college counselor or a personal trainer. I bet they did not have a café latte or even in many cases parents who were supportive of their education or development (2009). What they did possess was the ability to think outside the box and be open to collaborating with others in their fields, welcoming novel ideas. Developing a productive and effective individual or team is not any different from building a new invention; it takes people who are creating new paradigms and committed to learning from others' mistakes.

It is not a mystery that individuals build organizations. These individuals form the executive team, management structure, departments, groups, and teams within their organizations. There is no doubt among professionals that without motivated, self-aware, and competent individuals as executives or managers who would effectively manage the workforce, no organization would survive the ineffective and unmotivated employees or the massive turnover that might be the end of such an organization. To accomplish such a worthy task, businesses and organizations go through many change interventions. Some are small as part of the day-to-day business processes, and some are larger, what we know as organization development (OD) or a form of change management. This chapter will shed light on the foundation and the very first level of OD and change intervention, the individual intervention or, in our case, the executives' or managers' change intervention, which given organizations and teams are made of individuals, has direct influence on an organization's change, and ultimately the organization's effectiveness.

Definitions and Descriptions

To assure understanding and provide clarity of the main terminologies in this chapter, we are underlining several definitions, descriptions, and distinctions of this undertaking:

Individual Intervention: Individual-level intervention is one of the most used interventions by organizations, given the fact that individuals have the most influence and impact on making or breaking organizations. Some of the individual interventions are on the area of recruiting new employees, training and development of employees, replacement/displacement of employees, and providing coaching or mentoring for employees (Burke 2018; Rothwell 2015).

Executive Coaching: Executive coaching finds its place in leadership development programs within diverse industries around the world (Gan & Chong 2015). The executive coaching program is premeditated to transform executives' personal and professional views beyond current success and give them the tools to re-invent themselves continuously. They will be trained to invent a future that will pull them forth and inspire them and others around them (Bakhshandeh 2002).

Managerial Coaching: Among organizations, a managerial coaching approach to professional coaching is considered to be a forward motion leadership creativity that would enhance the manager, supervisor, and workforce relationship and empower strong mutual manager/supervisor and workforce exchanges (Hsieh & Huang 2018).

First Level of OD Intervention: The Individual Change

According to Rothwell et al. (2016), there are eight levels of organization change, which also define specialized professional OD practitioners involved with the change intervention. The first level is the individual-based change effort: a need to change among individuals.

Given that the nature of this chapter is about the process of individual intervention, we are only emphasizing the first level, the individual-based change efforts. Rothwell et al. (2016) gives us a clear definition of OD. "OD is usually known to mean bottom-up change effort focused on improving the interpersonal relationships of employees. OD usually involves internal or external consultants to facilitate the change process. These consultants apply the practical aspects of psychology, sociology, anthropology, and political science to organizational challenges" (9). We can see the importance of individuals throughout this definition of OD. Individuals make up teams and organizations; that is why *individual intervention* is the first level of a change effort. Individual development will give rise to OD through executives and managers using coaching as a means to self-development, which ultimately has a positive influence on their management and directing their staff, teams, and organization to a successful outcome.

As part of behavioral coaching, professional and trained coaches use the model of Person-Centered Psychology which is based on what is known as "holding up a mirror" (Rothwell 2016) for the individuals to get to know themselves on a much deeper level and get present to the history of their behavior and attitude development through the years. This is a very effective approach to an individual's self-awareness and self-realization because by conducting an inquiry with the coach's support, they will see through themselves. This way, they always remember their own process of self-realization because it had not been imposed on them by someone else.

What Is Coaching, and the Place of Coaching in the Business Environment

There are diverse definitions of coaching by different professional associations. For example, the Association for Talent Development (ATD) defines coaching as "Applying a systematic process to improve others' ability to set goals, take action, and maximize strengths" (ATD-Association for Talent Development 2014, 4), while the International Coach Federation (ICF) defines coaching as "Using an interactive process to help individuals develop rapidly and produce results, improving others' ability to set goals, take action, make better decisions, and make full use of their natural strengths" (Arneson et al. 2013, 45).

From this author's point of view and based on his 27 years in the field of personal and professional development, he would define coaching as "A highly effective tool for individuals and organizations" ("Primeco Education" n.d.). To go further, he can describe and explain coaching as an intimate, non-linear, but systematic approach and inquiry into our own authenticity and relationship to reality. "It is for healthy, ambitious, brave and open-minded people who strive for excellence" (Bakhshandeh 2009, 35).

Coaching is known, accepted, and widely used in many industries as a form of executive and manager coaching for OD individual interventions. Coaching is attracting attention in academic, scholarly, and professional practice-oriented articles, especially in HRD (Human Resources Development) management, change management, psychology, and training & development industries (Ellinger & Kim 2014). Coaching is also widely used by business consultants, performance consultants, and OD practitioners, assisting organizations in realizing their visions, formulating and achieving their goals, and removing obstacles (Vidal-Salazar et al. 2012).

Organizational Diagnosis Models and Relevancy to the Individual Intervention

In any organizational diagnosis, either conducted by internal resources (executives and managers) or by external OD practitioners, the OD practitioner uses conceptual diagnoses models and employed diagnosis methods to evaluate the organization's current situation and will determine approaches to resolve the pressing issues, enhance employees' performance and productivity, and help an organization to set new processors to empower HRD in the organization (Harrison 2005; Rothwell 2015). During this undertaking, they are always dealing with individuals, which makes individual intervention vital to the success of group/teams and organization-level interventions.

On the *Organization Level*, the OD practitioner is examining human capital; the organization's structure and hierarchy; HR and HRD practices; use of information technology; the organization's policies and practices; and its environment, norms, and culture.

On the *Group & Team Level*, the OD practitioner is examining the team format; team structure and hierarchy; team composition; relationship among the team and groups; team processes; their behavior, norms, and culture; the use of information and technology by teams; and HR & HRD policies concerning teams and groups.

On the *Individual Level*, the OD practitioner is examining individuals' behaviors, attitudes, values, principles, beliefs and characteristics, interests, self-awareness, communication style, and motivations.

The following diagnosis models are some of the popular models used by OD professionals to recognize an organization's issues, including issues that might be caused by individuals. In this section, we briefly explain these models for you to see the vital role of individuals (executives, managers, supervisors, technicians, and workers) in all aspects of presented models.

Individual and Group Behavior Model

This model was originally designed by Michael I. Harrison in 1985 and through the years has been modified and used on many editions of Harrison's work. According to Harrison (2005), this model's elements include the following:

- **Inputs**: Human capital, material, financial, intangible.
- **Outputs**: Goods, services, products, employees' well-being and satisfaction.
- **Organizational behaviors and processes**: Practices the organization has adopted to create outputs.
- **Technology**: Equipment, tools, and systems that would transform inputs into outputs.
- **Environment**: Close environment, such as an organization's competitors, customers, partners, suppliers, and investors. Remote environment, such as the political system, the economy, its social structures, and technological advances.
- **Culture**: Society's shared values, norms, beliefs, and behaviors. (Harrison 2005; French & Bell 1990; Rothwell et al. 2016).

The Great Place to Work Model

This model was designed by Michael Burchell and Jennifer Robin in 2011. According to Burchell and Robin (2011), this model includes the following elements of individual and group interactions and relationships:

- **Trust**: Respect and fairness among the members of an organization.
- **Credibility**: Open communication, competence, and integrity displayed by the members of an organization.
- **Respect**: support, collaboration, and caring for one another displayed by individuals among the groups, teams, and organizations.
- **Fairness**: Equality, impartiality, and justice in all levels of an organization.
- **Pride**: Individual achievement, team performance, and the company's status in the community.
- **Camaraderie**: Intimacy, hospitality, and a sense of community in the workplace (Burchell & Robin 2011).

SWOT Analysis

This model was originally designed by Albert S. Humphrey in 1960. According to Gupta et al. (2014), this diagnosis model includes the following elements:

- **Strengths:** Positive tangible and intangible attributes internal to an organization that are within the organization's control.

- **Weaknesses:** Factors that are within an organization's control that reduce from its ability to attain the desired goal.
- **Opportunities:** External or internal attractive factors that represent the reason for an organization to exist and develop.
- **Threats:** External or internal factors, which could place the organization's mission or operation at risk.
  (Gupta et al. 2014).

As you can see, without individuals' efforts and influences, no organizations can achieve strengths and opportunities. At the same time, individuals can have a major influence on creating weaknesses and threats for the organization.

Strategies or Tactics Needed for Successful Coaching Intervention

During the process of coaching as an individual intervention, besides using OD as a platform for gathering data, professional coaches and OD practitioners are using several strategies and tactics to deepen their understanding of coachees. These processes will assist them to reveal and recognize some personal elements of their personalities and characteristics that would determine their behavior and attitudes. Some of these strategies are as follows.

Self-Awareness Process

This author is a complete believer that when we alter our thinking and behaviors, we are altering our lives and our directions. He believes that who we are, what we do, and the way we do it all depend on who we are for ourselves, and how we see ourselves in the world. When we keep relating to ourselves as the power we possess and the possibility that we are, we can generate anything in our lives (Bakhshandeh 2009). The view of ourselves and others will control our awareness, and our awareness will become our new reality that naturally will determine our actions (Bakhshandeh 2015). Many psychologists define *self-awareness* as having a clear understanding and view of our personality and its traits, such as weaknesses, strengths, attitudes, motivations, beliefs, and emotions. The knowledge of our self-awareness gives us the access to create an opportunity to recognize and understand others, how they view us, how they perceive our attitude, and how we respond to them (Wayne 2019; Rothwell 2015; Stevens 2009). The level and depth of the group's self-awareness depend not only on their own awareness but also on the degree that they are consciously or intentionally hiding it from others. The self-awareness levels are as follows:

Identified—In this level, individuals are aware of one's emotions, thoughts, desires, attitudes, behaviors, and beliefs which are also known and understood by others. Being positive or negative, productive or damaging is not the point. The point is that they know them, and so do others around them in the personal or professional settings. This level considers an above-average level of self-awareness, given that individuals are able to recognize their emotions and are capable of controlling their thoughts and their actions (2019; 2015; 2009).

Blind Spot—In this level, individuals are not aware of their emotions, thoughts, and behaviors toward others around them but others can see and recognize the emotions and behaviors displayed by the unaware individuals. This situation is like a blind spot because individuals can't see what others are seeing about them (2019; 2015; 2009).

Concealed—At this level, individuals are very much aware of their emotions, thoughts, attitudes, and behaviors; however, for some reason or other, they are concealing these things from others so well that others are not aware of such emotions and thoughts, which leads them to believe things about those individuals that are not true (2019; 2015; 2009).

Unidentified—On this level of self-awareness, individuals are completely oblivious to their own thought process and emotional display, while at the same time, others are not aware of them either. In this level, their self-awareness is not identified by either themselves or others (2019; 2015; 2009).

Doing Versus Being

Trainers and consultants tend to emphasize the *Doing* part of the change, when what makes the biggest difference is the *Being* part of a person. Based on my experience, most executives and managers in organizations plan their individual, team, and organizational successes on just doing and not on both being and doing. What gives an individual the *Doing* is who he or she is *Being* at that given moment (Bakhshandeh 2009; emphasis added). I would say with absolute certainty that there are two sides to any individual change, team-building change, or organizational change. "The *Doing* side is about processes, measurements, tools, structures, and procedures. This side is about management. The *Being* side is about participation, commitment, attitude, creativity, overcoming resistance to change, and self-leadership. This side is about leadership" (Primeco Education, n.d.).

We are human beings, but most of the time all we do is human doings. When we pay attention to how we are, we can see that regardless of our age, gender, nationality, race, culture, or upbringing, we are aware that when others have some upsetting situation or when they are happy, we can identify their state of being even if they are not speaking or explaining their situation. We can recognize resentment, regret, unhappiness, and other ways of being in others. On the other hand, we can also identify someone being interested, engaged, committed, communicative, and results-oriented as well as being a leader. In the book *Being and Nothingness*, Jean-Paul Sartre, the French philosopher and ontologist, explained this phenomenon as "There is no being which is not the being of a certain mode of being, none which cannot be apprehended through the mode of being which manifests being and veils it at the same time" (Sartre 1943, 24–25). They don't need to do anything; even without them doing anything special, we can recognize those characteristics in them (Bakhshandeh 2009). "State of being is what makes us all do what we do, or even feel what we feel. It makes us interested in what we do, and it allows us to relate to others, or take ourselves away from them! It makes us succeed or fail, and it makes us love or hate ourselves and others!" (22).

Emotional Intelligence (EI)

Emotions have a direct impact on one's state of mind, and in some shape and form they are ruling everyone's day-to-day lives. We are making decisions based on what we are feeling at that time such as sad, angry, happy, frustrated, or bored; therefore, unconsciously we select activities correlated to the emotions we are inflaming (Hockenbury & Hockenbury 2007). According to Hockenbury and Hockenbury (2007), "An emotion is a complex psychological state that involves three distinct components: a subjective experience, a physiological response, and a behavioral or expressive response" (n. p.).

Coaches want to provide training for their coachees in a set of emotional intelligence knowledge and skills that will assist them not only in their personal intervention and development but also will add to their managerial skills, which will directly influence their team, group, or departments to work with better behavior and display positive and workable attitudes that will impact their productivity in a positive way. The following (Figure 5.1) are some of the most important and practical emotional intelligence that would

Category of Emotions	Displaying Qualities
Self-Awareness	Self-confidence. Self-assessment. Self-control. Self-disparaging humor.
Self-Regulation	Practicing integrity. Being accountable. Being at ease with uncertainty. Welcoming change.
Compassion	Active listening. Relating to other's issues. Looking for what is right. Being at ease with other's failures.
Empathy	Recognizing talent. Being sensitive to cross cultures. Understanding diversity. Being a service to others.
Motivation	Being for achievement. Displaying enthusiasm in the face of disappointment. Entertaining multiple perspectives on a situation. Awareness of differences among people.
Interpersonal Skills	Skillful verbal and nonverbal communication. Sensitivity to other's mode and temperaments. Entertaining multiple perspectives on a situation. Awareness of differences among people.
Intrapersonal Skills	Appreciation for oneself. Awareness of self-motivation/agenda. Display of self-discipline. Overcoming distractions.

Figure 5.1 Categories of Emotions and Their Displaying Qualities. Inspired and adapted from Wayne (2019); Stevens (2009); Hockenbury and Hockenbury (2007).

be very helpful to an executive or manager at work (Wayne 2019; Stevens 2009: Hockenbury & Hockenbury 2007):

To understand and have a benchmark for training and development of an executive or manager on emotional intelligence, this author has designed a rating system for evaluation of "Presence and Use of Emotional Intelligence at Work." The reader can use this tool, displayed in Table 5.1, and self-rate their own emotional intelligence (from 1 to 5, *1* being the lowest rate and *5* being the highest rate of presence and use of emotional intelligence) at the initial date of rating, and then continue rating themselves in six months and then a year after the initial rating.

Appreciative Coaching (AC)

In this section, we look at the principles and distinctions of *Appreciative Coaching* (AC), a coaching approach with a background in *Appreciative*

Table 5.1 Presence and Use of Emotional Intelligence at Work Rating System

Presence and Use of Emotional Intelligence at Work Rating System		
Date:	Participant:	Team:
Month:	Supervisor	Department:

Rating Scale: 1=Poor, 2=Marginal, 3=Acceptable, 4=Good, 5=Excellent

Categories	Descriptions	Qualities	Rating				
			1	2	3	4	5
Self-Awareness	One's capacity to identify and understand one's emotions, temperaments, and motives. Awareness of their impact on other people.	Have Self-Confidence					
		Have Self-Assessment					
		Display Self-Control					
		Display Self-Disparaging Humor					
Self-Regulation	One's ability to recognize & redirect distracting impulse & temperament. A tendency to defer immediate judgment and to apply considerations before acting against others.	Practicing integrity in all matters					
		Being responsible & accountable					
		Being at ease with unknown					
		Being open to necessary changes					
Compassion	One's ability to show kindness and understanding for others in the time of their hardship and sorrow. A consciousness of feeling others' distress and desire to relive their pain.	Listen actively without judgment					
		Relating to others' issues as real					
		Looking for what is right with others					
		Being at ease with others' failures					

(Continued)

TABLE 5.1 Presence and Use of Emotional Intelligence at Work Rating System (Con't)

Presence and Use of Emotional Intelligence at Work Rating System

Empathy	One's aptitude to recognize and understand others' emotional status. Competence in dealing with people according to their current state of feelings and emotions.	Recognizing and retaining talent				
		Having sensitivity to cross cultures				
		Understanding & welcoming diversity				
		Being at service to others				
Motivation	One's desire to work for personal and inner motives beyond monetary status, which are external rewards. The inclination to follow their goals with high energy and perseverance.	Having a formidable motive for success				
		Enthusiasm in the face of defeat				
		Displaying forward motion activities				
		Positive attitude for productivity				
Interpersonal Skills	One's interest and ability to understand, relate, intermingle, and effectively interact with others. A powerful skill for creating cooperation and building relationships with others.	Displaying communication skills				
		Being sensitive to others' moods				
		Entertaining multiple perspectives				
		Noticing differences among people				
Intrapersonal Skills	One's ability to distinguish and understand one's thoughts, emotions, and feelings. A skill for planning and directing one's life, personally and professionally.	Appreciation for oneself				
		Awareness for self-motivation				
		Being self-disciplined				
		Facing & overcoming distractions				

(Continued)

TABLE 5.1 Presence and Use of Emotional Intelligence at Work Rating System (Con't)

Presence and Use of Emotional Intelligence at Work Rating System
Two actions for this month that would bring up my 3 lowest emotional intelligence ratings by at least 1 point on the next month rating:
Action 1:
Action 2:

Note: Adopted from: Wayne (2019); Stevens (2009); Bakhshandeh (2009); Hockenbury and Hockenbury (2007).

Inquiry (AI). (You can see more information and details about AI in Chapter 2 of this book.) We will explain the AC process and principles and demonstrate a set of questions designed for walking clients through the AC process.

The Five Principles of Appreciative Coaching

Five fundamentals and basic principles are the core philosophy for AC (Oren et al. 2007):

Constructive. Throughout the coaching sessions, the coaches should look for statements by the coachees about their understanding of themselves and their perspective and fabric of their lives, their families, and their careers. Make sure to point out their strengths, their gifts, and their abilities (2007).

Positive. The coaches should keep focusing on presenting or emphasizing the positive effects around coachees' strengths and achievements. Keep changing the coachees' language by redirecting their problem-indicating language to resolution-related language (2007).

Poetic. The coaches must pay close attention to the coachees' stories that they are saying about themselves. Encourage them to rewrite elements of their stories by establishing themselves in positive ways and transforming their problems into strengths (2007).

Simultaneous. The coaches should keep in mind to continue their inquiry as the source of awareness that would guide the coachee to the change. The appropriate questions are helping the coachees see their present challenges or hardships in a new perspective (2007).

Anticipatory. The coaches could be very instrumental in assisting the coachees to generate positive and empowering views of themselves via self-declarations and visions for their future (2007).

Practical Process Model for Appreciative Coaching (AC)

There have been many models proposed to define how the AC process works, and what process to follow to make sure all five stages of AC are implemented to provide a quality AI process for clients. The following is a five-step practical model for implementing the AC process (Rothwell 2016):

Establish Rapport and Build Trust with the Client. As coaches, this is the most important aspect of building an effective process with less resistance. Without trust and relatedness, nothing would work.

Assist the Client to Pinpoint the Main Issue in the Way. As coaches, it is our job to assist the clients to get to the primary and key issues in their way in order to create a powerful vision for their future, personally and professionally.

Promote and Empower Clients to View the Desired Future. As hard as it might get, as their coaches it is our commitment to empower them to see their possible and predictable future based on what they are envisioning about themselves and their lives, at home or at work.

Encourage and Build Up the Clients' Engagement with the Design. We have to make sure that the client is the one who is working on designing and building their future and to make sure they are encouraged, empowered, and acknowledged for their hard work.

Assist the Clients to Design an Action Plan to Fulfill the Vision. This is all about action plans and managing black and white steps to implement and fulfill their vision. We as the coaches have to assist our clients to stay focused on designing their purposeful action plan and desire to make it recognized.

Stages of Appreciative Coaching (AC)

According to Cooperrider et al. (2003), "The Appreciative Inquiry, 4-D Cycle is a dynamic, iterative process of positive change" (p. 101). Besides the philosophical nature of AI, it is also an attempt to make a personal and professional change. Please note that later on the fifth stage, the Define stage as the first stage of the process, was added to the original 4-D Cycle (Discovery, Dream, Design, and Destiny) to make it a 5-D Cycle (Watkins et al. 2011).

During coaching sessions with a client, the coaches will guide clients through the main five stages of AI and ask a set of questions designed to walk them through the 5-D process. Coaches will assist clients in getting present to their dreams and desired future from an empowering perspective versus trying to overcome a possible failure. Basically, they will look at what is working versus what is wrong. We have included a series of questions as a model for implementing each phase of AC which could be used for empowering and encouraging the client to think deeper and be more at ease in participating. You can see the relationship between the stages in Figure 5.2.

Define Stage. In this stage, the coaches assist the coachees in defining their interests and desired topics for the coaching relationship. In this stage,

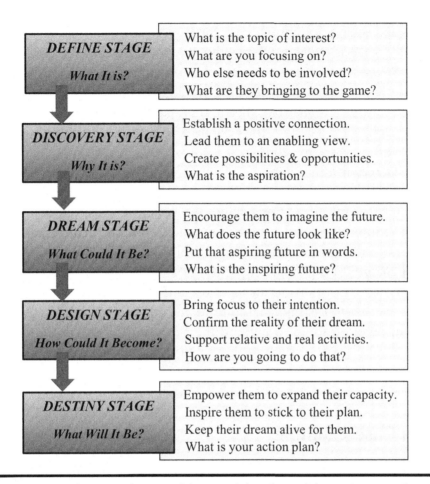

DEFINE STAGE *What It is?*	What is the topic of interest? What are you focusing on? Who else needs to be involved? What are they bringing to the game?
DISCOVERY STAGE *Why It is?*	Establish a positive connection. Lead them to an enabling view. Create possibilities & opportunities. What is the aspiration?
DREAM STAGE *What Could It Be?*	Encourage them to imagine the future. What does the future look like? Put that aspiring future in words. What is the inspiring future?
DESIGN STAGE *How Could It Become?*	Bring focus to their intention. Confirm the reality of their dream. Support relative and real activities. How are you going to do that?
DESTINY STAGE *What Will It Be?*	Empower them to expand their capacity. Inspire them to stick to their plan. Keep their dream alive for them. What is your action plan?

Figure 5.2   Appreciate Inquiry Coaching Model. Adopted from Oren et al. (2007), 109. *Appreciative Coaching: A Positive Process for Change.* **San Francisco, CA: Jossey-Bass; Rothwell, William, J. (2015), 28. edit.** *Organization Development Fundamentals: Managing Strategic Change.* **Alexandria, WV: ATD Press.**

the coaches encourage the coachees to come with ideas of who else needs to be involved and what they need to bring to the game to accomplish their intention and the topics they are focusing on. The main inquiry in this stage is all about "what is it?" and "who is involved?" (2003).

Discovery Stage. In this stage, coaches establish a positive connection between themselves and coachees and lead the clients to an empowering view by confirming the wisdom of what is possible and looking at the best aspects of what is available at this moment. This is the stage for assisting the coachees in creating possibilities and seeing opportunities for themselves and their future. The primary inquiry in this stage is "why are things the way they are now?" (2003).

Dream Stage. In this stage, the coaches encourage the clients to generate empowering images of possibilities by inviting them to express and share their desired future. The main inquiry in this stage is "what could it be?" In this stage, the coaches are assisting the coachees to put their aspiring futures into words and verbalize them (2003).

Design Stage. In this stage, the coaches would support their coachees to bring their desired dream or future into light and focus by asserting the reality of their dreams or futures. At this stage, the coaches assist the coachees to focus on their intentions and confirm the reality of their dream by supporting the coachees to design an action plan established on reality (2003).

Destiny Stage. In this final stage, "the goal is how to empower, learn and adjust/improvise" (Cooperrider et al. 2003, 101). At this stage, the coaches help their coachees to distinguish their dreams and realize them in the present time, by empowering them to expand their capacity to create the desired future and inspire them to stick to their action plan. The main inquiry at this stage is "what will it be?" (2003).

Business Case Example

In this section, we will present an example of an executive/manager coaching that will highlight the first level of OD intervention, the individual intervention, based on a need for the improvement of the individual approach, behavior, and attitude, following the standard process of an OD intervention.

An OD intervention with an individual intervention followed by a team-based change intervention is one of the best investments an organization can provide for its stakeholders, management team, and their workforce. When individuals are present and aware, and teams work cohesively and in sync with their management's vision and organization's mission, naturally the level of production, collaboration, and communication will increase. This, in turn, will cause the turnover and dissatisfaction among the workforce to decrease. This balance of events will directly provide higher profitability for the organizations, which will have a direct positive influence on the quality of the workplace and result in increased compensation and benefits for their employees. Individual intervention on the executives' and managers' level creates a win-win-win situation for individuals (management), teams (workforce), and organization.

Background

Mrs. Mary Johnson was the VP of Education and Training and member of the executive team and partial stockholder for Visionaries, Inc., a training company located in San Diego, operating internationally. Mary oversaw the designing and implementing of training programs for training and developing small businesses which were owner-operated or run by a manager. At the time of our involvement with her as the OD practitioner for the individual intervention, Mary was directly accountable for managing, training, and developing six trainers who were providing training services for over 25 accounts, six of which were directly managed by Mary herself. The Visionaries training company was in business for five years at the time of our involvement with the individual intervention. During the five years of operations, the training company has used our consulting services for conducting a series of trainings on team building, effective communication, and customer service. Given their overall satisfaction with our services and positive impact of our trainings on their staff and contractors, they asked us to get involved with their needs for this individual intervention under the umbrella of executive coaching and managerial training.

The following is what we used as a step-by-step explanation and demonstration of how to conduct an effective and long-lasting individual intervention, using Rothwell's (2015) general approach:

Preparation. Setting up the approach, having a contract/agreement, and explaining the process.

Set-Up and Data Collection. Setting up for observations, document reviews, and one-on-one and focus group interviews.

Data Analysis. Collecting, organizing, and analyzing the data to locate problems and come up with solutions to the problems using interviews for collecting resolutions.

Feedback. Providing feedback to the management/owners about data analyses and findings.

Action Planning. Managing and assisting the team to come up with their action plan for resolving their team issues.

Follow-Up. Continuing following up on the implementation of the team's action plan and providing needed coaching or mentoring.

Step 1: Entry

According to the company's CEO and President, Mary's department was not providing effective and influential services and was operating in a stagnant position and hitting a plateau. The following evidence supported his claim: a) lack of growth and expansion of accounts, b) decrease on the rating of customer satisfaction, c) drop in repeat business or referrals from existing accounts, and d) turnover of trainers and coaches.

The CEO expressed his satisfaction for our previous services and asked us to get involved with resolving their organization issues involving what they believe was Mary's lack of effective involvement in developing and expanding her department. Before the first in-person meeting with the executive team and Mary, we emailed our intentions and explained some key principles in our approach to conduct this individual intervention as follows:

- What is OD?
- What is individual intervention?
- What is executive coaching?
- What is AI?
- What is AC?
- What is the Action Research Model (ARM)?

Step 2: Start-Up

We set up the initiation meeting with the executive team: the CEO, COO, VP of Finance and Budgeting, and Mary (the VP of Education and Training). We established the primary purpose of the meeting to empower Mary to establish a powerful structure for her operation and fulfill her vision for her career. We made sure that Mary knew that the undertaking project was not about fixing Mary, blaming her, or pointing the finger at her as the source of the problems, but to empower her to operate with freedom, self-expression to conduct her work with fun, freedom, and joy, which ultimately will produce much higher results and provide a positive outcome for her, her team, her clients, and her organization.

As OD practitioners, we offered the company executive coaching as our approach instrument, using AC empowered by the distinctions, principles, procedures, and design of AI to assist Mary to open up and feel safe to communicate her possible reservations, resentments, and upsets. We used the ARM as a processing platform for managing the process and reporting the progress and feedback to the CEO. Everyone asked questions, expressed their concerns and desires while we answered all their questions and concerns. By the end, we agreed to the contract's terms and conditions, and we started to plan our approach and structure our process of executive coaching with Mary.

Stages of Appreciative Coaching

We explained that during the process of AC (Figure 5.2) we would support, coach, and guide Mary through the following stages, according to Watkins et al. (2011, 39):

1. ***Define Stage.*** Choosing the positive approach—"what is working?"—which works well with Mary's productivity and working style as the focus of inquiry.
2. ***Discovery Stage.*** Inquiring into stories of forces which give life to what Mary was dealing with.
3. ***Dream Stage.*** What are Mary's dreams for her life and career? Locating the themes that appear in Mary's stories and selecting empowering topics for further inquiry.
4. ***Design Stage.*** Creating shared images with Mary for a preferred future, personally and professionally.
5. ***Destiny Stage.*** Guiding Mary to find innovative ways to create her designed and desired future.

ARM Process Plan

We presented the following stages of the ARM as our main platform for managing the processes of the individual intervention change effort with Mary (Table 5.2):

Table 5.2 Action Research Model (ARM) Process

Steps	Category	Actions
Initiation	Initial Meeting	■ Create rapport. ■ Ask about apparent issues. ■ Discuss the intervention. ■ Explain the process and what you would do.
Contract	Official Agreement	■ Identify the sponsor, client, and participant. ■ Explain the scope of work. ■ Indicate the approach and processes. ■ Include dates, locations, and compensation. ■ Identify the contact person.
Designing Plan and Needs Assessments	Knowledge & Skills	■ Determine what type of data must be collected. ■ Determine the source of data. ■ Examine the purpose of this assessment. ■ Identify the type of data collecting methods.
	Job & Task	■ Identify high performance. ■ Refine job responsibilities. ■ Identify job tasks. ■ Identify training and non-training requirements.
	Competency	■ Review competency standards of the organization. ■ Establish parameters. ■ Identify key players and their influences. ■ Collect, organize, and analyze the data.
	Strategy	■ Gather information about the current situation. ■ Examine the external & internal environment. ■ Conduct a root cause analysis.
Collecting Data on the Current Condition	Knowledge & Skills	■ Review available documents and historical records. ■ Conduct one-on-one interview with the coaching client's superior. ■ Conduct one-on-one interview with the coaching client.

(Continued)

TABLE 5.2 Action Research Model (ARM) Process (Con't)

Steps	*Category*	*Actions*
	Job & Task	■ Identify standards. ■ Make observations. ■ Distribute job analysis questionnaires.
	Competency	■ Review the competency standards of the organization. ■ Interview coaching client's superior on required competencies, defining incompetence, and expected behaviors. ■ Interview coaching client on required competencies, defining incompetence, and expected behaviors.
	Strategy	■ Interview coaching client's supervisor. ■ Review historical records. ■ Review the organization's current strategies. ■ Conduct SWOT analysis of internal and external environments' influences on the client.
Feedback	Findings	■ Conduct a feedback session, and present the findings of the needs and potential issues/problems to executives. ■ Propose a timeline to present potential action plans for each need's category.
Action Plan	Proposal Based on Findings (see Table 5.3).	■ Collaborating with the client and the organization, design an action plan to implement the intervention. ■ Include a set of action plans for each need's category.
Coaching Intervention	Appreciative Coaching. See Step 5, and Table 5.4 for more details.	■ *Define Stage.* Choose the positive as the focus of inquiry. ■ *Discovery Stage.* Inquire into stories of life-giving forces. ■ *Dream Stage.* Locate the themes that appear in the stories, and select topics for further inquiry. ■ *Design Stage.* Create shared images for a preferred future. ■ *Destiny Stage.* Find innovative ways to create that future.

(Continued)

TABLE 5.2   Action Research Model (ARM) Process (Con't)

Steps	Category	Actions
Evaluation	Appraising the Intervention	■ Design evaluation forms. ■ Receive feedback and evaluation from the client. ■ Receive feedback and evaluations from the coaching client's superior.
Coach Departure	Intervention Completed	■ Organize all the process documentation for the client. ■ Be available for phone calls and follow-up needs. ■ Complete the relationship with the client and the organization's executives.

Step 3: Assessment and Feedback

After completing the administration side of the engagement, such as signing the contract and all the necessary HR paperwork and arrangements to give us permission to conduct the data gathering and needs assessment process, we start collecting data concerning what the organization is expecting from Mary as the VP of Education and Training. Also, Mary needs to distinguish her view of her position by herself and what she thinks the organization is expecting from her and what she thinks she is providing. We want to make sure there is a good and sufficient connection between what the organization's views and interests are and what Mary's reality is about what she is providing. So, within this domain of comparison, we collect the data in the following areas: 1) Knowledge & Skills, 2) Job & Task, 3) Competency and 4) Strategy as the details are mentioned in the above Table 5.2 and Step 2: Set-Up.

1. ***Review Documents.*** We reviewed some historical documents provided by the organization's HR office, such as:
   • Mary's employment history and productivity.
   • Organization's HR policies and operational standards and expectations.
   • Mary's job description, including her responsibilities and accountabilities.
   • Mary's potential promotions or disciplinary notices.

2. ***Interview with the CEO.*** We interviewed Mary's direct supervisor, which in this case was the company's CEO and President. This interview was to shed light on the following issues:
   - What the CEO and the organization were expecting from Mary's performance and productivity.
   - How the CEO is rating Mary's performance and productivity.
   - What the CEO's perspective is about the apparent problems Mary is facing.
   - What kind of knowledge, skills, and competencies the organization is looking for in the position of VP of Education and Training.
   - What the CEO sees as Mary's strength and weakness.
   - What the organization's plans are for Mary's position and accountabilities in the future.

3. ***Interview with Mary.*** We conducted an in-person interview with Mary about the following issues:
   - What she was expecting from the organization and her position.
   - What she thinks about her performance and productivity, and how she rates her own performance.
   - What her perspective is about the apparent problems she is facing.
   - What she thinks about the organization's strengths and weaknesses.
   - What kind of knowledge, skills, and competencies she is looking for in the position of VP of Education and Training.
   - What her plan is for her position in the organization and accountabilities in the future.

After collecting all the above data, we conducted a data analysis and needs assessment process and prepared a detailed report about our analysis, our findings, and our general proposed plan to resolve the issues facing Mary as one of the organization's executives. This feedback report was presented to the CEO and Mary in a private and closed-door session with prior permission from Mary. The feedback session was effective and productive and welcomed by both parties as a good platform to start the action plan to enter the intervention phase.

Step 4: Action Planning

Given the nature of the individual intervention, it is much easier to create an action plan, given it is only engaging one person, which makes the planning much easier compared with team intervention or the organization level intervention. With collaboration from Mary, her schedule and availability, the HR department policies

Table 5.3 Creating an Action Plan for the Individual Intervention

Categories	Actions and Tools
Set-Up and Schedule	■ Establish a rapport with Mary, and set up roles and expectations of the coaching relationship. ■ Schedule in-person, confidential weekly coaching sessions with Mary. ■ Schedule meetings with Mary's supervisor.
Review the Findings	■ Review and conduct a deeper cut on our findings, analysis, and viewpoints after interviews. ■ Conduct a needs assessment process relevant to Mary's position and accountabilities. ■ Review and discuss the results of the SWOT.
Discuss KSAs, Behavior, and Attitude	■ Review and create her needed knowledge, skills, abilities, and competencies for high-performance management and productivity. ■ Discuss how Mary is viewing a change, how she is relating to potential change, and if she is resisting a change. ■ Review how Mary's is using interpersonal and intrapersonal skills.
Tools to Use	■ 360-Degree Feedback process between Mary and her direct supervisor. ■ "Presence and Use of Emotional Intelligence at Work" rating. ■ "Leadership Qualities of an Effective Manager" rating. ■ "Great Place to Work" model of diagnosis of Mary's relationship with the organization and others. ■ "SWOT Analysis" of Mary's behavior and attitude. ■ Using Appreciative Coaching.
Coaching Instruments, Models, and Approaches	■ Plan for conducting coaching instruments and models, such as self-awareness and Appreciative Inquiry. ■ Pinpoint all of Mary's disempowering behaviors and attitudes and replace them with workable mindsets and behaviors. ■ Assist Mary to invent a personal vision statement. ■ Assist Mary to create new practices for her role as an executive.

concerning Mary's availability and time off, and the CEO's support, we designed an action plan to implement the intervention (see Table 5.3):

Step 5: Coaching Intervention

Like any other intervention projects, individual intervention (in the form of executive coaching or managerial coaching) also has stages for developing an individual through coaching. According to Rothwell (2016), the following stages are mainly adopted from and based on one of the main OD intervention models, the ARM, with some substages for supporting the readers to understand when and what they need to implement during this intervention.

Please note that the following structure and table is a representation of stages and steps for conducting the actual coaching process within the individual intervention, while all the information and details of related steps are mentioned on the above-mentioned steps: Steps 1: Entry, Step 2: Set-Up, Step 3: Assessment and Feedback, and Step 4: Action Planning. This step-by-step approach could be easily modified to a customer intervention plan for team intervention as well as an organization intervention.

The following Table 5.4 is representing step-by-step actions needed for conducting an actual coaching process during the intervention. This is a very effective way to support OD practitioners on their approach to the individual intervention.

It is a good time to mention Mary's results of her executive coaching and what she accomplished in participating in this coaching as a form of her individual intervention. As we mentioned in the background section, Mary was directly accountable for managing, training, and developing six trainers who were providing training services for over 25 accounts, six of which were directly managed by Mary herself. After one year of direct coaching with Mary, and another year of maintaining and providing coaching support for her and her ICA (Internal Change Agent), Mary was overseeing training services for over 70 accounts, 21 of which were managed by herself. She expanded her trainers' body from 6 to 18 trainers, plus she is managing the entire training program. Mary got married, bought a house for herself to start a family, and also purchased three other properties as an investment. That was not bad for a person who was complaining of not having time or money. That is what is possible from participating in executive coaching and taking on one's life in both personal and professional domains while being happy, fulfilled, expressive, and productive beyond what you thought was possible. She demonstrated the power of having a vision and committed to achieving it! That is the power of overcoming one's resistance to be the best you can become and the power and magic of turning yourself into someone who is there unconditionally to support you when you are going where you thought was not possible—your coach!

Step 6: Evaluation

The most frequently used definition of evaluation, according to Trochim William and Donnelly (2008), is "The systematic assessment of the worth or

Table 5.4   Step-by-Step Actions to Conduct a Coaching Intervention Using Appreciative Coaching Supported by Appreciative Inquiry Model

Initiation and Set-Up
■ Create a background of relatedness.   ■ Establish coaching, roles, policies, and structure with the coachee.   ■ Establish coach and coachee's relationship and expectations from both ends.   ■ Get coachee's commitment to the process.   ■ Express your commitment to the process and your coachee's success.   ■ Review the findings, analysis, and assessments.   ■ Explain the OD model, especially the individual level.   ■ Conduct a self-awareness inquiry.   ■ Use the Practical Model for Implementing Appreciative Inquiry Process.   ■ Explain and use the Appreciate Inquiry Coaching Model.   ■ Define the coachee's interest and desire.   ■ Keep the coachee's commitment alive and in front of the conversation.
Tools and Instruments to Use
■ 360 Feedback.   ■ "Present and use of Emotional Intelligence at Work" rating. Use Table 5.1.   ■ "Leadership Qualities of an Effective Manager" rating. Use Table 5.2.   ■ Appreciative Inquiry Model.   ■ Appreciative Coaching Approach.   ■ Organization Diagnosis Model. Use Figure 5.1.   ■ Self-Awareness Model. Use Figure 5.2.
Define Phase
■ What are we focusing on?   ■ Who else needs to be involved?   ■ What do we need to bring into this game?   ■ What is the actual accomplishment and outcome of this game?
Discovery Phase
■ Lead the coachee to an empowering view.   ■ Confirm the wisdom of what is possible.   ■ Create possibilities and opportunities.   ■ Ask empowering and uplifting questions.   ■ What is the aspiration?   ■ What else is possible?   ■ What is predictable out of our undertaking?   ■ Who are your role models?   ■ What attributes of these role model inspires you?   ■ What are your top five accomplishments?
Dream Phase
■ Encourage coachee to imagine and visualize their future.   ■ Put the aspiring future at work to make it real and possible.   ■ Ask questions that lead your coachee to see their future.

(Continued)

TABLE 5.4 Step-by-Step Actions to Conduct a Coaching Intervention Using Appreciative Coaching Supported by Appreciative Inquiry Model (Con't)

■ What does your future look like? ■ Who are the people who would support you in creating that future? ■ What are the top three things you would change in your life? ■ What are the top three adjectives that best describe you? ■ What would you like to achieve in the next three years? ■ What would you like to accomplish in the next six months? ■ Who else would benefit from your success and that inspiring future?
Design Phase
■ Bring focus on intentions. ■ Confirm the reality of their dreamed future. ■ Support relative and realistic activities. ■ Ask questions that would support the real black and white activities and practices. ■ How are you going to do that? ■ What would energize and move you forward? ■ What might undermine you and our actions? ■ What are the top ten actions you need to take on during the next two months? ■ Who can support you with your action plan and be your partner? ■ What would you consider as a new practice you have never completely implemented?
Destiny Phase
■ Encourage and empower the coachee to expand their capacity. ■ Empower them to stick to their plan. ■ Keep their dream and desired future in front of them. ■ Ask questions that would keep them focused. ■ What are you currently doing that is not aligned with your designed future? ■ How would you alter your schedule to achieve your action plan? ■ What daily routine needs to change to help you accomplish your plan? ■ What activities might you consider, and what would you not consider doing? ■ How disciplined are you about following your plan?
Review the Results
■ Review the coachee's progress and results monthly. ■ Compare the actual progress with the intended outcomes monthly. ■ Continue correcting the course of action.
Maintenance and Mentorship
■ Keep the coachee's vision and future in front of them. ■ Keep reviewing the coachee's action plan and potential obstacles in their way. ■ Encourage the coachee's self-realization and self-awareness. ■ Keep checking the coachee's emotional intelligence and self-rating. ■ Promote self-discipline and accountability. ■ Continue working on the leadership quality rating. ■ Present it to the coachee and the client.

Note: Adopted and inspired by Rothwell et al. (2016), Bakhshandeh (2009), and Cooperrider et al. (2003).

merit of some object" (352), or "The systematic acquisition and assessment of information to provide useful feedback about the object" (352). The main goal of evaluation of our coachee was to provide a practical view of the coachee's progress and feedback on her development to the client (sponsor) and to the coachee herself. We decided to provide our evaluation on two general categories, formative and summative forms.

Formative Evaluations. The formative evaluation will reinforce or improve the object or topic that was evaluated; the formative evaluations will help researchers or OD practitioners in assessing the program delivery or technology and the quality of their application (Trochim William & Donnelly 2008). This author has used the following three formative evaluations during this individual intervention process: a) *Needs Assessment Evaluation,* b) *Implementation Evaluation,* and c) *Process Evaluation.*

Summative Evaluation. Summative evaluation is assessing the effect or outcome of an intervention, program, or technology by describing what happened as an outcome or result, following the delivery of the intervention, program, or technology (Trochim William & Donnelly 2008). This author has used the following two summative evaluations during this individual intervention process: a) *Outcome Evaluation* and b) *Impact Evaluation.*

Step 7: Adoption

During the individual intervention and implementation of executive coaching, Mary had some insights and realizations about who she was being and how she operated in her work. She looked at what kind of attitude and behaviors she had displayed and took ownership of her part in her team's dysfunctions, conflicts, turnover, and decreased productivity. This eye-opening awareness caused her to apologize to her team and her supervisor for what she had done (continuously or unconsciously), and she came with 1) self-awareness of her behaviors, attitude, emotional intelligence, and self-recognition, and 2) a new set of promises concerning her new commitment to herself, her team, her department, and her organization (Rothwell et al. 2016).

Step 8: Separation

This is the time that the OD practitioners or practitioners are concluding the individual intervention with the coachee and are leaving the organization. However, this does not happen before they make sure the selected internal change agent or team leaders are powerfully and entirely in action for the change intervention to resume work after they leave (Rothwell et al. 2016). We had a decision-making meeting with the coachee and her direct supervisor (the CEO) to assign one person as the Internal Change Agent (ICA) in charge of overseeing the coachee's action plan and all procedures resulting from the individual intervention. The ICA can be situated to manage the change implementation process while the senior management team controls the content (Sullivan, Rothwell & Balasi 2013).

Key Lessons Learned

Out of the work we have done with organizations on their needs for individual intervention and an executive coaching approach, we found the following distinctions to be vital to the success of any change intervention, including the individual intervention change effort:

- ▪ ***Trust the Process.*** As a coach, we shall inform, support, and encourage our clients to trust the process of coaching and apply the distinctions, practices, and methods that are designed to empower them and allow access to effective ways of living and working (Bakhshandeh, 2009).
- ▪ ***Relatedness Is the Key to Trust and Rapport.*** Effective coaches will not act as if they are better than or above their coachees. They will display respect, empathy, and compassion for where the coachees are at that particular time and location of their career or of life in general (Bakhshandeh 2009, 2015).
- ▪ ***OD Practitioner as a Coach and Instrument.*** OD practitioners have a relatively big influence on their coaching clients while conducting an individual intervention. They can provide their knowledge, abilities, and skills to direct, consult, support, and advise in order to be an effective instrument of the individual intervention change effort (Cheung-Judge 2012).
- ▪ ***Authority Versus Leadership.*** Running an organization as an authority figure, such as an executive or senior manager, is one of the oldest models of management that is still used by many businesses and organizations. Unfortunately, research has shown that this good old management style is producing more resistance versus engagement and participation (Satell 2014).

Discussion Questions

In the end, we are asking you to look into the following discussion questions and express your perspective of what the individual intervention and coaching processes are, and some best practices you can implement to conduct a practical OD individual change intervention.

1. Has your organization used any individual intervention change approaches in its attempt to improve someone's performance and productivity?
   If Yes, was the approach successful? Why? What was the experience for the individual and the organization?
   If No, what was standing in the way of your organization implementing the individual intervention and change approach?
2. From your point of view, in your organization, is there a strong relationship between the top management team and the organization's hierarchy?
   If Yes, what do you think is causing such strengths?
   If No, what do you think is interfering with or causing a weak relationship?
3. How do you describe your relationships with your supervisor?
4. How do you rate your own performance and productivity at your management position?
5. Have you ever been involved with any dysfunctions and conflicts with your supervisor or a subordinate?
   If Yes, what was the dysfunction or conflict, and how was it resolved?
   If No, what would you attribute to a dysfunction-free operation?
6. From your point of view, what are the most important values or principles that would strengthen and build a strong bonding between you and your supervisor or your subordinate?
7. What would be the most destructive behavior or attitude that would cause un-workability in an organization's management process?
8. Considering what you have read in this chapter about individual intervention (in executive and managerial coaching format), what else would you suggest adding to elements of individual intervention? What was missing?
9. Do you think professional coaching and OD consulting would make a difference for establishing strong and cohesive executives and managers?

References

Arneson, J., W. Rothwell, and J. Naughton. 2013. "Training and Development Competencies Redefined to Create Competitive Advantage." *T + D* 67 (1): 42–47.

ATD-Association for Talent Development. 2014. "ATD Competency Model: Talent Development Redefined. ATD Competency Model Graphic and AOE.pdf." Retrieved from http://www.tdcascadia.org/assets/2014/12/ATD-Competency-Model-Graphic-and-AOE.pdf

Bakhshandeh, Behnam. 2002. *Executive Coaching: For Those of You Who Have Arrived*. Unpublished workshop on coaching executives. San Diego, CA: Primeco Education, Inc.

Bakhshandeh, Behnam. 2009. *Conspiracy for Greatness; Mastery on Love Within*. San Diego, CA: Primeco Education, Inc.

Bakhshandeh, Behnam. 2015. *Anatomy of Upset: Restoring Harmony*. Carbondale, PA: Primeco Education, Inc.

Burchell, Michael, and Jennifer, Robin. 2011. *The Great Workplace: How to Build It, How to Keep It, and Why It Matters*. San Francisco, CA: Jossey-Bass

Burke, Warner. 2018. *Organization Change: Theory & Practices* (5th ed.). Los Angeles, CA: SAGE Publication, Ltd.

Cheung-Judge, Mee-Yan. 2012. "The Self as an Instrument: A Cornerstone for the Future of OD." *Journal of the Organization Development Network* 44 (2): 40–47. https://cdn.ymaws.com/www.odnetwork.org/resource/resmgr/odp/vol_44_no2.pdf

Cooperrider, David L., D. Whitney, and J. M. Stavros. 2003. *Appreciative Inquiry Handbook: For Leaders of Change* (2nd ed.). Brunswick, OH: Crown Custom Publishing, Inc.

Ellinger, A. D., and S. Kim. 2014. "Coaching and Human Resource Development: Examining Relevant Theories, Coaching Genres, and Scales to Advance Research and Practice." *Advances in Developing Human Resources* 16(2): 127–138. doi: 10.1177/1523422313520472.

French, W., and C. Bell, Jr. 1990. *Organization Development: Behavioral Science Interventions for Organization Improvement* (4th ed.). Englewood Cliffs, NJ: Prentice-Hall.

Gan, G. C., and C. W. Chong. 2015. "Coaching Relationship in Executive Coaching: A Malaysian Study." *The Journal of Management Development*. doi: 10.1108/JMD-08-2013-0104

Gupta, K., C.M. Sleezer, and D. F. Russ-Eft. 2014. *A Practical Guide to Needs Assessment* (3rd ed.). San Francisco, CA: John Wiley.

Harrison, Michael I. 2005. *Diagnosing Organizations: Methods, Models, and Processes* (3rd ed.). Thousand Oaks, CA: Sage Publisher, Inc.

Hockenbury, Don H., and Sandra E. Hockenbury. 2007. *Discovering Psychology*. New York, NY: Worth Publishers.

Hsieh, Hui-Hsien, and Jie-Tsuen Huang. 2018. "Exploring Factors Influencing Employees' Impression Management Feedback-Seeking Behavior: The Role of Managerial Coaching Skills and Affective Trust." *Human Resources Development Quarterly* 29(2): 163–180. doi: 10.1002/hrdq.21311.

Oren, Sara, L. Jacqueline Binkert, and Ann L. Clancy. 2007. *Appreciative Coaching: A Positive Process for Change*. San Francisco, CA: Jossey-Bass.

Primeco Education, Inc. (n.d.) website. "Team and Organizational Training." Accessed February 10, 2020. www.PrimecoEucation.com.

Rothwell, William J. 2015. edit. *Organization Development Fundamentals: Managing Strategic Change*. Alexandria, WV: ATD Press.

Rothwell, William J. 2016. "Penn State Course Commentary. OD&C Program." WFED572- Foundation of Organization Development, The Pennsylvania State University.

Rothwell, William J., Jacqueline M. Stavros, and Roland L. Sullivan. 2016. *Practicing Organization Development: Leading Transformation and Change* (4th ed.). Hoboken, NJ: John Wiley & Sons, Inc.

Sartre, Jean-Paul. 1943. *Being and Nothingness: A Phenomenological Essay on Ontology*. Translated by Hazel E. Barnes. New York, NY: Washington Express Press.

Satell, Greg. 2014. "To Create Change, Leadership Is More Important Than Authority." *Harvard Business Review*. Harvard Business School Publishing Corporation.

Stevens, R. 2009. *Emotional Intelligence in Business: EQ, The Essential Ingredient to Survive and Thrive as a Modern Workplace Leader*. Middletown, DE.

Sullivan, Rothwell and Balasi. 2013. "Organization Development (OD) and Change Management (CM): Whole System Transformation." *Development and Learning in Organizations* 27 (6): 18–23. doi:10.1108/DLO-08-2013-0060

Trochim William, M. K., and James P. Donnelly. 2008. *The Research Methods Knowledge Base* (3rd ed.). Mason, OH: Cengage Learning

Vidal-Salazar, M., V. Ferrón-Vílchez, and E. Cordón-Pozo. 2012. "Coaching: An Effective Practice for Business Competitiveness." *Competitiveness Review* 22(5): 423–433. doi: 10.1108/10595421211266302.

Watkins, Jane, M. Bernard Mohr, and Ralph, Kelly. 2011. *Appreciative Inquiry: Change at the speed of imagination* (2nd ed.). San Francisco, CA: Pfeiffer.

Wayne, Jenny. 2019. *Emotional Intelligence 2.0. A Guide to Manage Anger, Overcome Negativity ad Master Your Emotions*. Middletown, DE.

Chapter 6

Individual Interventions: Mentoring and Sponsorship (Levels of Advocacy)

Leila Farzam and Jamie Campbell

Contents

Overview

As longer serving generations are leaving the workforce, younger cohorts are entering with a new vision in mind. It is time to understand the importance and necessity of individual interventions such as mentorship and sponsorship, and the positive impact on the future. Individual interventions are a way to support the next generation of leaders in the workplace. These types of interventions also allow for the organization to show its commitment to the employees within the company. Mentoring and sponsorship give the company not only the opportunity to promote from the ground up, but they also show the employees that they are valued pieces of the organization. As more positions open up, it is imperative to realize that to be effective at succession planning, there must be confidence in the younger generations to step up and stand motivated to be engaged to bring innovative ideas to the table. The other factor to this equation is using individual interventions to teach, guide, and influence the mentee. As the generational shift starts to take place with five generations in the workforce, it is the perfect time to take advantage of the positive impacts of individual interventions to increase the success of personal and professional productivity. Also important is the ability to ensure there is no brain-drain as the more experienced employees and leaders exit the workplace, as well as guarantee the business continuity, which is a fundamental platform for the new and emerging talent coming in to learn; assess; bring creativity, resiliency, and simplification to the business; and take it to the next stage of success. In this chapter, the objectives are as follows:

- Individual interventions are explored as well as the four categories that individuals providing the services fall into, which are Advocate, Champion, Sponsorship, and Mentorship.

- Though there are many types of individual interventions, for the purpose of this chapter, four categories are used as the necessary levels of personal interventions.
- The framework for this model derives from the Human Process Intervention model, and our model was created with the mentality of Maslow's Hierarchy of Needs (shown in Figure 6.1).
- Practical tools and activities are provided to guide the implementation of individual interventions.

The Four Basic Levels of Individual Interventions

Our model regarding the levels of practitioners conducting individual interventions was created with the mentality of Maslow's Hierarchy of Needs. Maslow (1943) produced a hierarchy of needs model that identified five essential human needs, which were self-actualization, esteem needs, belongingness and love needs, safety needs, and physiological needs. Maslow (1943) described that once an individual meets a certain level of need, naturally the person desires to move to the next level of need. According to Maslow (1943), "when a need is fairly well satisfied, the next ... 'higher' need emerges, in turn, to dominate the conscious life and to serve as the center of

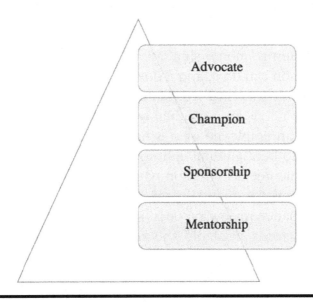

Figure 6.1   Four Levels of Individual Interventions. Copyright by Leila Farzam and Jamie Campbell.

the organization of behavior" (395). Maslow's hierarchy of needs gives us a general idea of what we need in life to survive as engaged human beings. In Maslow's theory, each level represents a higher stage of development. Our model of individual interventions, shown in Figure 6.1, can be viewed in the same way.

These same levels can also apply to individual interventions. It is vital to continuously take the pulse of the four levels of personal interventions established and continued within an organization to create an inclusive working environment, and increase and diversify learning and development programs to embed excitement as employees grow and diversify their portfolio. To do so, organizations can use an expanded, diverse, and inclusive approach and tools to explore the relationship between different elements within mentoring and sponsorship.

The Relationship Between the Levels

Each of the terms listed above can be very easy to consider as synonymous. However, that is not the case! This section will attempt to give you a more profound definition of each term and show their interconnectedness *and* their differences as well.

Mentorship

As we understand all these terms, we must start at what can be considered the foundation for all terms, mentorship. Mentorship is the foundation for these terms as every person can do it, and it does not cost a great deal to perform. It does not require individuals to work in the same unit, company, or line of business. It simply needs an individual who is *willing* to share with either a new employee or an employee who is having difficulty performing a given task, or is willing to be a guiding light to provide give-forward and be a confidant for the mentee. The reason why *willing* is emphasized when discussing mentorship is that many organizations make mentoring a mandatory part of the performance review process. Rothwell and Chee (2013) share that "the willingness factor is, arguably, the most important ingredient in the decision-making mix. Among the three—ability, experience, and willingness—it is the one that will most likely get you to say yes to a mentoring relationship" (30). Individualistic and competitive notions of social stratification embedded in functionalist perspectives imply that those who succeed have done so solely through their efforts (Darwin 2000) and may not be as keen to help anyone else advance their careers. Many organizations feel the need to develop their next generation of leaders, but the current generation of leaders may see this group as a threat to their position. Companies recognize this and have, in some instances, made the coaching of younger employees a path to the career advancement of middle managers. Hence, these managers will "take on" a mentee but not provide any real support.

Think of it this way; remember when you were asked to watch younger siblings or other younger family members. Better yet, remember when you were *told* to do it for some type of payment. Be honest, how good of a job did you do? Sure, you did not let them jump off a roof (or maybe you did), but being forced to do it was not the same as when you volunteered to take on the task. Being a mentor takes on that same type of aspect. Remember, one of the critical elements of being a mentor is willingness to be one. It is about having the confidence and generosity to see others succeed, owning the success of others, and taking pride in it (Ballaro & Polk 2017). Just like when you are forced to do something that you do not want to do, mentorship cannot be a forced or strongly suggested occurrence. Mentorship at its lowest level must have an individual (the mentor) who is willing to provide support without being concerned if their help will jeopardize or help their personal gains. A mentor has an inherent responsibility to share wisdom or knowledge with another person. Any instance of a forced march can impede that transfer of knowledge. Mentors can also be from fields that are not directly aligned with the mentee's career path or business. Mentors can provide support to their mentees due to their various experiences.

Although these experiences may not be the same as the mentee's, there could be some parallels in personal backgrounds, especially around competencies such as values, ethics, collaboration, and innovation. These experiences can provide the mentee with direction and guidance. Most importantly, the experiences of the mentor can help prevent the mentee from making costly mistakes. More recently, many diverse organizations are now promoting reverse mentoring, which excites the mentor and mentee to exchange knowledge, share their know-how, and create a collective forum for success. How does this work? The newly joined employee will bring to the table new approaches to interventions, modern design thinking, and technology application to the business complemented by the longer serving employees sharing the company purpose, its inner workings, the do's and don'ts, and sectoral connection within the service organization provided to its clients. The organizational capacity will need to accept failures and successes (Chin et al. 2016). The fundamental question is if everyone can be a mentor, should they?

Sponsorship

The next level of personal intervention or individual intervention is sponsorship. It is important to note at the onset of this discussion that persons who are invested have some type of *power*. Using the term *power* is an attempt to explain the ability of individuals (sponsors) to place others (the sponsored) in the position to advance their careers. This advancement comes from the ability to provide *access*. Access means meetings, projects, conversations, and opportunities that the sponsored individual would not have the ability to be invited to be part of under normal circumstances. Think of it this way; sponsors openly use their creditability to create a pathway for those who have not established themselves. These persons may need a push that a mentor cannot or may not be able to provide, as they do not possess enough of a reputation to open doors for the person that they would like as a sponsor. For example, in just about every coming of age movie, especially those of the high school variety, there is a sponsor (the "Cool Kid") and the sponsored (the "Outcast") who have come together to join forces for some life-affirming situation. The Cool Kid takes the Outcast under their wing, and now the Outcast becomes accepted by all the people (for the most part) in the town, school, athletic team, or theatrical production. The Cool Kid did not put any monetary support in the community, but they did put their name on the line for the Outcast. They do this without concern for how much of their creditability is impacted. They do it because they have seen the Outcast as a person with skills and talents that had not been recognized by the community as a whole.

In the real world, sponsorship works the same way. A sponsor provides light to be shined on an individual that would be overlooked due to their current level/status in the organization. Sponsorship comes in three levels. These three levels are (in no particular order) intermediate (hybrid), personal, and official (Comings & Cuban 2002). The intermediate (individual or hybrid) sponsor serves as both a friend and a coach. The hybrid sponsor can be someone who works with the organization but also is someone that could be considered a friend. The personal sponsor is more in line with a mentor that is a family member, but their primary role is to provide emotional support and guidance for how to deal with different personal issues in the workplace through their past experiences. Lastly, there is the official sponsorship. This type of sponsorship is from someone within the organization who has identified the sponsored individual as a talent but has not yet been allowed to show their skills. This person is not a friend, but is a supervisor within the immediate unit or a leader in a parallel line of work.

Champions

Everyone needs a hero, right? In the workplace, a champion becomes that hero. Have you heard the phrase "championing a cause"? The champion is the person that can sing the praises of the person that the individual intervention is being provided for. The champion will not only invite individuals to the table and use their intellectual capital to open doors, but they will *place* the individual in a leadership position. Again, just as in the case of a sponsor, there is a power dynamic included here. However, the champion's superpower is the ability to place other persons in positions of power or leadership (Choudhury & Baines 2012). Champions can create space for individuals to grow and demonstrate their abilities on a larger scale while still guiding, supporting, and advancing the individuals' career they are championing.

Advocates

Lastly, there is an advocate. The advocate is the combination of the three previous levels with a few significant differences. The first one is the power of the advocate. Similar to the champion, the advocate can place budget with words. Whereas the champion can provide a seat, the sponsor can make a suggestion, and the advocate can put the individual in a leadership position with little to no resistance *and* provide budget resources to the project. The advocate can also act as a protector for the individual. In this protector position, the advocate can advise how to miss potential pitfalls and unintentional mistakes. The advocate serves as a pivotal component to career advancement for the individual undergoing the intervention (Silliman et al. 2016). In many organizations, the ability to be responsible for personnel and budgets is a significant factor for being eligible for a promotion. These experiences give the individual the ability to take on new roles and provide inspiration for others. Since the advocate can provide both, they have the ability to be the gate opener for the individual.

How Does It All Work in Practice?

In most organizations, these four roles can be and often play out by one person, the mentor, a term used interchangeably for the four roles described above and shown in Figure 6.2. Why? Once a mentor and mentee are matched, there begins a sense of ownership of success and desire to

Figure 6.2   Interchangeable Interventions. Copyright by Leila Farzam and Jamie Campbell (2020).

succeed, while evolving over time (Zerzan et al. 2009). Effective mentorship takes on a role of sponsor, champion, and advocate when the mentee innovates. The mentor moves to centerstage focus to the mentee when he or she applies for other positions. The mentor begins to champion for the mentee's intellectual capacity and competencies in support of the mentee's personal and professional success. If the mentor has the budget and position, the mentor very willingly will allow the mentee to advance given the interest in the mentee's abilities and potential. The practical implementation of individual interventions can create an environment through an organization's culture of growth while reaping benefits and incentives to all involved in the development.

For the Organization

- Rapidly integrate new employees
- Capture experience and knowledge of departing employees
- Increase understanding of the organization's business direction, priorities, and plan
- Encourage intellectual capital
- Accelerate staff learning
- Build confidence in handling internal and external relationships
- Provide cost-efficient delivery of career guidance to new and longer standing staff

For Mentors

- Contribute to increase an organization's intellectual capital
- Create space for generative conversations and reciprocal learning
- Build mentoring communities in the organization
- Form partnerships that promote further learning

For Mentees

- Acquisition of technical and organizational knowledge to more effectively navigate the organization and learn about the business
- A better understanding of working in a complex organization and the agility that is required to be successful
- Improve interpersonal skills
- Receive guidance to foster the development
- Create personal reflective space
- Appreciate the opportunity to reflect and learn from an experienced colleague

What Does All This Mean?

Each of the levels of individual intervention has different roles and responsibilities for the individual receiving and implementing the intervention. The most important to understand is the ability and limitations that the person providing the intervention is constrained. Individual interventions provide support, advancement, and development for the person(s) undergoing them (Dziczkowski 2013). These interventions can dictate the success or failure of the organization. Individual interventions serve as a potential spark for leadership. Even within those levels that do not have a great deal of power, they may have substantial levels of influence that can help the individual get ahead in their career.

Tips for Making the Most of the Individual Intervention Relationship

It is essential to capitalize on valuable individual interventions and understand how to make the best of the knowledge exchange while strengthening the connection and collaboration. Following are various guidelines to follow as you create the identified individual relationship:

- Set meeting times in advance.
- Agree on parameters of the relationship.
  - Format for meetings, confidentiality, and developmental needs
- Set objectives in the areas of broadening or developing technical knowledge, understanding the organizational culture, increasing interpersonal effectiveness, and creating improved short- and long-term career and learning goals.
- Keep in mind "elements of success".
  - Shared responsibility, mutual trust and respect, clear expectations and focus, and confidentiality
- Keep expectations realistic.
  - Mentees should not expect:
    - Solutions to all problems
    - Unlimited access to his or her mentor
    - Special favors or expectations of promotion
  - Mentors should not expect:
    - Full responsibility for the mentees' performance
    - Life-long gratitude
- Create a comfortable environment that encourages openness, trust, and transparency, while setting boundaries to provide structure and clarity.
- Listen actively.
- Be non-judgmental and genuine.
- Consider the message received in an objective way.
- Emphasize the positive.
- Provide activities or take-aways.

Case Study

The following case study focuses on a millennial employee who has recently accepted a position at an organization, while exploring the following eight steps of organization development (OD) interventions.

Step 1: Entry

Jasmine, a junior OD practitioner, was recently hired to analyze the effectiveness of OD interventions in various departments within the organization. The organization is a multinational environment that promotes the elimination of hunger around the world. The CEO of the organization recently implemented an initiative for employees that focuses on mentorship between longer serving employees and new hires. This initiative is based on an extensive climate survey led by the OD department due to challenges within the organization of newer employees not fully understanding the whole system and its impact on people they serve.

Step 2: Start-Up

Though Jasmine has extensive education and training in OD, she struggles with understanding the various department and organizational matrix structures. Through the new initiative formed by the CEO, she was partnered with Amir, the Vice President of Engineering, who has been with the organization for 15 years and has led many mentoring workshops. Many employees in the organization use Amir as an example when it comes to institutional knowledge.

Step 3: Assessment and Feedback

As Jasmine got settled in her new position, she decided to reach out to Amir in an effort to build the mentor and mentee relationship. Within two hours, Amir sent a positive and welcoming note to Jasmine and suggested meeting the following day for lunch and a tour. Though Amir was quite busy, he spent three hours with Jasmine to clarify organizational structures, institutional history, various sectors that come together to provide a holistic service to clients, and learn more about Jasmine's personal and professional background.

Step 4: Action Planning

As the initial meeting went very well, they decided to meet monthly to do continuous check-ins. During the following monthly meetings, Amir took a crystallized approach to draw on the various department relationships and interactions and provided a possible critical path for Jasmine to use as a guide. He also guided Jasmine to think carefully about the importance of professional reputation as a basis for success and failure as the organization was not a very forgiving kind of firm. This means if the OD intervention missed critical elements to the road to recovery, or there were mishaps in the implementation, there would always be an association of failure to Jasmine.

Step 5: Intervention

With that critical guidance, Jasmine ensured and forced herself to be super careful and staged all her diagnosis and recommendations on fact-based data and information and left nothing for individual interpretation. Given her positive experience with Amir, she began observing and working more closely with longer serving employees for a self-assessment purpose, as she wanted to focus on and learn from the successful and respected employees to deeply understand their behaviors at work and their interactions with superiors/peers/juniors. She made her connections and began mimicking the same actions. In a concise period, she learned very effectively from these longer serving employees, who were not necessarily on the organization chart but carry heavy organizational weight, and demonstrated humble behaviors needed to lead in this type of organization. Before Jasmine knew it, she was very much welcomed and included in that group, and her learning curve was expanded.

Step 6: Evaluation

As she continuously reflected on her behavior and how best she could contribute to the organization, Jasmine noticed she created a feed-forward loop for herself to ensure continuous learning, ask for guidance without shame, and allow for mistakes to occur in a sandbox format. Five months later, Jasmine presented her six-month review from her supervisor to Amir.

Step 7: Adoption

As he was beyond impressed with her evaluation, Amir decided to put her name forward for the OD Manager position within the Engineering department. Though he was not on the search committee for the position, he provided his opinion on the matter in his role as Vice President of Engineering. Amir often used this experience in his speeches to indicate that learning from each other is a gift and a very complex competency to build as it requires a very high level of confidence, humility, and generosity to self and others.

Step 8: Separation

Jasmine, as an OD practitioner, took the opportunity to create a hands-on learning event led by Amir for emerging leaders to learn these critical competencies and ensure the organization has a succession planning process put in place. This intervention created a very positive and virtuous cycle leading to extraordinary employee motivation, commitment to excellence, and collegiality.

Reflection Questions

As the reflection process takes place, consider the following questions:

1. How did the four various levels of individual interventions occur during this case?
2. With such interventions, would you consider this company to be a learning organization? And if so, can you expand on why it is and name the characteristics of it.
3. Would this intervention be a value or hindrance to succession planning and exchange of knowledge?

Mentee and Mentor Journal Tool

Activity: Use the Mentee and Mentor Journal Tools, shown in Figures 6.3 and 6.4 in a mentorship session as a guide to collect personal thoughts and provide a guided conversation.

The mentee journal provides systematic thinking through developed questions for the mentee.

The mentor journal offers guided questions created for a mentor during interactions with the mentee.

Mentee Journal

1. *Record your top three questions:*
   1. _____
   2. _____
   3. _____

2. *Share your experience thus far in the organization.*
   _____
   _____
   _____
   _____

3. *Discuss your top three challenges at work:*
   1. _____
   2. _____
   3. _____

4. *Ask for feedback on competencies and behaviors.*
   _____
   _____
   _____
   _____

5. *Invite your mentor to give you feed-forward comments in area of needed improvement or development.*
   _____
   _____
   _____
   _____

Figure 6.3   Mentee Journal. Copyright by Leila Farzam and Jamie Campbell (2020).

Mentor Journal

1. *Record the top three mentors or leaders in the organization you admire(d):*
   1. _____
   2. _____
   3. _____

2. *Share your experience thus far in the organization.*
   _____
   _____
   _____
   _____

3. *When you first started at the organization, what were your top three challenges at work?*
   1. _____
   2. _____
   3. _____

4. *Ask how best can you guide your mentee.*
   _____
   _____
   _____
   _____

5. *Additional notes:*
   _____
   _____
   _____
   _____

Figure 6.4   Mentor Journal. Copyright by Leila Farzam and Jamie Campbell (2020).

Johari Window

In addition to the forms above, another tool used for an individual intervention is a Johari Window, as shown in Figure 6.5. A Johari Window can assist an individual with understanding who they are, what they know, and how they can better themselves with the knowledge they already have. Still, the knowledge or ability is not being presented. As defined by Luft and Ingham (1961, 1), the four spaces are:

1. **Open or Free Area**—what is known by the person about him/herself and is also known by others.
2. **Blind Area**—what is unknown by the person about him/herself but which others know.
3. **Hidden Area**—what the person knows about him/herself that others do not know. It is also called the façade.
4. **Unknown Area**—what is unknown by the person about him/herself and is also unknown by others.

Approach the use of a Johari Window the same way you use strength, weakness, opportunity, threat, or SWOT analysis. The main difference with a Johari Window is that it gives the individual a genuine chance to review their current skill set. You can use this to learn about the individual and get a brief assessment of their skills.

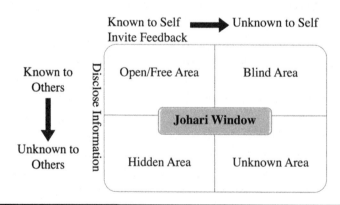

Figure 6.5   Johari Window. Adopted from Luft and Ingham (1961).

Key Lessons Learned

In this chapter, the four levels of individual interventions—mentorship, sponsorship, champion, and advocate—were discussed. These four levels can be used interchangeably, or in an evolving fashion, to help individuals in the workplace foster an environment of continuous interpersonal improvement. Each level can expand into the next level as individuals grow within their positions. Individual interventions are essential as they can not only provide development opportunities for employees, but they also offer the organization with the ability to remain sustainable in their corporate arena.

Discussion Questions

1. In your words, define the four levels of individual interventions. Discuss the positives and negatives in your explanation.
2. What individual interventions and roles have you been able to experience in your professional capacities? Explain how you used your abilities in each instance.
3. If an intervention were provided for you by your organization, at which level would you like the person providing the intervention?
4. Can individual interventions be provided for all persons?
5. How can be individual interventions be implemented?

References

Ballaro, Julie M., and Laura, Polk. 2017. "Developing an Organization for Future Growth Using Succession Planning." *Organization Development Journal* 35(4): 41–59.

Chin, Jean Lau, Lyne, Desormeaux, and Katina, Sawyer. 2016. "Making Way for Paradigms of Diversity Leadership." *Consulting Psychology Journal: Practice and Research* 68(1): 49.

Choudhury, Barnie, and David, Baines. 2012. "We Are the Champions: Mentors Ease Newcomers into the Net." *Ethical Space* 9(2/3): 74–85.

Comings, J., and S. Cuban. 2002. "Sponsors and Sponsorhip." *Focus on Basics: Connecting Research & Practice* 6(A): 1–7.

Darwin, Ann. 2000. "Critical Reflections on Mentoring in Work Settings." *Adult Education Quarterly* 50(3 May): 197–211. doi: 10.1177/07417130022087008

Dziczkowski, Jennifer. 2013. "Mentoring and Leadership Development." In *The Educational Forum* 77(3): 351–360. Taylor & Francis Group.

Luft, Joseph, and Harry, Ingham. 1961. "The Johari Window." *Human Relations Training News* 5(1): 6–7.

Maslow, A. H. 1943. "A Theory of Human Motivation." *Psychological Review* 50(4 July): 370–396. doi: 10.1037/h0054346

Rothwell, W. J., and P. Chee. 2013. *Becoming an Effective Mentoring Leader: Proven Strategies for Building Excellence in Your Organization*. McGraw Hill Professional.

Silliman, Benjamin, Pennie, Crinion, and Thomas, Archibald. 2016. "Evaluation Champions: What They Need and Where They Fit in Organizational Learning." *Journal of Human Sciences and Extension* 4(3): 22–45.

Zerzan, Judy T., Rachel, Hess, Ellen, Schur, Russell S. Phillips, and Nancy, Rigotti. 2009. "Making the Most of Mentors: A Guide for Mentees." *Academic Medicine* 84(1): 140–144.

Chapter 7

Small-Group Interventions: Achieving Effectiveness Through Interpersonal Training

Marie Carasco

Contents

Overview

This chapter introduces common types of small-group interventions and highlights the benefits of interpersonal training on team effectiveness. It also provides a brief overview of some important theoretical concepts of group dynamics and development which are essential for practitioner success. The chapter takes *the participant action research* approach where "the people who are to take action are involved in the entire research and action process from the beginning. This involvement increases the likelihood of carrying out the actions once decided upon, and keeps the recommended actions feasible" (French & Bell 1999, 137). The chapter discusses the following concepts:

- Theoretical perspectives on small groups and group processes
- Historical development of interpersonal training
- Small-group interventions
- T-groups/Training groups/Sensitivity training/Encounter groups
- The Tavistock Method

- Group development
- Group dynamics
- Emotional intelligence
- Self-awareness
- Communication skills
- Experiential learning

Many organizations are comprised of teams where individuals are brought together to achieve specific tasks. These groups, which can be as small as a dyad, are often expected to be more effective than an individual's solo working effort. Depending on the project or task, effective teams have the following characteristics: clear purpose, informality, participation, listening, civilized disagreement, consensus, open communications, clear roles and work assignments, shared leadership, external relations, style diversity, and self-assessment (French & Bell 1999, 157). Moreover, effective teams are able to harness the power of diversity in ideas and skills towards not only successful completion of their work, but also outstanding outcomes that would be impossible out of a group. Yet, most teams are unable to navigate the challenging interpersonal dynamics required to maximize team effectiveness. As businesses continue to rely on team-based collaborations, the use of small-group interventions are increasingly important since they are designed to address the unique circumstances that can often get in the way of achieving desired team outcomes.

Theoretical Perspectives on Small Groups and Group Processes

Before we explore the common types of small-group interventions and the benefits of interpersonal training on team effectiveness, it is important to understand some theoretical concepts of groups, group dynamics, and group development. Why is understanding and exploring theory important to be an effective practitioner? Well, "Kurt Lewin, the founder of modern social psychology...felt that without a bridge between theory and practice, theorists would develop theory that would have no application and practitioners would engage in action uninformed by theory" (Schmitt 2012, 7). Therefore, it would be a mistake to assume that learning a few techniques to facilitate small-group interventions is sufficient for successful outcomes without a baseline understanding of the theoretical underpinnings at play.

Defining Groups

A *group* is comprised of "several individuals who come together to accomplish a particular task or goal" ("Group Dynamics" 2019, 494). These can be formal groups (put together by someone with authority over those selected to be in the group, and participation in compulsory) or informal groups (voluntary participation). Some examples of formal groups that come together to accomplish a task or goal are project teams, task forces, or working groups in organizations. An example of an informal group is one comprised of friends seeking to organize a surprise birthday party. However, beyond assembling people for the purpose of completing a task, groups are also defined by commonalities in identity. In fact "a group [also] exists when, two or more individuals…perceive themselves to be members of the same social category" (Brown and Pehrson 2019, 1). Moreover, this "[s]ocial identity is based on attributes shared among members of particular social groups and categories. The approach holds that people categorize themselves and others according to salient differences in a social comparative context" (Abrams et al. 2004, 99–138). This categorizing can be based on demographic categories such as age, gender, race, national origin, ethnicity, marital status, occupation, and education etc. Categories can also be based on ideologies, belief systems, and points of view. "Thus, categorization implies shared membership at a particular level of inclusiveness, and it is applied flexibly to maximize the comparative and normative fit of individuals to their categories" (Abrams et al. 2004, 99–138).

Nine High-Level Theoretical Lenses to Support Small-Group Interventions

Poole et al. 2004 inform us that when it comes to research on groups, there is a fragmentation that exists in individual disciplines and as a whole, and few attempts have been made to integrate theory and research across disciplines (1). However, the work of Poole and Hollingshead (2004), which was the culmination of a National Science Foundation supported project to promote integrative thinking about group theory and research, provides a summary of the current state of group theory and research outlining nine theoretical perspectives on small groups that can be useful in supporting practitioners' understanding of group dynamics and development. See Table 7.1 for a summary of each theoretical perspective listed alphabetically.

Table 7.1 Summary of Nine Theoretical Perspectives on Small Groups

Theoretical Perspective	Description
Conflict-power-status perspective	This perspective explains group dynamics in terms of authority, position/rank, resources, and social relationships and group structures.
Feminist perspective	This preventative examines at how power and privilege are authorized through interactions that favor a specific gender.
Functional perspective	This perspective takes a process approach that describes inputs and outputs that can help or hinder performance.
Psychodynamic perspective	This perspective explores the relationship between consciousness, emotions, and logical processes of interpersonal interaction.
Social identity perspective	This perspective explains groups in terms of belonging and the dynamics of ingroups and outgroups.
Social network perspective	This perspective examines the configurations and patterns in relationships.
Social-evolutionary perspective	This perspective asserts that group patterns imitate aspects of the theories of evolution.
Symbolic-interpretive	This perspective focuses on the meanings that groups hold towards other members.
Temporal perspective	This perspective explains groups in terms of transformations that occur over time.

"A group of strangers, meeting for the first time, has within it many obstacles to valid communication…The problems of understanding, the relationships that develop in any given group are from one aspect a unique product of the particular constellation of personalities assembled" (Bennis & Herbert, 1956, 416). Since group dynamics and development come with their own complexities, theoretical perspectives can be particularly useful for practitioners to gain a deeper understanding of the dynamics occurring in groups and subsequent selection of appropriate interventions. In fact, the field of organization development (OD) has an extensive number of interventions that can be classified based on the focus (individual/group/organization) and the goal (desired objectives). In general, small-group interventions can fall under a number of classifications, but are closely aligned to team-building activities, intergroup activities, and education/ training activities. Interpersonal training as a small-group intervention is best classified under education/training activities that are "designed to improve individuals' skills, abilities, and knowledge…in isolation from his or her own work, or one can be educated in relation to the work group)" (French & Bell 1999, 151). The irony to improving team effectiveness is in making the intervention at the individual level either before, in conjunction with, or after team-building activities. With this understanding and awareness that groups can be formal, informal, task/goal focused, and/or have some shared social identity, practitioners and scholars should begin their evaluation of a particular group-based interventions' appropriateness from these basic considerations.

Burke (2013) asserts that although there is no all-encompassing theory of OD there are several theories that are related or connected to aspects of OD. "From a *group* perspective, Kurt Lewin's work on norms and values, the work of Chris Argyris on interpersonal competence and organizational learning, and Wilfrid Bion's theory on the collective unconscious undergird OD practice" (543). In the next section, we will explore the historical development of interpersonal training from the humanistic and psychodynamic theoretical perspectives, then introduce common types of small-group interventions, their expected outcomes, and benefits on team effectiveness.

Historical Development of Interpersonal Training: National Training Laboratories (NTL), a Humanistic Perspective

One of the most well-known small-group interventions is the T-group, which is an abbreviation for Training Group, that is experienced by in individual in isolation/away from his or her place of work and among strangers. This intervention has roots in social-psychology and was developed in the mid-1940s by the work of Kurt Lewin, Kenneth D. Benne, Leland Bradford, and Roland Lippitt. During a two-week workshop that was focused primarily on discussions involving ethnicity, the foundational approach to the T-group experience was cultivated and ultimately refined by the National Training Laboratories Institute for Applied Behavior Science (NTL) (Cooke 1999, 3–4). T-groups quickly became one of *the* most trusted methods of personal and professional development for both individuals and OD practitioners alike. Early on "[i]n the United States, these [trainings] occurred at the National

Training Laboratory in Group Development at Bethel, Maine; Western Training Laboratory in Group Development at the University of California, and the Research Center for Group Dynamics at the University of Michigan" (Sher 2004, 611).

The approaches used in T-groups are humanistic in nature as opposed to psychoanalytical. "The chief difference between the humanistic and psychoanalytic approaches is that the humanistic approach focuses on the unleashing of potential rather than the curing of pathology" (McLeod & Kettner-Polley 2005, 63–99). In fact, NTL became the organization most closely associated with humanistic approaches. Over time, NTL workshops were known by number of the labels including human relations training, sensitivity training, and encounter group training, and most recently, human interactions lab (HI labs). As the movement grew in the 1960s and 1970s, there was not a clear distinction in methodology or approach to T-groups due to the increased number of independent consulting practices around the United States, and there were controversial issues regarding the T-group sessions being perceived and possibly experienced as therapy sessions.

Historical Development of Interpersonal Training: The Tavistock Institute for Human Relations, a Psychodynamic Perspective

While NTL was developing one approach to group dynamics and development in North America with its T-groups, across the pond in the United Kingdom, the *human relations* conference was developing in Tavistock Institute in London in 1946 with financial support from the Rockefeller Foundation (Sher 2004), built largely on the work of the Tavistock Clinic founded in 1920—an outpatient psychotherapy clinic based on treating psychosis in World War I (French and Bell). According to Neumann (2005), there were three key founders "Eric Trist (a clinical and social psychologist), Wilfred Bion (a psychiatrist) and Jock Sutherland (a psychologist and psychoanalyst)—wanted to foster peace-time applications of war-time advances in 'social psychiatry'" (120). "The theoretical father and founder of the T-group was Lewin, whereas the *human relations* conference's theoretical father and founder was Bion" (Burke 2013, 545). In fact, "[h]is theory and method have been applied to groups of all sizes, within just about every setting imaginable. The most widely taught and cited theories of group development...are built on the skeleton of Bion's theory" (McLeod & Kettner-

Polley 2005, 63–99). Moreover, "Bion's experiments with conducting psychotherapy in group settings, which eventually became known as 'the Tavistock method,' began at a British military hospital with neurotic patients" (McLeod & Kettner-Polley 2005, 63–99). "The Tavistock Institution predated NTL by nearly 20 years, and we know that the NTL founders were influenced by Bion's work. There is also evidence that the Tavistock practitioners knew of and respected the work of the early NTL contributors, Kurt Lewin in particular" (McLeod & Kettner-Polley 2005, 63–99). In the United Kingdom, the Tavistock Institute of Human Relations worked in conjunction with "the University of Leicester though the establishment of a series of residential conferences to study group dynamics, and with the European Productivity Agency, which was concerned with improving industrial training methods" (Sher 2004, 611–612).

.The assumptions associated with psychodynamic perspectives for which the Tavistock Institute are tightly associated posit that "emotional and nonconscious processes exist within all human groups, and despite the fact that these processes are largely outside of group members' conscious awareness, they nevertheless affect the quality of interpersonal interaction and task performance, no matter the specific domain or definition of the task" (McLeod & Kettner-Polley 2005, 63–99). Bion described two types of cultures: one where groups come together to do logical tasks and another where groups come together for reasons other than completing a task (McLeod & Kettner-Polley 2005). His contribution to the development of the Tavistock method is built on these assumptions "to provide a way of treating the group-as-a-whole, in contrast to treating individuals within a group setting" (McLeod & Kettner-Polley 2005, 63–99). It should be noted that unlike NTL whose workshops came to be known by number of the labels, Tavistock groups remained closely affiliated with the Tavistock Institute (McLeod & Kettner-Polley 2005).

Other Theoretical Aspects Connected to the Tavistock Institute: Socio-technical Design

It's important to note that the Tavistock Institute for Human Relations is credited with "originating the concept and practice of socio-technical systems (STS) design in the 1940s, although the institute is still active…STS design, together with social psychology and social ecology, were the three major foci of the institute's concern with improving relations between people who were seen as 'dehumanized' by modern industrial society" (Scacchi 2004, 656).

Despite the theoretical differences, "the Tavistock Institute and the NTL share the psychodynamic focus on emotions and nonconscious processes in groups and the notion that an explicit focus on these processes is beneficial for the development of groups" (McLeod & Kettner-Polley 2005, 63–99). There has also been some cross-pollination, since "the design of the early T-groups certainly borrowed some of the techniques from Bion's Tavistock method. The consulting practice of the Tavistock Institute, in turn, was influenced by Lewin's action research techniques" (McLeod & Kettner-Polley 2005, 63–99). Moreover, both versions of these interpersonal trainings focused on an individual's changes and learning occurring within the context of a group of 8 to 12 people who are also learning and changing as group members themselves (Burke 2013). "A major difference between the two versions is that the T-group's focus is on interpersonal relations and individual feedback whereas the human relations." It could be argued that that both T-groups and the Tavistock Method are types of group relations conferences. Group Relations Conferences "offers to its participants an opportunity to study what happens in and among groups at the same time that it is happening…The aim is to bring together experience and thought, emotion and intellect, without neglecting one for the other." Moreover, "[t]he design of the conference is such that a number of aspects of authority can be examined in a variety of contexts" (Banet Anthony & Hayden 1977, 159). "Role behavior is prescribed for the staff, in order to define its authority structure…However, no rules are made for the members; they are free to experiment with any behavior that they believe will enhance their learning" (160). We now turn to a discussion on common types of small-group interventions.

Common Types of Small-Group Interventions for Interpersonal Development

Within the categories that exist for OD interventions, *small-group interventions* at the core are structured activities, actions, and strategies selected for learning or change in among 15 people or less (French & Bell 1999; "Small Groups" 2009). When placed in the context and goal of achieving effectiveness, in this chapter, a subset of small-group interventions falls under education and training activities that are designed to improve technical or interpersonal skills, knowledge, and abilities (SKAs) (French & Bell 1999). This can be accomplished either by being "educated in isolation from his or her own work group (say, in a T-group comprised of strangers), or one can be educated in relation to the work group (say, when a work team learns how better to manage interpersonal conflict)" (French & Bell 1999, 151). When it comes to interventions designed to improve effectiveness in teams and groups this chapter focuses on two interpersonal trainings that take *the participant action research* approach: T-groups/Training groups—also known are sensitivity training and encounter groups, and the Tavistock Method.

T-Group Training

Earlier in the chapter we discussed the humanistic underpinnings T-groups developed by NTL. In fact, ""T-group training," sometimes referred to as "encounter-group training" or "sensitivity training," traditionally took the form of closed-door intensive and unstructured events away from the workplace" (Bokeno et al. 2008, 438). More specifically, *encounter groups* are a "[g]roup of individuals who engage in intensive and psychotherapeutic verbal and nonverbal interaction, with the general intention of increasing awareness of self and sensitivity to others, and improving interpersonal skills" ("Encounter Groups" 2001, 220). *Sensitivity training* was a precursor to team-building that evolved in the 1950s and 1960s, focused on increasing sensitivity and awareness to the feelings and sentiments of others. This training was "initially designed as a method for teaching more effective work practices within groups and with other people, and focused on three important elements: immediate feedback, here-and-now orientation, and focus on the group process" ("Sensitivity Training" 2019, 971). "[T]he objective of T-groups is not to solve specific problems. Rather, individual group members learn to take what they have learned from the T-group experience to solve their problems for themselves" (McLeod & Kettner-Polley 2005, 15). Moreover, T-group experiences aimed to facilitate an environment where participants engage in self-disclosure and are able to give and receive feedback (Bokeno et al. 2008), all of which are foundational to the awareness needed for interpersonal development. It should be noted that NTL adopted the term Human Interactions Lab (HI lab) for their T-group trainings.

The Mechanics of T-groups

The first T-groups consisted of groups of 10–12 people with two practitioners. "A format particularly popular during the height of the T-group encounter movement in the 1960s and 1970s was the 2- to 3-day marathon session, with

T-group experiences interspersed with other learning activities such as lectures" (McLeod & Kettner-Polley 2005, 63–99). T-groups would meet at various locations around the country, and in the early days, participants were afforded the kind of anonymity the facilitated freedom to share and respond to each other in an unfiltered way because they did not know each other.

Groups consist of a diverse array of individuals by age, race, occupation, and social status and meet in a private room for several hours going through many of Tuckman's (1965) stages of development. Sessions had no agenda, and the participants are given space to engage in conversations based on anyone's interest. "T-group training involved participants sharing information about themselves and each other with a view to learning more about themselves, other group members, and the dynamics of the group" (Bokeno et al. 2008, 438). Moreover, Bradford et al. (1964) help us understand the T-group learning experience when they assert "[t]he data [exchanged] are the transactions among members, their own behavior in the group, as they struggle to create a productive and viable organization, a miniature society; and as they work to stimulate and support one another's learning within that society" (1). They go on to say "T-Group members must establish a process of inquiry in which data about their own behaviors are collected and analyzed simultaneously with experience which generates the behaviors" (2). There is an interplay between the individual and collective experiences that are grounded in an awareness and understanding of feedback from these interactions. "[T]he objective is to mobilize group forces to support the growth of members as unique individuals simultaneously with their growth as collaborators" (2).

If there are multiple T-groups being held in the same location, between group sessions, there are larger plenary gatherings with other HI labs. In those larger sessions, T-group practitioners or NTL staff lead presentations on concepts that will be experienced by participants, especially those covered in the NTL publication the *Reading Book for Human Relations Training*. There are breakout sessions, and other subgroups called support groups are formed to provide opportunities for participants to ask questions of each other.

The Role of the Practitioner/Facilitator in T-groups

Marshak (2009) informs us that "the role of the OD practitioner is to collaborate or partner with the subject system by facilitating, coaching, or otherwise supporting self-directed change…[In fact,] the first and most essential ingredient is to operate from a client-centered, collaborative, and facilitative mind-set" (9). In the T-group, "practitioners are usually called *trainers*, emphasizing their role of education and development" (McLeod & Kettner-Polley 2005, 63–99). At the core, trainers are there to support the participants in navigating the group dynamics and to manage the emotions that will come up during a given session. Depending on the style of the NTL trainer, he or she accomplishes this by referencing plenary material, offering reflections on group dynamics, sharing observations, and asking questions of an individual or to the group. There have also been times NTL trainers insert him/herself into the group dialogue.

Challenges with T-group Training

In recent years, T-groups, or HI labs by NTL, are far from anonymous. When participants are grouped together their full names are shared and remain visible for the duration of the training. Email correspondence to participants is also unfiltered. This lack of anonymity will undoubtedly impact the level of vulnerability, candor, and authenticity of the experience of some participants that come expecting anonymity. Participants in current NTL HI labs are also encouraged to define and share their goals for attending the training. These goals are also visible to all in attendance. "Unfortunately, not everyone appeared to benefit from T-group training. The open and direct feedback that is an integral element of this form of training exposed some participants to feelings and experiences that they simply could not handle" (Bokeno et al. 2008, 438). In addition, the validity of the experience to the workplace was not always clear to participants given the unstructured nature of the experience (Bokeno et al. 2008). Moreover, "the use of T-groups has declined as an OD intervention and have mainly been replaced with less touchy-feely team-building activities" (Bokeno et al. 2008, 438). The modern changes of the T-group experiences offered by NTL may be working against the original intention. By eliminating anonymity, introducing support groups (which could turn into gossip sessions), and having trainers engage as participants instead of practitioners has disrupted the development of an ideal environment where participants can more fully engage in the self-disclosure pivotal to maximizing the T-group encounter.

The Tavistock Method

The Tavistock Method at its core seeks to support participants in navigating unconscious individual-level processes that are manifested in a group context (McLeod & Kettner-Polley 2005). In fact, in the Tavistock approach, the individual's significance is not elevated except in relationships with others (Sher

2004). "The individual is a creature of the group, the group a creature of the individual. Individuals, according to their capacity and experience, carry within themselves the groups of which they have been and are members" (613). Moreover "[u]nderstanding groups was the principal research preoccupation of the early pioneers of the Tavistock Clinic and the Tavistock Institute of Human Relations" (Sher 2004, 611). In fact, the primary objective of the Tavistock Institute has been to create a unified theory that could explain unconscious relationships between multiple levels in society (Sher 2004).

The Mechanics of the Tavistock Method and the Role of the Practitioner/Facilitator

The most impactful contribution made by Wilfrid Bion to the Tavistock method was to "provide a way of treating the group-as-a-whole, in contrast to treating individuals within a group setting" (McLeod & Kettner-Polley 2005, 73). In almost direct contrast to T-group practitioners as trainers, "Tavistock group practitioners usually are referred to as *consultants*, emphasizing their role of diagnosing and helping to solve problems" (McLeod & Kettner-Polley 2005, 73). Referencing the work of Whitman (1964), McLeod and Kettner-Polley (2005) inform us that when it comes to the Tavistock method "[t]he consultant decidedly does not act as a leader, organizer, or practitioner of the group. The ambiguity inherent in the situation that ensues is central to the technique" (78). The consultant, who attempts to keep a very emotionally neutral posture, will ultimately make interpretations about group behavior (even those stemming from a single group member) built on evidence-based observations and consider how to allow group members to recognize what he or she has observed (McLeod & Kettner-Polley 2005). Moreover, these interpretations are always focused on solving a specific problem, and in that way, the Tavistock approach is prescriptive.

From a participant perspective, Banet Anthony and Hayden (1977) give us some basic premises that start with the notion that an aggregate collection of individuals "becomes a group when interaction between members occurs, when members' awareness of their common relationship develops, and when a common group task emerges" (156). However, more importantly, the vital aspect of the Tavistock Method is the "belief that when an aggregate becomes a group, the group behaves as a system—an entity or organism that is in some respects greater than the sum of its parts—and that the primary task of the group is *survival*" (156). Understanding the group as an entity requires "a *perceptual shift* on the part of the observer or consultant, a blurring of individual separate ness. and a readiness to see the collective interactions generated by group members" (156–157). Once individuals make the shift to group membership, they adopt a collective identity and change in behavior to reflect that new identity (Banet Anthony & Hayden, 1977).

Challenges with The Tavistock Method

While the Tavistock Institute has maintained a strong reputation and consistent methodology and offerings, they are not as well-known as NTL in the United States. Additionally, the Tavistock Method gives more focused attention on the group experience rather than that of the individual. There is a clear benefit to understanding the interplay of the individual and group experience, which can be lost with the Tavistock Methodology.

Expected Outcomes, Benefits and Competencies Developed Through Interpersonal Training

French and Bell (1999) make an important point about interventions when they said "interventions *do* different things; they *cause different things to happen*…These *differential* results are often exactly what is needed to produce change in the particular situation" (149). Through experiential learning, such as interpersonal trainings, OD practitioners that serve as trainers, consultants, and practitioners of interpersonal training should aim to support participants towards outcomes that include: personal development, group development, group dynamics, emotional intelligence, self-awareness, and communication skills.

An individual participating in an interpersonal training can expect the following seven benefits:

- Enhanced awareness and discernment of emotional responses in self and others
- Ability to learn from and leverage feedback, including one's actions and the actions of others
- Ability to clarify and confront previously unknown inconsistencies in one's values
- Theoretical concepts to help make sense of the experiences
- Increased effectiveness in interpersonal dynamics in one's environments
- Opportunities to apply new behaviors after the training has ended
- New understanding of how to learn

Although the seven benefits noted above are mainly individual outcomes, teams can also reap the same benefits when they allow team members to be part of the same interpersonal training experience like a T-group but more so with the Tavistock approach, which emphasizes interpretations about group behavior over individual behaviors.

Ethical Considerations

As with most helping professions such as psychiatry and social work, OD practitioners should operate from a place of ethos that seeks to support positive outcomes and not harm. Unlike the discipline of engineering, for example, that has a National Society of Professional Engineers (NSPE) and a clear code of ethics, or the physician's oath to "Do No Harm," there is no universal ethical standard for the field of OD. This is in part due to the lack of distinctions around what OD is and what it is not.

However, Banet Anthony and Hayden (1977) outline four boundaries that can serve as ethical requirements for OD practitioners serving as consultants, trainers, or practitioners in group relations conferences. They begin be stating "[b]oundaries are both physical and psychological… A fundamental precept of group relations maintains that work is not possible unless some boundaries that are known to all members are established and maintained" (163). Moreover, "[b]oundaries must be strong enough to maintain the integrity of what is contained inside, but also permeable enough to allow transactions between the inside and outside environments to occur" (163).

From an ethical standpoint, "[t]he group relations conference staff maintains strict boundary functions in four different areas" (see Figure 7.1 below):

1. **The "Input" Boundary**. This is an issue of regulating participation by having individuals apply for participation in a conference.
2. **The Task Boundary**. This ensures that no events are competing with each other and one task occurs at a specified time.
3. **The Role Boundary**. This requires that the practitioner or consultant remains in his or her role for the entire duration of the conference.
4. **The Time Boundary**. This requires all events begin and end on time.

Given the intense vulnerability that can emerge between participants and trainers, practitioners, or consultants, it should be added that OD practitioners maintain a professional distance from participants *after* the group

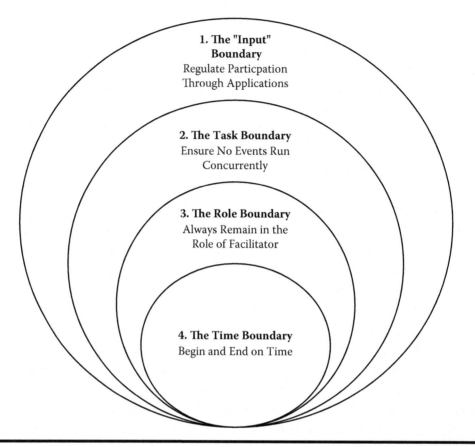

1. The "Input" Boundary
Regulate Particpation Through Applications

2. The Task Boundary
Ensure No Events Run Concurrently

3. The Role Boundary
Always Remain in the Role of Facilitator

4. The Time Boundary
Begin and End on Time

Figure 7.1 Summary of Group Relations Staff Boundary Functions. Author's original creation.

relations conferences have ended and refrain from personal contact. It is also important to maintain confidentiality of participant experiences after the facilitation has ended.

Business Case Example

Samantha, a mid-level engineer in a large electronics firm was asked by her manager to sign up for an NTL HI Lab. Her first thought was "Why should I waste my time with this touchy-feely stuff? I have a ton of work to do, and I'm going to fall behind on my projects if I take a week off." Samantha asked her manager if attending the NTL Lab was a requirement and expressed that she'd rather focus on making progress on her projects. While acknowledging Samantha's concern for her project work, her manager explained that the team had a plan for the work to continue in her absence. Samantha's manager informed her that although she did great technical work, there has been feedback that her interpersonal and communication skills on project teams needed improvement. This was not the first time that Samantha received this feedback. In fact, Samantha was made aware during her performance appraisal last year that if she wanted to become a project lead, she'd have to develop different skills to move beyond the work and role of an individual contributor, which includes her approach to communication. The company was known for promoting from within the business so Samantha knew the feedback about her future there was important. Although she didn't want to go, Samantha signed up for the six-day training in Washington, D.C. While she appreciated the company's willingness to invest in her development, Samantha was still skeptical that spending a week with strangers would do anything for her.

The following will describe some high-level steps in leading a T-group facilitation with some elements of Samantha's experience noted.

Step 1: Entry

The T-group experience for all parties involved begins before any face-to-face interactions. For the trainers, there are preparation meetings that include deciding who will lead plenary sessions and which colleagues will be paired together as co-trainers, as well as discussions on when reminders to the group might be necessary. Training administrators, such as the Dean of the training, typically contact participants via email ahead of the face-to-face meeting to share information to help in preparation for the HI Lab, including: a) letter from the Dean with an overview of the HI Lab with a schedule, self-assessment, and ways to make the most out of your experience; b) an article defining a T-Group; c) T-group guidelines; and d) conditions for lab learning.

In the case of participants like Samantha, the Dean's message included a special note to those who were "sent" to the NTL T-group. The essence of this message is that the participant still has a choice about how he or she can use this opportunity and encourages experimenting with a different kind of learning among strangers.

Step 2: Start-Up

Trainers in NTL T-groups have specific development and training required by NTL to facilitate trainings on behalf of the organization, including but not limited to going through an NTL T-group experience as a participant and apprenticeship where they learn T-group facilitation; how to navigate diversity dynamics; awareness, prevention, and response to distress reactions; and experiential learning, design, and delivery. During the first introductory plenary face-to-face sessions of the T-group experience, participants learn about logistics, key concepts, the various reasons people participate in T-groups, and what to expect emotionally, and they engage in a number of small-group activities that allow the trainers to learn more about the participants. By the end of Day 1, the trainers will have observed enough to determine how to best assign participants to groups to achieve diversity in age, gender, race, and role seniority. The full names of all participants, and their practitioners, are then listed by group numbers, which is shared on a butcher block paper for reference.

Trainers should aim to create ideal conditions for laboratory learning. These conditions help participants to play a part in their learning and the learning of others, and to identify and determine alternative behavior choices. Trainers frequently "interrupt" participants to remind them to stay in the "here-and-now," if they spend significant time talking about the past. "It is this experience that is immediately relevant to members of the group, not what has transpired previously. T-group learnings can [also] be transferred to other situations, of course, either on behavioral or emotional levels" (Golembiewski 1999, 185). Ideally, there should be space for experimentation as a means to practice and apply new behaviors in an atmosphere of trust. This can only be developed though the group's own dynamics.

Step 3: Assessment and Feedback

Although there were some preliminary assessments made about the participants for the sake of group assignment via the self-assessment questionnaire sent prior to the first face-to-face session, and observations on
Day 1, T-group trainers are not there to provide that feedback to participants in the typical ways that change agents would. Feedback, if provided, is given after the trainer has some time to make observations of patterns within the group. When he or she shares those observations, it is—or should be—presented with the caveat that the observation is information for the group to decide what to do with it. The group can either ignore the feedback or act. What often happens when feedback from a trainer is shared is one person might ask the other group members, "What should we do?" or the person might try to follow what he or she believes was implied by the feedback.

The primary source of feedback in the T-group should be from the participants to one another. It is often in the form of a reaction to a statement, silence, or body language. It may be helpful for trainers to model effective feedback if/when a participant's approach may create more barriers than bridges. For example, Samantha received feedback from other participants that the questions she was asking came across as accusatory and not curious. This feedback brought out a defensive reaction from Samantha, who said that she was just trying to understand. While this was her intention, she was not aware of how her approach to questions and the type of questions she raised invoked defensiveness in others. A T-group trainer intervened during this tense exchange and asked those giving feedback to Samantha to do so by saying, "When you say_____, it makes me feel_____, and my wish for you is _____." This approach was helpful for those giving Samantha feedback and for Samantha to get clarity on how she was coming across and what she could do instead.

Step 4: Action Planning

Early plenary sessions of the NTL T-group allow the participants to outline personal goals and outcomes in attending the HI Lab. These are essentially action plans for the week. The trainers work with the participants to help them to shape their goals. The goals are written on a large sheet of paper that remains on the wall of the room that the participants' T-group will meet in for the week. Any additional action plans are determined by participants at the end of the HI Lab. Given that Samantha was required to attend the HI Lab, her goal for the week was to "see what the T-group was all about."

Step 5: Intervention

Given that training and practice are required to facilitate a T-group, the following only presents a high-level overview of what trainers might be expected to do. Keep in mind that their style of intervention and choice to intervene at all is completely subjective, so the content in Tables 7.2 and 7.3 is not prescriptive but summative.

Step 6: Evaluation

At the end of a T-group, the participants are provided with an electronic survey to assess the plenary practitioners and their own T-group trainers. This is how the OD practitioner will know the impact of his or her presence on the participants.

Table 7.2 Possible Recursive Approaches Taken by T-Group Trainers During Each Session

Step	Action	Responsibility
1	**Examine your biases, understand your triggers, prepare to manage your emotions and reactions, and adhere to confidentiality:** ■ The effectiveness of a T-group trainer begins with his or her own personal development and use-of-self during a facilitation. ■ Developing an awareness of biases, triggers, or even unresolved trauma is imperative and can be accomplished through counseling, individual therapy, group therapy, coaching, and encounter groups such as a T-group, Tavistock Method, or Gestalt OSD training programs (see Chapter 4). ■ Without personal development prior to facilitating a T-group, a trainer's presence and interventions can be ill-timed, inappropriate, offensive, or in the interest of the trainer's emotional needs. ■ Trainers must also manage their reactions to T-group participants, since comments and interactions will invoke an internal reaction. Managing reactions includes an awareness of facial expressions, body language, staring, and verbal responses. ■ T-group facilitators are stewards of vulnerability and should not discuss the content disclosed in the T-group sessions outside of the parameters outlined in the training, namely with other faculty.	OD Practitioner
2	**Set the stage:** ■ Connect with your co-trainer before the session and discuss when/if either of you will intervene. ■ Determine seating that makes sense so that you can make clear visual contact with your co-trainer. ■ Remind participants of what is common in the T-group (e.g., there is not agenda, this is an opportunity to get feedback and to experiment). ■ Reiterate concepts that were covered in the plenary session.	OD Practitioner
3	**Determine the type of conversations occurring:** ■ Listen and observe the type of conversations occurring. ■ Are participants in the "there-and-then" or "here-and-now"? ■ Is the conversation aimless and more small-talk related? ■ Consider how long you'll "allow" the small-talk to continue.	OD Practitioner

(Continued)

TABLE 7.2   Possible Recursive Approaches Taken by T-Group Trainers During Each Session (Con't)

Step	Action	Responsibility
	■ Determine if a reminder about the "here-and-now" might be helpful now or later.	
4	**Observe the dynamics developing in the group and consider if intervening with feedback on any of the dynamics will be helpful to the group:** ■ What norms are developing?/What is recurring? ■ Are there any leaders emerging? ■ Who is more vocal? Who is quieter? ■ Where are there conflicts? ■ Where are there compromises? ■ Where are participants struggling? ■ How are emotions being expressed? ■ What are the power dynamics? ■ How are decisions made?	OD Practitioner
5	**Based on exchanges between participants, provide feedback on helpful interpersonal behavior that encourages:** ■ Using "I" statements. ■ Providing examples in lieu of generalizations. ■ Expressing feelings, thoughts, and reactions. ■ Sharing feedback with others. ■ Participating and not just observing. ■ Avoiding over-analyzing.	OD Practitioner
6	**Carefully support participants experiencing strong emotional reactions:** ■ Encourage them to breathe/take a beat. ■ Ask them if them are OK. ■ Ask what they need, or how you/the group can support them. ■ Allow them to sit in silence if needed. ■ Provide a "hand on shoulder" (if close by) and/or tissue. ■ Encourage all participants to journal about their experiences. Keep in mind that this is a very brief list of possible responses to emotional reactions. Training is needed to provide the right level of support without potentially harming the participant or observers in the group.	OD Practitioner
7	**Take care of yourself <u>during every break</u> from the T-group:** ■ Make time to decompress. • Spend time away from the group alone.	OD Practitioner

(Continued)

TABLE 7.2   Possible Recursive Approaches Taken by T-Group Trainers During Each Session (Con't)

Step	Action	Responsibility
	• Journal your thoughts and feelings experienced. • Connect with other T-group faculty to share reactions you were unable to display in the room during your facilitation. ■ Connect with other T-group faculty for guidance on challenges you are experiencing in the group facilitation. ■ Recognize that you will experience both positive and negative emotions1 as a facilitator from the first session to the last.	
8	**Maintain ethical boundaries with participants:** ■ Due to the intense emotions often expressed during T-group sessions, participants are vulnerable due to the trust established in the group. ■ It is advisable that trainers maintain a professional distance from participants and refrain from personal contact after the T-group has ended.	OD Practitioner

Long-term effectiveness can be evaluated from the perspective of multiple stakeholders, including the participant and his or her family, friends, and colleagues.

Step 7: Adoption

Given that participation in a T-group is an individual intervention, the ownership for the change was Samantha's. In the months ahead, she received positive feedback from her manager on improvements she made in her communication style, namely asking questions out of curiosity and having a more personable approach to her team members. She is well on her way to developing the kind of competencies expected in project team leaders.

Step 8: Separation

A final plenary session is held to facilitate closure, or what is often referred to as "re-entry." Plenary sessions tend to warn participants about the potential emotional upheaval of going back to their normal lives, and participants are often admonished not to make major life decisions for at least six months. Small-group as well as large-group activities can be designed to allow for sharing aloud or written reflections on the experience. One such activity can be to write down a short list of things to try when you return to your home or place of work. Another is to write down the key takeaways that were gained about oneself from the experience. Finally, it can also be helpful to think through how you will explain your experience to those who ask about it. Some NTL T-group experiences encourage participants to stay in touch, which is an option that many exercise in this new un-anonymous approach to T-group participation.

Key Lessons Learned

- Since group dynamics and development come with their own complexities, theoretical perspectives can be particularly useful for practitioners to gain a deeper understanding of the dynamics occurring in groups and subsequent selection of appropriate interventions.
- One of the most well-known small-group interventions is the T-group, which is an abbreviation for Training Group, that is experienced by an individual in isolation/away from his or her place of work and among strangers.
- The Tavistock Method at its core seeks to support participants in navigating unconscious individual-level processes that are manifested in a group context.
- Through experiential learning, such as interpersonal trainings, OD practitioners that serve as trainers, consultants, and practitioners of interpersonal training should aim to support participants towards outcomes that include: personal development, group development, group dynamics, emotional intelligence, self-awareness, and communication skills.

Discussion Questions

1. What are the advantages and disadvantages of adopting one or more of the nine theoretical perspectives on small groups before, during, or after an intervention?
2. Which small-group intervention would you deem the most important for an OD practitioner to enroll in as a participant to be more effective? Explain.
3. Compare and contrast the humanistic and psychodynamic approach to group-based interventions. Identify at least one situation where one approach would be more appropriate over another.

4. Are small-group interventions sustainable for long-term team effectiveness? Why or why not?

5. Under what circumstances would the Tavistock Method be more appropriate than a T-group?

6. Given the impact of COVID-19 on social interactions, what are some new ways of building the competencies expected from small-group interventions?

Tools

Table 7.3   T-Group Trainer Preparation and Break-Time Checklist

Directions: Read this checklist to increase your awareness of areas to give attention to as a T-group trainer before facilitations, during any breaks, and after the training conferences have ended as a baseline barometer to evaluate your effectives.

Have you...			Yes	No
			☒	☒
1	Worked on Your Self-Awareness	■ Examined your biases? ■ Gained an understanding of your triggers? ■ Prepared to manage your emotions and reactions? ■ Prepared to adhere to confidentiality during and after the training experience?	☐	☐
2	Set the Stage	■ Connected with your co-trainer before the session and discussed when/if either of you will intervene? ■ Determined seating that makes sense so that you can make clear visual contact with your co-trainer? ■ Reminded participants of what is common in the T-group (e.g., there is not an agenda, this is an opportunity to get feedback and to experiment)? ■ Reiterated concepts that were covered in the plenary session?	☐	☐
3	Listened Closely	■ Determined the type of conversations occurring? ■ Determined if a reminder about the "here-and-now" might be helpful now or later?	☐	☐

(Continued)

TABLE 7.3   T-Group Trainer Preparation and Break-Time Checklist (Con't)

4	Observed the Dynamic Developing	■ Considered if intervening with feedback on any of the dynamics will be helpful to the group? ■ Observed what norms are developing? What is recurring? ■ Recognized if there are any leaders emerging? ■ Noticed who is more vocal? and who is quieter? ■ Noticed where there is conflict? ■ Noticed where there are compromises? ■ Observed where participants are struggling? ■ Observed how emotions are being expressed? ■ Understood what the power dynamics are? ■ Understood how decisions are being made?	☐	☐
5	Provided Feedback on Helpful Interpersonal Behavior	■ Encouraged using "I" statements? ■ Provided examples in lieu of generalizations? ■ Encouraged expressing feelings, thoughts, and reactions? ■ Encouraged sharing feedback with others? ■ Encourage participating and not just observing? ■ Kindly admonished avoiding over-analyzing?	☐	☐
6	Carefully Supported Participants Experiencing Strong Emotional Reactions	■ Encouraged participants to breathe/take a beat? ■ Asked participants if they are OK? ■ Asked the participant what they need, or how you/the group can support them? ■ Allowed the participant to sit in silence if needed? ■ Provided a "hand on shoulder" (if close by) and/or tissue? ■ Encouraged all participants to journal about their experiences? Keep in mind that this is a very brief list of possible responses to emotional reactions. Training is needed to provide the right level of support without potentially harming the participant or observers in the group.	☐	☐

(Continued)

TABLE 7.3   T-Group Trainer Preparation and Break-Time Checklist (Con't)

7	Taken Care of Yourself During Every Break from the T-Group	■ Made time to decompress? ■ Connected with other T-group faculty for guidance on challenges you are experiencing in the group facilitation? ■ Recognized that you will experience both positive and negative emotions as a facilitator from the first session to the last?	☐	☐
8	Maintained Ethical Boundaries with Participants	■ Maintained a professional distance from participants? ■ Refrained from personal contact after the T-group has ended?	☐	☐

References

Abrams, Dominic, Michael A. Hogg, Steve, Hinkle, and Sabine, Otten. 2004. "The Social Identity Perspective on Small Groups." In *Theories of Small Groups: Interdisciplinary Perspectives*, edited by Marshall Scott, Poole and Andrea B. Hollingshead, 99–138. Thousand Oaks: SAGE Publishing.

Banet Anthony Jr. G., and Charla, Hayden. 1977. "A Tavistock Primer." In *The 1977 Annual Handbook for Group Practitioners*, edited by John E. Jones and J. William Pfeiffer, 155–167. La Jolla, California: University Associates, Inc.

Bennis, Warren G., and Herbert A. Shepard. 1956. "A Theory of Group Development." *Human Relations* 9(4 November): 415–437. doi: 10.1177/001872 675600900403

Bokeno, R. Michael, Christopher J. Rees, David L. Bradford, W. Warner Burke, Lisa K. Gundry, Kim-Chi Wakefield Trinh, and Michael A. Roberto. 2008. "Organization Development and Change in the 21st Century." In *21st Century Management: A Reference Handbook*, edited by Charles Wankel, 423–479. Thousand Oaks, CA: SAGE Publications. Gale eBooks.

Bradford, Leland P., Jack R. Gibb, and Kenneth D. Benne. 1964. "Two Educational Innovations." In *T-Group Theory & Laboratory Method: Innovation in Re-education*, edited by Leland P. Bradford, Jack R. Gibb, and Kenneth D. Benne, 1–14. New York: John Wiley & Sons, Inc.

Brown, Rupert, and Samuel, Pehrson. 2019. *Group Processes: Dynamics within and Between Groups* (3rd ed.) Hoboken, NJ: John Wiley & Sons.

Burke, Warner W. 2013. "Organizational Development." In *Encyclopedia of Management Theory*, edited by Eric H. Kessler, 542–547. Vol. 2. Thousand Oaks, CA: SAGE Reference. Gale eBooks.

Cooke, Alfred. 1999. "About the Work." In *Reading Book for Human Relations Training*, edited by Alfred L. Cooke, Michael Brazzel, Argentine Saunders Craig, and Barbara Greig, 3–4. Virginia: NTL Institute for Applied Behavioral Science.

"Encounter Group." 2001. In *The Gale Encyclopedia of Psychology* (2nd ed.), edited by Bonnie Strickland, 220–221. Detroit, MI: Gale. Gale eBooks.

"Experiential Learning." 2008. In *International Encyclopedia of Organizational Studies*, edited by Stewart R. Clegg and James R. Bailey, 487–492. Vol. 2. Thousand Oaks, CA: SAGE Publications. Gale eBooks.

French, Wendell, and Cecil, Bell. 1999. *Organization Development: Behavioral Science Interventions for Organization Improvement*. Upper Saddle River: Prentice-Hall.

Golembiewski, Robert T. 1999. "Perspective on the T Group and Laboratory Learning." In *Reading Book for Human Relations Training*, edited by Alfred L. Cooke, Michael Brazzel, Argentine Saunders Craig, and Barbara Greig, 185. Virginia: NTL Institute for Applied Behavioral Science.

"Group Dynamics." 2019. In *Encyclopedia of Management* (8th ed.), 494–499. Vol. 1. Farmington Hills, MI: Gale. Gale eBooks.

Marshak, Robert. 2009. *Organizational Change: Views from the Edge*. Bethel: The Lewin Center.

McLeod, Poppy Lauretta, and Richard, Kettner-Polley. 2005. "Psychodynamic Perspectives on Small Groups." In *Theories of Small Groups: Interdisciplinary Perspectives*, edited by Marshall Scott Poole and Andrea B. Hollingshead, 63–99. Thousand Oaks: SAGE Publishing.

Neumann, Jean E. 2005. "Kurt Lewin at The Tavistock Institute." *Educational Action Research* 13(1): 119–136.

Poole, Marshall Scott, and Andrea B. Hollingshead. 2004. *Theories of Small Groups: Interdisciplinary Perspectives*. Thousand Oaks: SAGE Publishing.

Poole, Marshall Scott, Andrea B. Hollingshead, Joseph E. McGrath, Richard, Moreland, and John, Rohrbaugh. 2004. "Interdisciplinary Perspectives on Small Groups." In *Theories of Small Groups: Interdisciplinary Perspectives*, edited by Marshall Scott Poole and Andrea B. Hollingshead, 1–20. Thousand Oaks: SAGE Publishing.

Scacchi, Walt. 2004. "Socio-Technical System Design." In *Berkshire Encyclopedia of Human-Computer Interaction*, edited by William Sims Bainbridge, 656–659. Vol. 2. Great Barrington, MA: Berkshire Publishing, 2004. Gale eBooks.

Schmitt, Bernd. 2012. "Bridging Theory and Practice." In *Cracking the Code: Leveraging Consumer Psychology to Drive Profitability*, edited by Steven S. Posavac, 3–20. Armonk, NY: M.E. Sharpe. Gale eBooks.

"Sensitivity Training." 2019. In *Encyclopedia of Management* (8th ed.), 970–974. Vol. 2. Farmington Hills, MI: Gale. Gale eBooks.

Sher, Mannie. 2004. "Group and Systems Theory." In *Encyclopedia of Leadership*, edited by George R. Goethals, Georgia J. Sorenson, and James MacGregor, Burns, 611–617. Vol. 2. Thousand Oaks, CA: SAGE Reference, Gale eBooks.

"Small Group." 2009. In *The SAGE Glossary of the Social and Behavioral Sciences*, edited by Larry E. Sullivan, 474. Thousand Oaks, CA: SAGE Reference, Gale eBooks.

Tuckman, Bruce W. 1965. "Developmental Sequence in Small Groups." *Psychological Bulletin* 63, 384–399.

"Types of Organization Changes/Interventions: Human Process Interventions." 2013. In *Gale Business Insights Handbook of Cultural Transformation*, edited by Miranda Herbert, Ferrara, 163–174. Detroit, MI: Gale Business Insights. Gale eBooks.

Whitman, Roy M. 1964. "Psychodynamic Principles Underlying T-group Processes." In *T-group Theory and Laboratory Method: Innovation in Re-education*, edited by Leland P. Bradford, Jack R. Gibb, and Kenneth D. Benne, 310–335. New York: John Wiley.

Chapter 8

Small-Group Intervention: Team-Building

Behnam Bakhshandeh

Contents

Overview

This chapter is about the elements of team-based change intervention in organizations, as the third level of intervention. Team-level interventions attempt to enhance and improve a group or team performance by building strong interpersonal relationships and interdependency among the team members. This effort could include problem-solving activities, designing outcomes and team strategies, setting goals as a team, or effectively communicating each team member's roles and responsibilities. As Rothwell William (2015) has mentioned, the possibilities that could arise because of team-building interventions are nearly unlimited. Furthermore, he mentioned, "Like a great orchestra or a medal-winning soccer team, individual participation is not nearly as effective as a team whose members demonstrate the commitment to the goal and each other" (92).

In this chapter, readers will become familiar with definitions, characteristics, and processes of team-building intervention, along with some useful information about how team members relate to their team and its structure. Chapter 8 covers the following areas:

- Some definitions related to team-building change intervention
- Key aspects, principles, and stages of team-building
- Team's place and relevancy to the organization's culture
- Team members' competencies
- Role of the team leader
- Effective practices to build and strengthen a team
- Team-building practices and exercises
- Step-by-step on how to conduct a team-based change intervention

It is not a mystery that individuals build organizations. These individuals form departments, groups, and teams within their organizations, regardless of their size and dimensions. There is no doubt among professionals that without motivated individuals and an effective team, no organizations would survive the fierce competition to hold on to their market shares and plans for a healthy expansion of their operations by effectively increasing their production and service. To accomplish such a worthy task, businesses and organizations go through many change interventions. Some are small as part of the day-to-day business processes, and some are larger, what we know as organization development (OD). This chapter will shed light on one of the most important aspects of OD and change intervention, that being the team and team-building, which has direct influence and will make or break any organization. To point out the importance of team-building and to have an effective team, Rothwell William (2015) gives us a clear definition of OD. "OD is usually known to mean bottom-up change effort focused on improving the interpersonal relationships of employees. OD usually involves internal or external consultants to facilitate the change process. These consultants apply the practical aspects of psychology, sociology, anthropology, and political science to organizational challenges" (9).

Definitions and Descriptions

To assure understanding and provide clarity of the main terminologies in this chapter, we are underlining several definitions and distinctions of this undertaking:

Team—Levi (2016) defined a team as a particular kind of group formed of individuals who work interdependently to achieve a common goal. Businesses and organizations use several distinct types of teams to work on a variety of objectives (2016).

Team-Building & Team Intervention—Team-building change intervention is one of the most popular types of OD change interventions among organizations. Professional OD practitioners and consultants consider the interpersonal relationships among team members to be a vital element of a team-building process that needs close attention, given that team cohesiveness and closeness are critical to the success of this level of change (Rothwell William 2015; Rothwell William et al. 2016).

The 4Cs of Team-Building

There are four key aspects in team-building that need to be addressed and make sure they are handled, and all their relevant elements are in place to ensure effectiveness and strength of the team-building undertaking. They are the team context, the team composition, the team competencies, and the change management skills of the team (Dyer Gibb et al. 2013; Rothwell William et al. 2016). These four aspects are also known as the 4Cs of team-building and include context, composition, competencies, and change. These 4Cs determine the quality of team performance (Dyer Gibb et al. 2013; Rothwell William et al. 2016).

Team Context

The team context element of team-building is about establishing the situations and conditions that team members would. The team context is about organizational factors, such as organization culture, structure, level of leadership, operational systems, and processes that support teams. The use of this factor and leadership attention to the quality of these factors directly determines the level of an organization's support for teams, its team members, and the team's desire to grow and be productive (Dyer Gibb et al. 2013; Rothwell William 2015; Rothwell William et al. 2016). According to Dyer Gibb et al. (2013) effective and high-performance teams manage their team context by:

- Forming clear, precise, measurable, and attainable goals for their team performance.
- Emphasizing critical elements of cohesive teamwork as the foundation.
- Creating an incentive reward system that would praise the team accomplishment.

- Reducing barriers to teamwork that might be generated by restrictive organization rules.
- Creating an organizational culture that encourages and promotes teamwork.
- Designing and establishing an information system that supports team's decision-making.
- Instituting human resource processes and procedures that support team development.

Team Composition

The team composition is comprised of the team members, their attitudes, behaviors, and how well they conduct their team tasks while working together. Team composition is consistent with team size; team members' skills, abilities, and work experience; and team members' motivations (Dyer Gibb et al. 2013; Rothwell William et al. 2016). As Dyer et al. described the importance of team composition, "You have to have the 'right people on the bus' to make things happen as a team and achieve top performance" (15). To accomplish such tasks for establishing an effective team composition, the organization's management should conduct the following questions as a form of inquiry to having the right people on their teams (Dyer Gibb et al. 2013):

- Do the team members have the necessary technical skills needed for the team task or job?
- Do the team members have the essential interpersonal skills and understand effective communication to collaborate with the rest of the team?
- Are the team members displaying a positive attitude, motivation, and commitment to the team's goals?
- Are the team members showing interest in effectively conducting their jobs and tasks?
- Do we have the right size team for achieving our goals?

Team Competencies

The team competencies concern the team and its members' ability and competence to deal with a variety of issues and conflicts and how they resolve the problems, make decisions, and deal with issues in front of them. Team competencies are about the team's ability to collectively work together to accomplish their team's goals and to keep the team members motivated and focused on their desired outcomes (Dyer Gibb et al. 2013; Rothwell William et al. 2016). According to Donahue (2018), the term *competency* has become something like a buzzword people are throwing around as something pointless. On the contrary, in today's OD efforts, competency-based development, and education are regarded as the pathway to the future of education/learning, team-building, and OD. "Competencies are the measurable and observable knowledge, skills, attitudes, and behaviors (KSABs) critical to successful job performance" (21).

The following are examples of the applicability of the Teamwork and Cooperation competency pertaining to the team leader's KSABs (Donahue 2018):

- Establishing team structure, members' responsibilities, and clarifying members' tasks.
- Creating a team's purpose that is linked to the organization's vision, mission, and values.
- Facilitating team development activities and processes.
- Acting as a team member and participating in team-building processes and activities.
- Implementing an environment of cooperation, collaboration, and teamwork.
- Establishing and encouraging team members' accountabilities linked to team goals.
- Promoting critical thinking and creativity among team members.
- Establishing individual and team rewards and recognitions.
- Creating a healthy environment of open and honest communication.
- Inventing, and developing a problem-solving culture.

Team Change Management

Teams who are performing at high-performance levels know this essential fact; they must be open to change and adapt to new environmental conditions caused by the shifting markets, fluctuating economy, and changing laws and regulations to stay effective and be relevant in their market. These changes include but are not limited to their team context, composition, and competencies (Dyer Gibb et al. 2013; Rothwell William et al. 2016). "A team that is able to monitor its performance and understands its strengths and weaknesses can generate insights needed to develop a plan of action to continuously improve" (Dyer Gibb et al. 2013, 18). In this regard, an effective and productive team has established its capacity to change by (2013):

- Creating team-building methods and procedures that promote systematic evaluation of the effectiveness of their team context, composition, and competencies.
- Promoting the fundamental philosophy of "change is necessary and good" as part of their organization culture among their teams.

Stages of Team-Building

Like any other development and building projects, team-building requires development stages. According to Rothwell William (2015), there are six main stages in a team-building program which are designed based on the OD main intervention models, the Action Research Model (ARM). We will distinguish and explain all the following stages in more detail (as part of the eight stages of team-building intervention) in our case study, the *Business Case Example* of this chapter:

1. ***Preparation.*** Setting up the approach, having a contract/agreement, and explaining the process.
2. ***Set-Up and Data Collection.*** Set up for observations, document reviews, and one-on-one and focus group interviews.
3. ***Data Analysis.*** Collect, organize, and analyze the data to locate problems and come with solutions to the problems using interviews for collecting resolutions.
4. ***Feedback.*** Provide feedback to the management/owners about your data analyses and findings.
5. ***Action Planning.*** Manage and assist the team to come with their action plan for resolving their team issues.
6. ***Follow-Up.*** Continue to follow up on the implementation of the team's action plan and provide needed coaching or mentoring.

Key Principles of Team-Building

Any organization or group of people who are in the process of placing individuals in a team needs to follow some essential standards and clearly generated team-building principles (Levi 2016). In a professional domain, a team is considered being an organization by itself which depends on and is governed by the notion of interdependency. A team can only be distinguished as such when the individuals who form it are willing to work with each other to complete a set of tasks and achieve some agreed upon goals or mutual outcomes. In this section, we are looking at the necessary conditions for building a real team that could work in synchronicity. The prerequisite elements need to be in place before the team-building process and the basic components of team-building.

Conditions for Building a Real Team

Hackman Richard (2002) offered the following five distinctive classifications as basic conditions which must be present if a group considers being a *team*:

1. **Real Existence.** Teams cannot occur just in name only; real teams are a group of individuals who truly work together to accomplish common goals or objectives, not just call themselves a team member.
2. **A Compelling Direction.** Team members need to comprehend and support a collective purpose.
3. **Enabling Structures.** Teams include the appropriate numbers and types of individuals who are focused on the appropriate tasks, governed by the correct norms and collective values.
4. **A Supportive Organization.** Every structure, movement, process, action, and system of a real team must accelerate success.
5. **Expert Coaching.** A real team engages with knowledgeable leadership as an essential element of its success.

The Prerequisites for Team-Building

These important principles can help design and build a stable and strong team that is positioned for fulfilling a specific business and organizational need and requirement, compared to a team that works with uncertainty about its direction and purpose, which would be an indication of the team's weakness (Levi 2016; Bakhshandeh 2008; Bakhshandeh 2001):

- **Purpose.** The process of team-building starts from having a clear and precise team purpose that is accepted and supported by all the team members and the organization.

- **Specificity.** From the beginning, the functions of each team member should be clarified. This process will guide the team members both individually and as a whole through a productive and effective process of identifying specific issues and its related problem-solving actions.
- **Competencies.** It is essential to establish a set of competencies as the minimum requirement to be part of the team (based on the purpose and main objectives of the organization) and locate the individuals with such competencies to fill the team.
- **Guidelines.** In the beginning, the team should follow a set of guidelines which is formulated for the team-building process and assists in restructuring the team in the future.
- **Authority.** The level of the team's management and the hierarchy of authority over the team should be established at the beginning of the team-building process and approved by the organization's senior management.
- **Category.** Establishing the category in which the team will fit in the organization is important to the productivity of the team. The team needs to know if they work independently or in collaboration with other existing groups or teams.
- **Structure.** Any successful team needs a clear structure for the chain of command, channels of communication, and the hierarchy of leadership.

Organization and Team Culture and Norms

Organizational culture has been defined in different ways. Most authorities on the subject, however, would agree that "Culture consists of the behavioral patterns, concepts, values, ceremonies, and rituals that take in an organization.… Cultural values provide employees with a sense of what they ought to be doing, and how they should behave to be consistent with organizational goals. Culture represents the emotional, intangible feeling which is a part of the organization" (Daft 1983, 482). Organizational culture manifests itself in only one way and definition but in at least three different levels:

First Level. The first level of organizational culture is more than displaying and marketing the organization's slogans, logo, and vision statement. It also involves the physical aspects of the organization, and ultimately how employees are acting and behaving around the organization's executive and senior managers (Rothwell William & Sredl, 2014a).

Second Level. The second level of organizational culture is the organization's fundamental vision, mission, values, principles, and beliefs. "Experienced employees can usually describe those values and beliefs when prompted. The common patterns of employee responses to these items can provide clues to the second, deeper layer of organizational culture" (2014a, 306).

Third Level. The third level, which goes the deepest, is manifested by rituals, stories, vocabulary, and forms of dialogue. To have a better understanding of this level, we shall contemplate the common types of social activities in the organization and what these events signify, how the employees are explaining, describing, and telling stories about the organization's past events, or the way they are talking about and telling stories about the executives and senior managers or the ways they tell stories about all promotions/demotions, hiring/firing, and other potential issues with psychological and emotional charges (2014a).

The team's cultures are not separate from the collective culture of the organization and the totality of their influences and impacts on the nature of the team's operation and activities. One of the effective ways to recognize an organization or a team culture is to conduct what WLP professionals call a culture audit. This audit's results are compiled after an in-depth review of the current and existing culture, and comparison to a preferred or desired culture has been completed (2014a).

Team Norms. Team norms are referred to as a set of forces or rules that would shape people's behavior while they are participating in their team at the workplace, such as

- ***Performance norms,*** which inform or tell us how hard you should work at your position.
- ***Appearance norms,*** which inform or tell us how you should look at work.
- ***Social arrangement norms,*** which inform or tell us how you should act in your team.
- ***Resource allocation norms,*** which inform or tell us how and when the team's or organization's resources should be used.

We shall note that some of these norms are clear and obvious to everyone, and some are undeclared and just implied. All of the above team's norms combine and mix to form the team's culture (Levi 2016).

Role of the Team Leader as the Change Agent

As we all know, it doesn't matter if analyzing the performance problems is done perfectly, and the OD practitioner has selected a well-designed and relevant performance-improvement intervention for empowering the workforce to be productive. Change interventions will not work miracles if they do not fulfill the organization's desired outcome for the employees or a team's performance and behavior objectives. This phenomenon is one of the most disempowering reasons for change intervention failings: lack of follow-up and managing the change.

Similarly, organizational and team-change interventions can build a work environment where the appropriate individuals are chosen at the appropriate times and provided the appropriate tools and equipment while rewarded within a boundary of the rewarding system corresponding to their personal and team efforts. This vital approach and the essential role will be on the shoulders of a team leader and a change agent (2014b). A series of skills and competencies exists which would develop or enhance the team leaders' abilities to lead and facilitate their teams, especially in a diverse team environment:

- *Trust Building.* Building trust between the team leader and team members is one of the most important aspects of working with and leading any team. Regardless of any physical or virtual environment, a team's workability and productivity is built over trust. Trust-building can be achieved by team leaders promoting and displaying an example of being authentic with team members, being respectfully straight and sharing their strengths, weaknesses, and personal and professional experiences with one another (Kolb 2011; Bakhshandeh 2008; Bakhshandeh 2001).
- *Patience and Compassion.* We must remember that not all the team members are working with the same method and speed, especially when we are dealing with team members with different language, culture, or customs backgrounds. These differences are more apparent in virtual teams. Being patient, having compassion and empathy, and understanding others' differences is essential to the process of team-building and leading a team effectively (2011; 2008; 2001).
- *Active Listening.* The ability to listen without judgment, to be aware of one's bias, to stay away from interpretation and not have

attachments to the results, in addition to being patient and having compassion is the foundation of strong competency in active listening. Effective team leaders listen to communication like this is the most useful piece of information they are receiving, by listening while providing continuous attention to the speakers without interruption, and by allowing the speakers to complete their sentences (2011; 2008; 2001).

- **Time Management.** As a team leader, it is important to have an open mind about the process, the time to be allotted, and the goals to be achieved from this project. An effective team leader has a good understanding of the team members' skills, abilities, and time management. This practice can be achieved effectively by also being aware of all national and international holidays and events that might impact the project's timeline and by marking team members' vacations on the team calendar in advance to avoid gaps in the team's productivity (2011; 2008; 2001).

- **Express Empowerment and Promotion.** The team leader should make sure to be aware and acknowledge team members for their hard work and efforts with a simple "job well done" expression. Make sure to always use "please" and "thank you" in any written and oral communication; these are tax-free assets to be used without any hesitation or cost (2011; 2008; 2001)!

- **Sharing the Success.** A skillful team leader will make sure to include all their team members in the team's success and share the spotlight with them by always expressing the team effort and partnership in the team's accomplishments (2011; 2008; 2001).

Team-Building Exercises for Maintaining Team Effectiveness

Given the importance of building a strong and effective team and maintaining team members' cohesive relations, there are so many team-building practices available on the internet or from many different coaches and consultants, depending on the nature and design of teams. The following two simple but effective exercises are what this author has designed and used to bring team members to gather and create a long-lasting relationship among them.

Empowering Team Members to Invent Opportunities to Resolve Conflicts

Let's look at how to come up with new practices to empower teams for creating new opportunities for relatedness, cohesiveness, and collaboration. Let's look at the example of team-building. How could we empower our team-building process without any despair and resignation? (see Figure 8.1).

Get together with your team, and start brainstorming about all the opportunities your team can invent for what you all are doing about your responsibilities, your processes, and your accountabilities. Look at what is in the way of being more cohesive, having stronger bonds, effective communication, and every other aspect of the team you all desire. You and your team could plan to do this exercise on a monthly or quarterly basis and modify your new actions as needed.

Practices for Inventing New Opportunities

New practices we are inventing	Old practices we are eliminating
Opportunity #1:	
1. _____	1. _____
2. _____	2. _____
Opportunity #2:	
1. _____	1. _____
2. _____	2. _____
Opportunity #3:	
1. _____	1. _____
2. _____	2. _____
Opportunity #4:	
1. _____	1. _____
2. _____	2. _____
Opportunity #5:	
1. _____	1. _____
2. _____	2. _____

Figure 8.1 Practices for New Opportunities. Adopted from Bakhshandeh (2009, 350). *Conspiracy for Greatness; Mastery of Love Within.* **San Diego, CA: Primeco Education, Inc.**

Get your team's alignment with the top five opportunities (go through the process of elimination via democratic voting process), then write the top five opportunities, as shown in Figure 8.1, from #1 to #5 opportunities (on the left side). Then, start writing under the left column first, *"New practices we are inventing."* For each opportunity, come up with at least two NEW practices that you and your teammates have never done before or have not practiced for a very long time, maybe due to resignation and despair (Bakhshandeh 2009)!

Here is an example:

New practices we are inventing
Opportunity #1: Active Listening

    1. *I will not interrupt the speaker.*
    2. *I will ask if they would like to say more.*

These practices could be any opportunities you and your team might choose, but you have to remember this important fact; it doesn't need to be something so complicated! "Simple things make the biggest differences in the quality of our lives, the quality of our life experiences, and the quality of our relationships with others" (Bakhshandeh 2009, 347). After you and your team do that, go to the right column and work on the other side, the *"Old practices we are eliminating"* because removing what is not working is as essential as inventing new practices. These two sides will work hand in hand by empowering you to have the experience and the presence of your opportunities in your personal and professional aspects of your life (Bakhshandeh 2009).

Here is an example:

Old practices we are eliminating
Opportunity #1: Active Listening

    1. *Stop acting like I am so busy.*
    2. *Stop saying, "It was not like that."*

Place the two areas side by side in the format, as shown in the following example. After completing this exercise individually or as a team, you can see what needs to get practiced and what needs to be eliminated so that opportunities can be powerfully implemented. By doing this exercise, you are also building some team inspiration, team communication, and team bonding based on mutual respect and collaboration.

The final result of this exercise on opportunity #1 will look something like this:

<u>*New practices we are inventing*</u>
Old practices we are eliminating

  1. *I will not interrupt the speaker.*
  2. *I will ask if they like to say more.*

Opportunity #1: Active Listening

  1. *Stop acting like I am so busy.*
  2. *Stop saying, "It was not like that."*

Weekly Team-Building Discipline Rating

This exercise is designed to develop team members on a set of disciplines that has a positive influence on their day-to-day work and productivity and re-lationships with their team on an individual and team level. This process will be managed by team leaders or supervisors. It will be conducted on individuals who have some difficulty displaying discipline on their individual accountabilities and also not able to maintain the relationship with their team (Bakhshandeh 2008).

To start, the team leaders or supervisors need to set up the structure for the exercise by indicating to the individuals that there is nothing wrong with their performance, and this exercise is designed to develop their skills and enhance their team involvement and productivity. Explain the structure to complete the activity as follows (using Figure 8.2):

- The process will take at least three months.
- We need some track records and average ratings to assess the areas in need of development.
- You will submit this weekly rating to your team leader or supervisor every Monday morning.
- You are the judge and jury in this game; nobody else is rating you but you.
- The rating skill is from 1 (the lowest) to 10 (the highest) for the presence and practice of each discipline at work during the previous week.
- Every Monday morning before starting your work, you will rate your own discipline for the last week.
- Every Monday, you will total the raw numbers, divide them by 10, and write the weekly average.

Weekly Team-Building Discipline Rating						
Date:		Month:				
Participant:		Team:				
Team Leader:		Department:				
	Week Number	1	2	3	4	5
	Week Starting Date (Mondays)					
#	*Disciplines*	*Ratings from 1(lowest) to 10 (highest)*				
	As an Individua					
1	Apply & practice critical thinking method					
2	Display interpersonal skills					
3	Practice precise and clear communication					
4	Display professional behavior & attitude					
5	Show responsibilityfor his/her job & tasks					
	As a Team Member					
6	Use the problem-solving approach					
7	Maintaining relationships with teammates					
8	Learn from their team's success & failures					
9	Monitoring and practicing what works					
10	Communicate with other team members					
	Weekly Total					
	Weekly Average					
	Monthly Average					
Two actions for this week that would bring up my two lowest team-building disciplines' rating by at least 2 points next week:						
Action 1:						
Action 2:						

Figure 8.2 Weekly Team-Building Discipline. Adopted from: Bakhshandeh, Behnam. 2008 & Bakhshandeh, Behnam. 2001. *What Is Making a Great Team?* Unpublished workshop on team-building. San Diego, CA: Primeco Education, Inc.

- Every Monday, you will come up with two actions for the following week that will bring up your two lowest team-building discipline ratings by at least 2 points.
- By the end of each month, you will average the monthly rate and turn it in to your team leader or supervisor.
- Start the same process for at least another two months unless your team leader or supervisor wants you to continue this rating exercise for additional months.

- Your supervisor or team leader will manage the completion of your weekly action plan.
- With the supervisor's facilitation, every month the whole team will get together to share their experiences of this practice and share their action plans and results with the rest of their team.
- (Bakhshandeh 2008)

Business Case Example

In this section, we will present an example of a case study that will highlight the third level of OD intervention, the team-based change efforts, based on a need for the improvement of teams or groups, following the standard process of an OD intervention.

An OD intervention in general with a team-based change intervention in particular is one of the best investments an organization can provide for its stakeholders and their workforce. When teams work cohesively and in sync, naturally, the level of production, collaboration, and communication will increase. This, in turn, will cause the turnover and dissatisfaction among the workforce to decrease. This balance of events will directly provide higher profitability for the organizations, which will have a direct positive influence on the quality of the workplace and result in increased compensation and benefits for their employees.

Concerning the importance of the team-based approach and building strong and cohesive teams, Bersin et al. (2019), based on one of the research questions in the Global Human Capital Trends 2019 survey, reported that "Shifting to a team-based model improves performance." Moreover, 53% of participants reported significant improvements in organization performance, while 21% reported minimal improvement in the organization's performance, and 6% reported no change in the organization's performance. The 2019 survey showed the interest and support for transition from hierarchical to a team-operation format are high enough to increase the interest among the organization's C-Suite for preparing their organizations for the future of this team approach (Bersin et al. 2019).

Background

BMB is a successful and financially secure organization, operating in their industry, providing superior products since the late 1950s. BMB currently operates from several facilities and a workforce of over 400 employees, working together in the team-based format, including teams of management, administration, production, maintenance, sales, quality control, and shipping.

Step 1: Entry

The organization faced substantial turnovers and absenteeism, a lack of effective communication channels among their departments, the absence of teamwork and collaboration, and an overall high level of job/work dissatisfaction among their workforce. In 2017, BMB management expressed their desire to discover their organizational problems, find solutions, and implement action plans to resolve the issues they were facing. As their hired OD consultant, we planned a "Change Intervention Project" for BMB based on providing a sustainable team-building process to strengthen their team's productivity and collaboration, which would indirectly influence their workforce turnover.

Preparation Meeting

We were introduced to the organization based on work we had done with other organizations and one of the executive's knowledge of our consulting practices with companies having similar organizational issues. We had our initiation and preparation meetings with the key executives and senior managers and explained who we are, how we conduct our consulting and training programs, our history, and mainly how we hold a team-based intervention. We answered their concerns and questions; we talked about the details of our contract. We also took the time to explain *OD Intervention* and the *Action Research Model (ARM)* as the primary process of our team-building change intervention.

We explained the primary plan of action for conducting an effective OD change intervention and implementing the nuts and bolts of team-based intervention in two phases:

- **Phase 1:** Diagnosis and assessment of the situation to understand a) the reality of team conditions and impact of it on the organization and b) severity of issues they are facing. After completing this phase, the team themselves will come up with a plan of action, and with the assistance of the OD practitioner as the facilitator, they will decide what they want to do next in regard to setting up training and development workshops and how they will build up their team again.

- ***Phase 2:*** This phase is about conducting the team-building workshops and seminars to provide the training and development aspects of how to effectively work together as a team, and possibly come up with new processes, procedures, and structures that would support the team and benefit not only the organization but also the employees.

Step 2: Start-Up

During this step, we conducted several meetings with senior managers, junior managers, supervisors, and team leaders to provide information about what we planned to do and help them understand the reasons for the potential team-building process and its benefits to the organizations as well as the employees. We invited them all to express their knowledge of team-building and welcomed any input and perspectives for how they think the team-building program should progress (Rothwell William et al. 2016). This was a good relationship-building effort with all the management team. We made sure everyone understood we were coming in as a partner, not as an adversary. This way, we put their minds at ease and minimized their resistance to change, at least at this stage of the intervention. We listened to their views of what they thought or assumed to be the problems in their team's functioning.

We explained what would happen next during the 1) team-building diagnosis and assessment, and 2) team-building action planning and implementation, including interviews, data-collecting process, and analysis of the data. We described our role as the a) coach, and b) facilitator, and what we expected from them and their workforce as participants and our partners in implementing the successful intervention (2016). We asked the company's president and CEO to clarify the company's need for this team-based intervention and team-building and express his unconditional support and backing for this undertaking. His display of support and alignment caused deeper alignment from the rest of the management and leadership body.

To create a deeper team environment, we invited all managers and leadership bodies who were present at this meeting to go through a short brainstorming process and design a purpose statement for their team-based change intervention project. They came up with the following statement: "To give BMB access to empowering ways to view their current organizational breakdowns in the area of staff turnover, employee satisfaction, and team-building; and to provide an opening for BMB to create potential strategies and action plans for their success in areas as mentioned above." Having a common purpose was a great way to have a relationship with the management team based on partnership and a common goal.

Step 3: Data Gathering, Diagnosis, and Analysis of Problems

This step is about gathering information and data about what teams are dealing with. With the guidance of the OD practitioner as the change agent, team members will observe the results of the data gathering process and reflect on them by facing the actual issues in their team. This is the beginning of a team working together for a common goal and building stronger interpersonal relationships (Rothwell William et al. 2016). Furthermore, Cummings and Worley (2015) underlined the importance of the collaboration of organization members and its essential role in the success of the change effort and data-collecting activities as critical elements in action research model success. Rothwell William (2015) underlined data gathering to be one of the main aspects of OD as the process of collecting data as the foundation of planning a change intervention.

Diagnosis and Data Analysis Models

We used the Open System as the platform for diagnosing model for assessment and analysis of BMB during this project. According to Harrison (2005), there are many diagnosis models which treat organizations as an Open System (OS). These would assist OD practitioners in selecting topics for their diagnosis of organizations while developing criteria for assessing such an organization's effectiveness, collecting data from the organizations, conducting analysis and providing feedback. By the end of this cycle, practitioners can pinpoint the approach that will help their clients solve their organization's issues and improve effectiveness. Yoon (2017) explained how open systems work in a cycle of examining an organization's input, transformation, and output, "The output becomes the input for the next cycle and transformation occurs in an organization to produce a new output while interacting with the environment" (32). Yoon (2017) explained the basic features of the open system model and the five main key features in order of occurrence: 1) Environment, 2) Input, 3) Transformation, 4) Output and 5) Feedback and Congruence. For the purpose of diagnosing the organization issues, and using the OS as the

central platform, we used the following three diagnosis models:
a) Individual and Group Behavior Model, b) The Great Place to Work
model and c) the SWOT Analysis.

The first diagnosis model we used was the *Individual and Group Behavior
Model* which was originally designed by Michael I. Harrison in 1985, and
through the years has been modified and used on many editions of Harrison's
work. According to Harrison (2005) this model's elements include the
following:

- **Inputs.** Human capital (individuals, groups, teams, workers), material,
  financial, intangible, etc.
- **Outputs.** Goods, services, products, employees' (individuals, groups,
  teams, workers) well-being and satisfaction.
- **Organizational behaviors and processes.** Practices the organization
  has adopted to create outputs.
- **Technology.** Equipment, tools, and systems that would transform inputs
  into outputs.
- **Environment.** Close environment, such as organization's competitors,
  customers, partners, suppliers, and investors. Remote environments, such
  as the political system, the economy, social structures, and technological
  advances
- **Culture.** Society's (including local and organization's culture) shared
  values, norms, beliefs, and behaviors.
  (Harrison 2005; Rothwell William et al. 2016).

The second model we have used was the *Great Place to Work Model* to design
the interview protocol for the one-on-one and focus group interviews.
According to Burchell and Robin (2011), the six elements of a great place to
work are as follows:

- **Trust:** Trust involves credibility, respect, and fairness.
- **Credibility:** Credibility is achieved through open communication,
  competence, and integrity.
- **Respect:** Respect is reached through support, collaboration, and caring.
- **Fairness:** Fairness is achieved through equity, impartiality, and justice.
- **Pride:** Pride can be found in personal achievement, team performance,
  and the company's status in the community.
- **Camaraderie:** Camaraderie is built by facilitating intimacy, hospitality,
  and a sense of community in the workplace.

The third diagnosis model we used was *SWOT Analysis*. SWOT is a method of data collecting based on the influence of the internal and external environment in the organization. The origins of the SWOT analysis technique are credited to Albert Humphrey, who led a research project at Stanford University in the 1960s and 1970s using data from many top companies. The goal was to identify why corporate planning failed.

The research results identified four critical aspects of an organization or a team to explore:

- **Strengths.** Positive tangible and intangible attributes internal to an organization. They are within the organization's control.
- **Weaknesses.** Factors that are within an organization's control that reduce from its ability to attain the desired goal. Which areas might the organization improve?
- **Opportunities.** External or internal attractive factors that represent the reason for an organization to exist and develop.
- **Threats.** External or internal factors, which could place the organization's mission or operation at risk.
  ("SWOT Analysis" 2009)

After collecting the data and analyzing it based on the SWOT model, we asked all interview participants to brainstorm among themselves to express their perspectives and viewpoints based on their professional career and the time they participated with BMB to use the four main strategies of SWOT analysis findings to point out the following:

- **SO;** How to use strengths to take advantage of current and future opportunities.
- **ST;** How to use strengths to avoid current and future threats.
- **WO;** How to overcome weaknesses by using current and future opportunities.
- **WT;** How to minimize weaknesses to avoid current and future threats.

Data-Collecting Methods

We started the data-gathering process by implementing four data-collecting methods: Historical Document Review, Observation, One-On-One Interviews, and Focus Group Interviews. With the help of the Human Resources manager, we reviewed employment histories such as exit interviews, termination letters, disciplinary actions, and some other employment issues that might have something to do with employees' resentment toward managers, supervisors or teammates. This review gave us some perspective on the organization's culture and inner relationships.

With the cooperation of the management team, we scheduled to be present on several team meetings, including senior management monthly executive reports, bi-weekly production meetings with junior managers, and weekly meetings with supervisors and their team. Besides the team meeting, we spent four weeks just observing the workforce's production process while paying attention to their relationships with their supervisors and with each other. Their behaviors, their attitudes, and their responses during hard deadlines or their conflict with one another. We conducted six one-on-one interviews with the top senior managers, such as the CEO, VP, CFO, HR Director, and the Plant Manager. We tried to collect data from all the top managers to make sure we included their perspectives on the potential issues.

We also conducted five Focus Group interviews with six people in each group. This way, we covered almost all tiers of the workforce who were involved with the general floor production process.

According to McClelland (1994) concerning focus groups, on the one hand, group dynamics would be useful for gathering information and data about some specific issues. This approach can collect a wide range of insights and perspectives from group participation. At the same time, group dynamics can be harmful and ineffective to the purpose of data gathering if it is not done correctly. Specifically, this can occur when the influence of some participants' opinions causes other participants to take sides and form bias from their perspective (2). That being said, we, as the OD practitioners, have to be very careful about the design of the questions so they do not persuade participants' perceptions in either direction.

Step 4: Giving Feedback on Problems

This step is about the OD practitioner working with the team to give all interviewees (one-on-one or focus groups) feedback on the analysis of problems. It will be beneficial for the company to encourage all team members to provide their feedback to each other about the issues which were uncovered during the last step, the "Data Gathering and Analysis of Problems" process. The final outcome of this step is to get in alignment and agreement on which team problems to undertake now and which ones to solve in the long run (Rothwell William et al., 2016).

We gave our feedback report in two separate sessions, once for executives and senior managers, and again for managers, supervisors, and members of focus groups. After reviewing the entire process of collecting data, listening to individuals' concerns (most being symptoms of a problem), paying attention to the source of issues/problems, and reflecting on the future of BMB and its well-being, the team came up with 32 issues they wanted to address and resolve. However, we found the following to be the sources of the organization's issues:

- No vision, clear path, business planning/strategies or long-term planning.
- Uncertainty due to lack of succession planning, open communication, and planning the transition period.
- No employment accountability/growth structure and absence of technical and professional training and development.

These issues have caused the following among BMB's workforce:

- Having uncertainty about their future.
- Just surviving the day or an issue and "passing the buck."
- Being resigned about what is next for them.
- Not being motivated to build something but just going through the motions.
- Not taking ownership of the company.
- Not taking any responsibility on issues or being accountable for resolutions.
- Expressing their frustrations on others.
- Not feeling their efforts being appreciated.
- Developing an "us" versus "them" attitude.

We encouraged them to categorize the level of urgency and take on only three pressing issues during this team-based intervention change project and tackle the remaining issues quarterly or over semi-annual periods.

Step 5: Data Gathering and Alignment on Solutions

We went through the same set of one-on-one and focus group interviews with a different intention, to collect information about what the team thinks about solutions for these uncovered issues/problems. Each individual and focus group expressed their views of solutions for the list of issues.

We collected and organized the solution list and prepared a feedback report on solutions.

Step 6: Giving Feedback on Solutions

Once again, due to work responsibilities and production schedule, we gave our feedback report on solutions in two sessions, once for executives and senior managers, and once for managers, supervisors, and members of focus groups. Through the voting and elimination process, they got aligned with solutions for all 32 issues, including their solutions for the top three issues they wanted to attack during this team-based change intervention project.

Step 7: Action Planning

Action planning is illustrated and defines how the OD practitioner or change agent will work with the organization's senior management or decision-makers and stakeholders to create a plan of action on how to implement the desired changes and solutions or selected issues (Rothwell William et al. 2016). Simply said, an action plan represents the project team's alignment on what to do to implement the change. They are the plans for implementing the change effort and setting the team-building objectives for improvement. This plan needs to be designed in detail and with clear and precise activities, with the alignment of team members who are responsible for executing the action plan. After several drafts of action planning, reviewing with the HR department, other department managers, and team supervisors, we came with a comprehensive action plan designed to support the solutions for resolving the selected issues. As the final act, we obtained BMB's executive's stamp of approval for executing the action plan.

Step 8: Team-Building Intervention

The BMB production structure (several plants, each with two production shifts) was a planning challenge by itself. We had to spend many hours with the HR department to plan our workshops and training sessions to coincide with the production schedule to avoid interruption of the company's regular production. With the help of HR and department managers, we scheduled a team introduction at the beginning and then divided the teams into three groups. They participated in a series of workshops and developmental trainings on three afternoons a week (Mondays, Wednesdays, and Fridays) for four weeks and concluded a final session with the whole team at the end.

For team trainings to be conducted effectively, it is important for us to understand how teams are functioning and how they are learning. In most scenarios, team learning is similar to a social process when members develop learning, share what they have learned, while mixing their knowledge and shared experiences (Mosson et al. 2019). Through a process of observation and focus group interviews, we learn about how these teams work together, the level of their team relationships, and how they relate to one another. These aspects of team relationships influence how we conduct our intervention process.

Like any other intervention project, team-building also has stages for developing teams through workshops, seminars, exercises, and team coaching. According to Rothwell William et al. (2016), the following stages are mainly adopted from and based on one of the main OD intervention models, the Action Research Model (ARM), with some substages for supporting the readers to understand what they need to implement during this intervention.

Please note that the following structure and table is a representation of stages and steps for conducting the actual small-group intervention process, while all the information and details of related steps are mentioned above: Step 1: Entry; Step 2: Set-Up; Step 3: Assessment and Feedback; and Step 4: Action Planning. This step-by-step approach could be easily modified for another customer's team intervention plan as well as an organization intervention.

Table 8.1 represents step-by-step actions needed for conducting an actual small-group and team-change intervention and team-building process during the whole-intervention undertaking. This is a very effective way to support OD practitioners on their approach to the team-building intervention.

As a result of our meetings, workshops, seminars, and teamwork, the BMB team resolved many team issues they were facing for several years, and the new environment of team cohesiveness, empathy, and compassion for others and a common commitment to workability and accountability was created. The following is the Communication Charter, which was created as a result of team commitment to effective communication and breakthrough in managing communication channels.

Table 8.1 Step-by-Step Conducting the Actual Small-Group and Team-Change Intervention Process

Phase 1: Diagnosis and Assessments	
This phase is about entry and getting with the organization and their teams to set up for the process of data collecting, data analysis, and providing the feedback report.	
a. Introduction & Set Up	
1. Introduction by the organization	▪ HR department to send a general announcement via email or an internal memo, introducing the OD practitioner and the fact that you will see him/her conducting the data-collecting process.
2. Introduction by the Sponsor or the Client	▪ CEO or President to send an email or internal memo express his/her support of the process and what the OD practitioner is doing.
b. Diagnosis & Assessment Models	
1. **Open System** (OS as the primary model). Looking into and reviewing what would influence teams' working environment, their input & outputs regarding their productivity, and how they are communicating, using elements of:	▪ Technology ▪ Structure ▪ Culture ▪ Members ▪ Processes
2. **Individual and Group Behavior.** Reviewing team members' individual behavior and also their behavior in their team's environment about productivity and collaboration regarding:	▪ Inputs ▪ Outputs ▪ Organizational behavior & processes ▪ Technology ▪ Environment ▪ Culture
3. **Great Place to Work.** Concerning the team's cohesiveness and the degree of strength in their relationship and working together, collect information regarding elements of:	▪ Trust ▪ Credibility ▪ Respect ▪ Fairness ▪ Pride ▪ Camaraderie
4. **SWOT Analysis.** To understand and recognize the influences of internal and external environment on team operations and procedures, look at team's:	▪ Strengths ▪ Weaknesses ▪ Opportunities ▪ Threats

(Continued)

TABLE 8.1 Step-by-Step Conducting the Actual Small-Group and Team-Change Intervention Process (Con't.)

c. Data-Collecting Methods & Instruments	
1. **Historical Documents Review.** To understand the organization's HR policies and influence of systems operations and procedures, teams look into and review:	■ Recruiting and hiring policies and processes. ■ Company's policies on personal interactions. ■ History of HR policy changes and reasons. ■ History, trends, and reasons for turnovers. ■ Channels of communication. ■ Exit interviews and feedback. ■ Termination policies and letters. ■ Disciplinary actions. ■ Compliance of managers or supervisors. ■ Availability & history of HRD practices. ■ Privacy and confidentiality.
2. **Observation.** To understand the organization's and team's culture and how they relate to one another or how they are communicating, be part of their meetings, and also their processes such as:	■ Senior management meetings. ■ HR team meetings. ■ Supervisory meetings. ■ Production managers' planning meetings. ■ Day-to-day productions and processes. ■ Behaviors and attitudes toward other people and deadlines. ■ Relationship between supervisors and members. ■ Communication models of supervisors and members. ■ Communication style and model of team members. ■ Recognition of the team's culture and norms. ■ Observation of their work, task, and procedures without engagement or interference.
3. **One-On-One Interviews.** OD practitioner should collect data directly from top managers to make sure they include their perspectives and feedback on the team's potential issues, provide and sign "Confidentiality and Non-Disclosure Agreement" with the interviewee,	■ Senior Managers or Executives (CEO, VP, COO, CFO). ■ HR director or manger. ■ Plant managers, department managers or supervisors. ■ Junior managers who are directing teams. ■ Team leaders.

(Continued)

TABLE 8.1 **Step-by-Step Conducting the Actual Small-Group and Team-Change Intervention Process (Con't.)**

display respect by not adding or deleting information and data being provided, and finally interview one or more managers who have direct information about team's operations and productivity, such as:	
4. **Focus Group Interviews.** To collect data directly from floor employees who have hands-on experience in production and the following procedures:	■ Identify all the primary teams in the group/business. ■ Select between two to six teams (depends on the size of the organization and its units) to collect data. ■ Randomly select five to seven people from each team to be in each focus group. ■ Provide and sign "Confidentiality and Non-Disclosure Agreement." ■ Display respect and do not add or subtract anything to and from any information and data they are providing.
d. Feedback Report	
1. **Preparing the Report.** This is where the OP practitioner presents the complete report to the senior management team (sponsor and client) about:	■ The organization's initial perspective of issues. ■ What they uncovered and issues they find. ■ How they find the issues and how they diagnosed the issues. ■ The actual issues and what the symptoms of the issues were. ■ What they use for data collecting. ■ What the process of finalizing the findings was. ■ Providing the needs Assessment Evaluation (Formative Evaluation). ■ Requesting permission to share the findings and outcome of diagnosis and analysis with department managers, junior managers, and team leaders.
2. **Delivery of the Report.** Nature of the meeting and what to use for the presentation:	■ This is the sponsor or client's meeting, and it is closed to other people. ■ The content of this report is confidential.

(Continued)

TABLE 8.1   Step-by-Step Conducting the Actual Small-Group and Team-Change Intervention Process (Con't.)

	▪ Everyone in the meeting will get a complete copy of the report. ▪ Use PowerPoint Presentation for better explaining the process and findings. ▪ Receive feedback from the sponsor and client. ▪ Ask what they think they need to do at this point. ▪ What are the organization's options at this point? ▪ Acknowledge the opportunity for conducting this process and display your appreciation for their business.
Phase 2: Implementation	
This phase will be delivered after the organization has shown interest in using the OD practitioner to facilitate the actual implementation of team-building and change intervention.	
a. Setting Up	
Announcement by the organization:	▪ HR department on behalf of the organization and the CEO or President will send a general announcement via email or internal memo, introducing the OD practitioner and the fact that you will see him/her conducting the data-collecting process.
b .Workshops & Seminars (Training and Development)	
1. In-person Introduction	▪ Introduce yourself and speak on your commitment to serve them. ▪ Create a background of relatedness and rapport. ▪ Let them know why you are here and nothing is wrong with anything or anyone. ▪ Ask them what they are expecting from this process. ▪ Do not try to change their expectations, perceptions, or mistrust. ▪ Express your commitment to the process, your availability, and their success.

(Continued)

TABLE 8.1   Step-by-Step Conducting the Actual Small-Group and Team-Change Intervention Process (Con't.)

	■ Review the general findings, analysis, and assessments with them (with prior permission). ■ Briefly explain the process of team-building.
2. **Series of Training and Development Workshops.** This is the time that the OD practitioner uses a series of training and development workshops using and implementing proven methods and procedures that would allow for personal and team transformation and change in individual and group levels. Some potential training sessions for the purpose of team-building include:	■ Elements of 4Cs of Team-Building ■ Critical Thinking process ■ Problem Solving process. ■ Inventing New Opportunities ■ Emotional Intelligence ■ Self-Awareness inquiry ■ Team-Building Discipline ■ Personal Effectiveness approach ■ Effective Communication ■ How a Great Team Works
3. **Tools and Instruments to Use.** You can use the following models and instruments or come with any other proven technology that would support your implementation process:	■ Problem-Solving models. One or two of the following models can be used: Cause & Effect Analysis such as Ishikawa (fishbone), Force Field Analysis or Brainstorming process. ■ "Presence and Use of Emotional Intelligence at Work." Use Table 5.1 ■ "Self-Awareness Model." ■ "Elements of 4Cs of Team-Building." ■ "Practices for Inventing New Opportunities." Use Figure 8.1. ■ "Team-Building Discipline." Use Figure 8.2 ■ "Roll Play" exercise ■ "Critical Thinking" games and team activities. ■ "Team-Building" activities and exercises.

Communication Charter

- **Upsets.** Go to the persons you have an issue with within 24 hours to talk to them or to schedule a time to talk to them.
- **Coaching/Mentoring.** Coaching, mentoring, or providing feedback is done with permission only. Always give the other person the space to decline.
- **Promises and Requests.** When making a promise or request, always use the X (what) by Y (date, time), with a condition for fulfillment

formula (your required or desired outcome). Appropriate responses to requests are: Accept, Decline, Counteroffer (a promise to respond by a different day or time).

- ***Listening.*** a) Listen for the possibility or the unknown in what someone is saying. b) Listen for *your* "inner chatter" and what filter you are using while you are listening. c) Be responsible for who you are being and how you are listening.
- ***Being Your Word.*** Communicate specifically to the person you gave your word to immediately if you are going to break it and make a new promise. Always close the communication cycle.
(Bakhshandeh 2008)

Step 9: Evaluation

The main goal of evaluation of our team-building process is to provide a practical view of the team's progress and feedback on their development to the client (sponsor) and the team. We decided to provide our evaluation on two general categories, formative and summative formats (as has been mentioned in Chapter 5, the individual intervention).

It would be wise to mention that each OD practitioner should choose the category or format of evaluation suitable for each intervention project depending on the individual or team level of involvement with the organization and level of accountability and influence on the organization's processes and productivity.

Formative Evaluations

The formative evaluation will reinforce or improve the object or topic that was evaluated. It will also help researchers or OD practitioners in assessing the program delivery or technology, and the quality of their application (Trochim William & Donnelly 2008). This author has used the following three formative evaluations (Trochim William & Donnelly, 2008) during this team intervention process: a) Needs Assessment Evaluation, b) Implementation Evaluation, and c) Process Evaluation.

Summative Evaluation

The summative evaluation assesses the effect or outcome of an intervention, program, or technology by describing what happened as an outcome or result, following the delivery of the intervention, program, or technology (Trochim William & Donnelly, 2008). This author has used the following two summative evaluations (Trochim William & Donnelly, 2008) during this team intervention process: a) Outcome Evaluation, and b) Impact Evaluation.

Describing and providing a model of measurement evaluating the effectiveness of workshops or the whole intervention is critical to the credibility of the change agent or consultant as well as the change intervention project as a whole. We asked all participants to complete a short evaluation form with five questions based on the Linkert Skill evaluation, two Yes/No questions, and an opportunity for additional comment for each session of our workshop and seminars.

Step 10: Adoption

During the team-building workshops, team members, regardless of their position and hierarchy in the organization, had some insights and realizations about who they were being and how they operated in their work. They looked at what kind of attitude and behaviors they had displayed and took ownership for their part in team dysfunctions and team conflicts. This eye-opening awareness caused team members to apologize for what they had done or who they were being, and they came with a new set of promises concerning their new commitment to the team and organization (Rothwell William et al. 2016).

Step 11: Separation

This is the time when the change agents or OD practitioners are leaving the organizations, however, not before they make sure the selected internal change agent or team leaders are powerfully and entirely in action for the change intervention to resume work after they leave (2016). We had a decision-making meeting with the executive and senior management team to assign one person as the Internal Change Agent (ICA) in charge of overseeing the action plan and all procedures resulting from the intervention. The ICA can be situated to facilitate the change implementation process while the senior management team controls the content (Sullivan Roland et al. 2013). We set up supporting structure for the ICA during Step 12 of the intervention setting.

Step 12: Follow-Up

The follow-up sessions are essential to safeguard the new and exciting work environment and what is generated from the team-building effort and intervention. Follow-up keeps the results of the change intervention in place and creates longevity for the new processes and procedures (Rothwell William et al. 2016). We established a monthly meeting with the management team and the team leaders for the first three months after completing the intervention to review the progress and make any potential adjustments.

Key Lessons Learned

Out of the work we have done with organizations and teams, we find the following distinctions to be vital to the success of any change intervention, including the team-based change effort.

- *Not Taking Over the Power.* It is natural that during a change intervention, the organization's executive or senior managers feel they are relinquishing their power to the OD practitioner. This feeling will cause resistance to change and will influence the velocity and speed of change intervention (Worley 2012).
- *Looking into the Organization's Design and Culture.* It is a common practice for the OD practitioner to look into an organization and try to understand their design and figure out their strategies (Worley 2012). That starts with changing people's behaviors and attitudes, which determine their actions.
- *Role of Team Members in Change.* To be able to successfully implement a change intervention, an OD practitioner needs to understand the critical roles that the organization's members are playing in the change effort (Wittig 2012).
- *OD Practitioner as Self-Instrument.* No OD practitioner can be a perfect instrument in the implementation of a change effort without having mastery in all aspects of an OD intervention. We can be a vital part of the organization undertaking the change and discovering a new and empowering way to operate and to be productive (Cheung-Judge 2012).

Discussion Questions

Consider the following discussion questions to express your perspective on the team-building processes. What are the best practices you can implement to conduct a practical OD team-based change intervention?

1. Has your organization used a team-based approach in its attempt to improve productivity?
   If Yes, was the approach successful? Why? What was the experience?
   If No, what was standing in the way of your organization implementing the team-based approach?
2. From your point of view, in your organization, is there a strong relationship between teams and the organization's hierarchy?
   If Yes, what do you think is causing such strengths?
   If No, what do you think is interfering with or causing a weak relationship?
3. How do you describe relationships in your team (if you are a member of a team)?
4. Have you ever been involved with any team dysfunctions and conflicts?
   If Yes, what was the dysfunction or conflict, and how was it resolved?
   If No, what would you attribute to your team's dysfunction-free operation?
5. From your point of view, what are the most important values or principles that would strengthen a team-building process?
6. What would be the most destructive behavior or attitude that would cause un-workability in a team-building process?
7. Considering what you have read in this chapter about team-building, what else would you suggest adding to elements of team-building? What was missing?
8. Do you think professional coaching and OD consulting would make a difference for establishing a strong and cohesive team, or adding and expanding the knowledge of teams in your organization?

References

Bakhshandeh, Behnam. 2001. *What Is Making a Great Team?* Unpublished workshop on team building. San Diego, CA: Primeco Education, Inc.
Bakhshandeh, Behnam. 2008. *Bravehearts; Leadership Development Training.* Unpublished training and developmental course on coaching executive and managers. San Diego, CA: Primeco Education, Inc.

Bakhshandeh, Behnam. 2009. *Conspiracy for Greatness; Mastery on Love Within.* San Diego, CA: Primeco Education, Inc.

Bakhshandeh, Behnam. 2015. *Anatomy of Upset: Restoring Harmony.* Carbondale, PA: Primeco Education, Inc.

Bersin, J., B. Denny, Y. V. Durme, M. Hauptmann, I. Roy, J. Schwartz, and E. Volini. 2019 . "Leading the Social Enterprise: Reinvent with a Human Focus 2019. Deloitte Global Human Capital Trends." *Deloitte Insights. Organizational Performance; It's a Team Sport*, 53–58. https://www2.deloitte.com/content/dam/insights/us/articles/5136_HC-Trends-2019/DI_HC-Trends-2019.pdf

Burchell, M., and J. Robin. 2011. *The Great Workplace: How to Build It, How to Keep It, and Why It Matters.* San Francisco, CA: Jossey-Bass.

Cheung-Judge, Mee-Yan. 2012. "The Self as an Instrument: A Cornerstone for the Future of OD." *Journal of the Organization Development Network* 44(2): 40–47. https://cdn.ymaws.com/www.odnetwork.org/resource/resmgr/odp/vol_44_no2.pdf

Cummings, T. G. and C. G. Worley. 2015. *Organization Development & Change* (10th ed.). Stamford, CT. Cengage Learning.

Daft, Richard L. 1983. *Organization Theory and Design.* St. Paul, MN: West Publishing.

Dyer Gibb, W., Jeffrey H. Dyer, and William G. Dyer. 2013. *Team Building: Proven Strategies for Improving Team Performance* (5th ed.). San Francisco, CA: Jossey-Bass

Donahue, Wesley E. 2018. *Building Leadership Competence. A Competency-Based Approach to Building Leadership Ability.* State College, PA: Centerstar Learning.

Hackman Richard, J. 2002. *Leading Teams: Setting the Stage for Great Performances.* Boston, MA: Harvard Business School Press.

Harrison, M. I. 2005. *Diagnosing Organizations; Methods, Models, and Processes* (3rd ed.). Applied Social Research Methods Series, 8. Thousand Oaks, CA. Sage Publication.

Kolb, Judith A. 2011. *Small Group Facilitation: Improving Process and Performance in Groups and Teams.* Amherst, MA: HRD Press Inc.

Levi, Daniel. 2016. *Group Dynamics for Teams* (5th ed.). Los Angeles, CA: Sage Publications.

McClelland, S. B. 1994. "Training Needs Assessment Data-Gathering Methods: Part 3 - Focus groups." *Journal of European Industrial Training* 18(3): 29–32. doi: 10.1108/03090599410056586

Mosson, Rebecca, Hanna, Augustsson, Annika, Bäck, Mårten, Åhström, Thiele, Schwarz Ulrica von, Anne, Richter, Malin, Gunnarsson, and Henna, Hasson. 2019. "Building Implementation Capacity (BIC): A Longitudinal Mixed Methods Evaluation of a Team Intervention." *BMC Health Services0 Research* 19. doi:10.1186/s12913-019-4086-1

Rothwell William, J. 2015. edit. *Organization Development Fundamentals: Managing StrategicChange.* Alexandria, WV: ATD Press.

Rothwell William, J., and Henry J. Sredl. 2014a. *Workplace Learning and Performance: Present and Future Roles and Competencies* (3rd ed.). I. Amherst, MA: HR Press.

Rothwell William, J., and Henry J. Sredl. 2014b. *Workplace Learning and Performance: Present and Future Roles and Competencies* (3rd ed.). II. Amherst, MA: HRD Press.

Rothwell William, J., Jacqueline M. Stavros, and Roland L. Sullivan. 2016. *Practicing Organization Development: Leading Transformation and Change* (4th ed.). Hoboken, NJ: John Wiley & Sons, Inc.

Sullivan Roland L., William J. Rothwell, and Mary Jane B. Balasi. 2013. "Organization Development (OD) and Change Management (CM): Whole System Transformation." *Development and Learning in Organizations* 27(6): 18–23. doi: 10.1108/DLO-08-2013-0060

"SWOT Analysis." 2009 In *Encyclopedia of Management* (6th ed.). 915–918. Detroit, MI. http://link.galegroup.com/apps/doc/CX3273100290/GVRL?u=psucic&sid=GVRL&xid=1e641eb3

Trochim William, M. K. & James P. Donnelly 2008. *The Research Methods Knowledge Base* (3rd ed.). Mason, OH: Cengage Learning

Wittig, Cynthia 2012. "Employees' Reactions to Organizational Change." *Journal of the Organization Development Network* 44(2): 21–28. https://cdn.ymaws.com/www.odnetwork.org/resource/resmgr/odp/vol_44_no2.pdf

Worley, Christopher 2012. "Toward a Relevant and Influential OD." *Journal of the Organization Development Network* 44(2): 5–6. https://cdn.ymaws.com/www.odnetwork.org/resource/resmgr/odp/vol_44_no2.pdf

Yoon, H. J. 2017. Diagnostic models following open systems (Chapter 3). In *Assessment* and *Diagnosis for Organization Development: Powerful Tools and Perspectives for the OD Practitioner*, edited by W. J. Rothwell, A. L. Stopper, and J. L. Myers, 54–79. New York, NY: CRC Press, A Chapman & Hall Book. https://ebookcentral.proquest.com/lib/pensu/detail.action?docID=4831182

INTERMEDIATE AND LARGE INTERVENTIONS

## Chapter 9

Intermediate-Sized Interventions

MiJin Lee and Behnam Bakhshandeh

Contents

Overview

This chapter is about the organization development (OD) intervention change approach for intermediate-sized OD organizations. As Rothwell et al. (2016) underlined, OD practitioners often specialize on a certain level of change and OD interventions. Among the eight levels of organization change, the OD field can facilitate an organization in changes at any level: individual, team, department, organization, and society (Rothwell et al. 2016, 39). Intermediate-sized intervention is the fourth level of OD intervention. This intervention level is mostly used for departmental or divisions change efforts, with needs for a change in a department or division within the organization. That being said, in some cases, the intermediate-sized OD change effort has been used on the fifth level of OD intervention when the change is covering the whole organization. Clearly, that is related to the size and structure of such organizations.

In this chapter, the readers will become familiar with some definitions, characteristics, and processes of intermediate-sized interventions. This chapter covers the following areas:

- Intermediate-sized interventions approach to change
- What is different about intermediate-sized interventions?

- Variation of OD intervention activities and techniques used on intermediate-sized interventions
- Creating an action plan that supports intermediate-sized interventions
- Using online and virtual platform for intermediate-sized interventions
- Step-by-step on how to conduct intermediate-sized change interventions

The systems of the organization can be approached in five levels: individual, group, intergroup, organization, and organization environment (Jones & Brazzel 2014). Intermediate-sized interventions are also referred to as inter-group OD interventions. What distinguishes intermediate-sized interventions from small-sized or large-scale intervention is that the intermediate-sized intervention embraces the group of employees who belong to subgroups and different team dynamics within the group. One might ask, what is different about intermediate-sized interventions? The small-group intervention is designed for a team-sized intervention, and the large-scale intervention is designed for organization-wide interventions or department-wide interventions, depending on the size of the organization. The intermediate-sized intervention is more suitable for the group of people who share the same office space, common goals to achieve common practices, common norms, or communicate and collaborate often.

It would be useful to point out one of the most noticeable elements of this level of OD intervention, and that is the fact that given the involvement of responsible individuals and needs for working with influential stakeholders, the intermediate-sized level of OD interventions and change effort is using and mixing elements of other OD intervention levels, such as Level 1, the Individual Change; Level 2, the Dyadic and Triadic-Based Change Efforts, for change among two or three people; and Level 3, the Team-Based Change Efforts, when there is a need for change and improvement of teams or groups.

Purpose and Importance of Intermediate-Sized OD Interventions

Intermediate-sized OD interventions are suitable for large groups or teams in an organization or in society. Given the nature of this OD intervention, the OD practitioners have to get a large range of stakeholders to get involved with large gatherings and meetings to explain important issues or approaches, values, and processes to develop new and empowering ways of thinking and working. This approach is vital to the articulation of a new vision and direction of the organization, or at least resolves demanding and pressing organizational issues. Besides the importance of this potential achievement, the intermediate-sized OD intervention and change effort can provide organizations, businesses, and groups with the following results:

- Enhanced quality of workforce production
- Increased overall productivity in groups and their organization
- Continuous improvement of the organization's systems and processes
- Improved quality of the organization's products and services
- Enhanced competitive edge in their market
- Increased overall profitability
  (Rothwell et al. 2016; Cummings & Worley 2015).

OD Intervention Activities and Techniques

After conducting the necessary needs assessment, applying a proper and relevant OD diagnosis model and methods, and analysis of the findings, the OD practitioners can use and apply a variety of OD intervention techniques and activities. OD intervention activities and techniques are designed to assist and help participants to understand their current situation and develop new approaches that would empower their new committed interest to produce a long-lasting change, individually, in groups, or at the organization level as a whole.

Given the nature of intermediate-sized interventions that are a mix of individual, team, and group interactions, the following are 20 different variations of OD intervention activities and techniques (see Table 9.1) that could be used on intermediate-sized interventions or any other levels of OD change efforts.

Why OD Intervention Versus Traditional Training?

One might ask why not use traditional training for handling teams, groups, departments, or organization problems? According to Rothwell (2015), "traditional approaches to training can be fraught with problems in today's organizations" (7). These potential issues and difficulties can be categorized in the following four general classifications:

1. In a general sense, training efforts habitually lack focus and central aims.
2. Usually, training is not generating organizations' management support and backing.

Table 9.1 Variation of OD Intervention Activities and Techniques

#	Names	Descriptions
1	Needs Assessment	Finding disparity among the existing condition and the preferred condition (Sleezer et al. 2014).
2	Diagnostic	Finding the facts and reality of the client's current situation (Harrison 2005).
3	Executive Coaching	Individual interaction and intervention with a senior executive (Bakhshandeh 2002).
4	Team Building	Working with teams to enhance their team effectiveness and productivity (Levi 2017).
5	Intergroup	Working with interdependent groups to increase effectiveness and productivity (Cummings & Worley 2015).
6	Survey	Gathering necessary information to find problems and resolutions (Anderson 2015).
7	Training & Development	Improving individuals & teams' knowledge, skills, and abilities (Rothwell et al. 2016).
8	Techno Structure	Improving job design and organization structure effectiveness (Cummings & Worley 2015).
9	Work Design	Defining tasks, jobs, and the work for each position (Rothwell 2015).
10	Job Enrichment	Upgrading responsibilities, accountabilities, and scope of jobs (Cummings & Worley 2015).
11	Process Consulting	Improving job processes and production efficiencies (Rothwell et al. 2016)
12	Coaching & Consulting	Improving individual's and team's behavior and defining individual career goals (Bakhshandeh 2009).
13	Career Planning	Helping individuals to plan and focus on their career and overall future (Rothwell et al. 2016).
14	Third-Party Involvement	Bringing in a skilled consultant to manage some interpersonal conflicts (Rothwell 2015).
15	Planning & Goal Setting	Improving individual's and team's goal setting (Rothwell et al. 2016).

(Continued)

TABLE 9.1   Variation of OD Intervention Activities and Techniques (Con't.)

#	Names	Descriptions
16	Problem Solving	Improving individual's and team's problem-solving and conflict-resolution techniques (Levi 2017).
17	Creating a Vision	Assisting individuals and organizations to come up with an empowering vision for the future (Bakhshandeh 2008).
18	Strategic Management	Working on change management and fundamental long-term planning (Rothwell et al. 2016).
19	Organization Transformation	Implementing large-scale system change (Rothwell et al. 2016).
20	Organization Redesign	Redesigning the organization to reduce stress and redefine authority (Rothwell et al. 2016).

3. Characteristically, in many cases, training lacks advanced planning and is conducted systematically in correlation to the organization's vision and mission and is mostly related to technical issues.
4. Traditionally, training is not efficiently and effectively connected to other organizational initiatives.

"Each problem warrants additional attention because each may dramatize the need to move beyond traditional training—and training as a standalone change strategy—to focus on more holistic approaches to enhancing human performance" (Rothwell 2015, 7).

Use of Virtual Participation in Intermediate-Sized Intervention

Given the size and dimensions of a group, business, or organization, which is using the intermediate-sized OD intervention, it is expected that many of their meetings and discussions are conducted through virtual communication and video conferencing. In many cases, this approach is covering different office locations throughout a state, a country, or globally.

Communication technology has changed dramatically over the last several decades. Subsequently, online video conferencing and communication have grown in popularity among academics and business professionals. Online communication and connectivity has become an answer to concerns about time and financial restraints, geographical spreading, and people's physical mobility limitations (Janghorban et al. 2014). In today's technical advancement of communication technology, there are many audio and video conferencing platforms readily available to the public. Skype, Zoom, Go-To-Meeting, and FaceTime are four of the synchronous online services that offer organizations the freedom and possibility of conducting their business at a distance (Janghorban et al. 2014). Also, any verbal and nonverbal signals in online video conferencing are offering the same level of authenticity as an onsite interview (Sullivan 2012). Ethical issues in online video conferencing are considered to be the same as in traditional onsite conferencing (Cater 2011).

Online interventions are an effective way of helping the workforce manage stress and improve performance during an unexpected crisis. The online intervention can be provided through audio/video teleconference. The intermediate-sized interventions are appropriate as the intervention can be tailored to the target audience who share common goals and practices. Moreover, from the management's perspective, they can expect the maximized impact of OD intervention considering the budget, especially in global health and economic crises, by facilitating the right number of employees in one intervention.

The development of Information and Communication Technologies (ICT) has substituted in-person communication with high-touch engagement despite the challenges with maintaining high touch with high tech (Tenkasi 2018). The participants' convenience and instructors' efficiency promotes the online learning model continuously, and experts provide the contents in interesting ways through podcasts and webinars depending on the content and audiences' preference (Goodson 2019).

Action Planning for Intermediate-Sized Intervention: Breaking Silos

Action planning is "a collaborative process of systematically planning a change effort. When done effectively, it can mobilize people, improve the impact of a change, and accelerate the time needed to achieve results. When done ineffectively, action plans will generate little commitment, have a low probability of being implemented, and produce unintended negative side effects" (Rothwell et al. 2016, 184). Action planning is demonstrated and describes how the OD practitioner or change is working with the organization's management and stakeholders to create a detailed plan of action on how to implement the necessary changes and solutions on pressing problems (Rothwell et al. 2016). The action plan needs to be premeditated in clear and precise activities, with the alignment of management and direct stakeholders who are accountable for implementing the action plan.

Although the group of people within the same department or division communicate and collaborate more often than other departments or divisions, silos may exist among teams or even within the team. Silos hinder people from further collaboration or active cooperation by creating misunderstandings and communication gaps. Intermediate-sized groups which consist of teams and subgroups may face challenges occurred by silos within and among the teams and subgroups in their assigned intermediate-sized group as each team and subgroup has different expertise, tasks, and culture.

Recognizing and admitting these silos may be challenging, but well-designed action planning would maximize the effect of the intermediate-sized intervention and enable sustainable change by involving all stakeholders throughout the intervention. According to Rothwell et al. (2016), well-designed action planning processes include the following elements: a) involve key stakeholders, b) evaluate and prioritize data, c) agree on the changes to be made, d) develop a change strategy, and e) clarify roles and follow-through on responsibilities. We will elaborate on these elements of Action Planning in the Business Case Example section of this chapter.

Planning and Designing the Approach to an Intermediate-Sized OD Intervention

In this section, we cover methods and models of organization assessment, diagnosis, and instruments that were used for the data-gathering process that was used on the Business Case Example we are presenting to our readers. Accurate and relevant assessments and diagnosis can be accomplished only if the OD practitioners provide their clients with collected data, analyses, and relevant recommendations that are not only useful but also valid and reliable. To meet such standards, the OD practitioners must fulfill the constraints of the following three key facets: 1) process, 2) modeling, and 3) methods (Harrison 2005).

Process

Creating a trusting relationship between the OD practitioners and their clients is vital to the success of any intervention. Support of the intervention by the management team and supervisors makes the possibilities of change interventions a reality.

Model

One of the popular organization diagnosis models is the Open System (OS), which is proper for the intermediate-sized OD intervention. According to Harrison (2005), there are many diagnosis models which treat organizations as OS. These would assist OD practitioners in selecting topics for their diagnosis of organizations while developing criteria for assessing an organization's effectiveness, collecting data from the organizations, conducting analysis, and providing feedback. By the end of this cycle, practitioners can pinpoint the approach that will help their clients solve their organization's issues and improve effectiveness. Yoon (2017) explained how open systems work in a cycle of examining an organization's input, transformation, and output, "The output becomes the input for the next cycle and transformation occurs in an organization to produce a new output while interacting with the environment" (Yoon 2017, 32).

Diagnosing Individual and Group Behavior Model

While using OS, one of the important elements for understanding an organization is to understand the organization's input, output, and relationships with the social environment. Harrison (2005) provides the following definitions and descriptions for such elements:

- **Inputs.** Human, material, financial and intangibles.
- **Outputs.** Goods, services, products, employees' well-being and satisfaction.
- **Organizational behaviors and processes.** Practices that the organization has implemented to create and support output.
- **Technology.** Equipment, tools, and systems that would support transforming inputs to an output.
- **Environment.** a) Close environment: organization's competitors, customers, partners, suppliers, and investors. b) Remote environment: local and national political system, the economy and its relevant influences,

social structures based on norms and cultures, and technological advances in the market.

- **Culture.** Society's shared values, norms, beliefs, and behaviors that would impact and influence the organizational culture, such as a) how work is getting done by employees, b) what the model of communications is among organization, c) how employees are treating their customer, and d) the way the organization treats its employees.

Method

Given the nature of this type of intervention (groups, divisions, and departments), the Qualitative Research Method is the best research method to use in this case.

Qualitative Research Method

Given that the qualitative research method is exploratory in nature, qualitative data contains variables that are not in a numerical fashion but in the form of words, texts, sounds, photographs, and so on. In the qualitative method, research questions typically start with words such as "what" or "how," since these words suggest detection or exploration of the variables (Trochim & Donnelly 2008). As has been established, the qualitative research method, by definition, is exploratory. This method shall be used when the researchers are not sure about what to predict or expect in defining the issue at hand or creating an approach to the issue. The qualitative research method is used when researchers want to dig deeper into the subject matter's interest and investigate different potential aspects related to the investigated issues (Rothwell et al. 2016; Sleezer et al. 2014; Trochim & Donnelly 2008). In comparison to the quantitative research method, the qualitative research method is focusing on texts and words rather than numbers and investigating depth rather than scale (Trochim & Donnelly 2008).

The qualitative research method commonly uses the following techniques for data gathering and research: a) observation, b) historical document review, c) one-on-one interviews, and d) focus group interviews, while all the data come from the field, where the participants are in action, working in their natural environment (Sleezer et al. 2014; Trochim & Donnelly 2008). According to Trochim and Donnelly (2008), the researchers allow the collected data to speak for itself and formulate into a set of themes short of the researcher's potential bias or natural bias of an existing theory or public opinion.

The instruments used for the data-gathering section on our Business Case Example intervention include 1) Focus Group Interviews, 2) One-One-One interviews, and 3) Survey.

1. **Focus Group Interviews.** In this group interview method, individuals who have something in common (like departments, groups, or divisions) are brought together to answer a set of questions and express their ideas, perceptions, viewpoints, or opinions regarding a topic of interest or research. Different from one-on-one interviews, the focus group interview asks questions and gathers data that is not the only purpose of an interview, but observing the group dynamics and inner relationship among the team members are also the focus of the interviewer. Commonly the focus groups are made up of five to eight individuals (Sleezer et al. 2014). Stopper and Myers (2017) simplified the focus group, describing it as follows: "Think of a focus group as group interviews. Just as in informal interviews, informal focus groups are simply group conversations focused on a problem. Formal focus groups, like interviews, can be open-ended or closed-ended, and many of the same rules apply" (108).

2. **One-On-One Interviews.** Interviews can be in the form of a) structured (scripted), which list intentions that will determine the questions to guide the interview process, b) unstructured, which list intentions and objectives of the interview that are guiding the process, and for which questions are not determined or listed in advance or c) semi-structured, which initially list objectives and questions that are guiding the process, but will consider other undetermined questions that will arise about which the interviewer will spontaneously ask. The semi-structured interview model is one of the most popular interview methods (Sleezer et al. 2014). While vastly structured survey interviews and robust questionnaires are used in needs assessments and research, less formal and structured interview strategies are becoming more desirable to OD professionals and researchers (Deterding & Waters 2018; DiCicco-Bloom & Crabtree 2006). Spencer (2017) described one-on-one interviews as the data-gathering approach comprised of numerous bases of evidence, indications, and parallel lines of examinations.

3. **Survey.** Check and Schutt (2012) defined survey research as "The collection of information from a sample of individuals through their responses to questions" (160). This method of research provides an array of approaches to cause participation and gather data. The traditional

description of the survey is a quantitative method approach in the form of collecting information from participants by asking various survey questions (Trochim & Donnelly 2008).

Evaluation

One of the critical aspects of a change intervention is the evaluation of the change, which can be potentially conducted in phases such as before (pre-intervention), during (intra-intervention), and after (post-intervention) the change intervention (Connelly-Jones & Rothwell 2018). What is highly recommended is an integrated, multiphase approach to change evaluation where the OD practitioner or assigned change agent performs a series of evaluations as listed below:

- **Pre-Intervention Evaluation:** Used to discover and recognize the current state of the organization and what is needed to accomplish and implement as result of a change intervention.
- **Intra-Intervention Evaluation:** Used during the progress of the change intervention at a pre-selected time of the change process. This evaluation will assist the OD practitioner in making necessary adjustments to the change intervention process.
- **Post-Intervention Evaluation:** Used at the end of the intervention. This evaluation provides an assessment of the complete results of the change intervention.
  (Connelly-Jones & Rothwell 2018).

Business Case Example

Designing inter-group intervention is more complicated than when the target audience is as simple as a team or as large as a whole organization. The following case study presents how inter-group intervention was provided, given the circumstances and challenges with which the group is faced.

Background

The company, well-known for its leading technologies in the market, recently hired a new CEO. The new CEO reviewed all ongoing projects and decided to disband the innovation project group, Group X created by the former CEO.

Group X has three subteams led by Richard, the group leader. Team A consists of 12 staff members, Team B of eight staff members, and Team C of five staff members. The group members were proud of their initiatives, and they worked hard to achieve the goals. However, there were employees who were opposed to the projects led by Group X as some of the projects were seen as rather disruptive.

Step 1: Entry

When Richard was first told that his team might be disbanded in the coming months, he was concerned about his hardworking group members. He did not want them to be discouraged and not be able to complete the remaining projects. The group members also heard the rumor that their group might be disbanded as the new CEO did not like the ideas of the former CEO. The group members' morale dropped, and Richard was concerned about their performance. Richard decided to hire Rachel, a junior OD practitioner who recently facilitated OD interventions for tech companies and therefore organized a workshop for all group members as soon as possible.

Step 2: Start-Up

The need for the OD intervention was obvious. The group members were discouraged to hear the rumor that their group may be disbanded. They thought it could have been much nicer if they heard the news formally first and not by rumor. Moreover, the workloads were still overwhelming for the group, and there were lists of projects to finalize by the end of the year. As Rachel was informed of the situation briefly and asked by Richard to facilitate the workshop for his group, Rachel initially arranged three forms of data-collecting methods: 1) ffocus group interviews with all three teams at separate times, using Zoom video conferencing; 2) one-on-one phone interviews with each group members to build a rapport and clarify the problem by distinguishing the root cause from symptoms; and 3) survey, which was used later in the intervention.

The following questions were asked during the focus group and one-on-one interviews, and the preliminary findings of the interviews were shared with Richard:

- Can they introduce their work briefly?
- What made the group members achieve the goals so far?

- What distinguishes the group from other groups?
- What are the key achievements they think they achieved?
- How do they perceive the current situation?
- How do they feel about the new management approach?
- What do they anticipate from this OD intervention?
- What do they want to achieve through this OD intervention?

Step 3: Assessment, Diagnosis, and Feedback

After going through the focus group and one-on-one interviews, Rachel learned that there was a communication gap between the management and the group. For deeper assessment, she conducted a survey with the group. As focus group interviews and individual interview results and survey results indicated that the group members felt the new management did not appreciate the achievements made by the group, she suggested that Richard invite the new management to the workshop. The survey was designed to assess group members' views on recent changes and their thoughts on ongoing projects that needed to be completed. The survey was intended to get more genuine responses from the group members for the following questions, which could be rather sensitive to be mentioned during the focus group and one-on-one phone interview. The survey adopted the 5-point Likert Scale (1 = Strongly disagree, 2 = Disagree, 3 = Neutral, 4 = Agree, 5 = Strongly agree, please see Table 9.2). The anonymous responses were compiled, and the results of the online survey were shared with Richard and the new management, which substantiated the needs for the new management's participation in the OD intervention.

- Do group members consider current projects congruent with the goals of the company?
- Do group members perceive their projects have been successful?
- Do group members feel that their achievement was made by a group effort rather than an individual effort?
- Do group members feel that their individual efforts were a more critical factor for success?
- Do group members perceive their performance as a high achiever?
- Do group members feel that the company acknowledges their efforts and achievements properly?
- Do group members feel that they are engaged with Group X?
- Do group members feel that they are engaged with ongoing projects?
- Do group members feel that they are engaged with the company?

Table 9.2 Group Assessment Survey and Results

#	Items	Strongly Disagree (1)	Disagree (2)	Neutral (3)	Agree (4)	Strongly Agree (5)
1	Group members consider current projects are congruent with the goal of the company.					
2	Group members perceive their projects have been successful.					
3	Group members feel that their achievement was made by a group effort rather than an individual effort.					
4	Group members feel that their individual efforts were a more critical factor for success.					
5	Group members perceive their performance as a high achiever.					
6	Group members feel that the company acknowledges their efforts and achievements properly.					
7	Group members feel that they are engaged with Group X.					
8	Group members feel that they are engaged with ongoing projects.					
9	Group members feel that they are engaged with the company.					

(Continued)

TABLE 9.2   Group Assessment Survey and Results (Con't.)

#	Items	Strongly Disagree (1)	Disagree (2)	Neutral (3)	Agree (4)	Strongly Agree (5)
10	Group members consider new management's decision affected their performance.					
11	Group members think they can present a new agenda that could alternate the current decision.					
Total (all 11 rates)						
Average (Totals divided by 11)						

- Do group members consider new management's decision affected their performance?
- Do group members think they can present a new agenda that could alter the current decision?

Step 4: Action Planning

Given the nature of the intermediate-sized intervention, the OD practitioner requested three team leaders to create action planning for their own group intervention. With collaboration from team leaders, considering their schedule and availability, and using elements of Action Planning by Rothwell et al. (2016), the team of four designed an action plan to implement the intervention.

Involve Key Stakeholders

Involving key stakeholders is one of the most critical factors for the successful OD intervention as it involves the people who would think of change strategy, decide their roles, and implement the change efforts. The key stakeholders are the people who make change initiatives and make change efforts throughout the processes. The key stakeholders of the intermediate-sized group are the group members, group leaders, and senior management.

Checklist
- Is everyone who is impacted by the change efforts involved?
- Is every voice heard? Louder voices are easier to be heard and regarded as leading opinion. A breakthrough idea may be heard from smaller voices who tend to think more than speak.

Evaluate and Prioritize Relevant Data

Data-driven assessment and decision making help the stakeholders observe and assess their situation more objectively and move forward to the next step rather than relying on intuition or subjective observation. As an intermediate-sized group consists of several teams, an OD practitioner helps the stakeholders evaluate and prioritize data by facilitating meetings. During the meetings, the OD practitioner helps the stakeholders develop a process, clarify the purpose of the change efforts and the desired outcome, and help them understand the current status and desired future.

Checklist
- Do stakeholders have initiatives in providing relevant data?
- Are meeting plans shared prior to the meeting?
- Are stakeholders aware of the goals before starting the meeting?

Agree on the Changes to Be Made

The action plans that stakeholders discussed, developed, and agreed to have a longer impact on the changes and lead to a sustainable change. The detailed and clear actions specified help the stakeholders follow the action plans when the OD practitioner is left after the OD intervention. Once the stakeholders agree on the desired outcome that they imagined and developed together, they feel more responsibilities and obligations that lead them to be more proactive during the change process.

Checklist
- Are plans detailed enough that stakeholders can follow after the OD intervention?
- Are the timeline and milestones specified in the action plan?
- Are actions and roles specified in the action plan?
- Are the plans too ambitious? Fewer actions that can be accomplished are better than many actions that can be only partially achieved.

Develop a Change Strategy

The success of the OD intervention may depend on how a change strategy was developed. During the change process, a change strategy is a map that indicates the possible and effective way that helps the stakeholders achieve the desired outcome by the changes. A force-field analysis is one of the ways to develop a change strategy (Rothwell et al. 2016). A force-field analysis explains the change mechanism with driving forces and restraining forces (Lewin 1951). Market changes, new technology, a new leader, and stakeholders who lead the change initiatives, talents, competencies, and a new generation of the workforce could be driving forces. On the other hand, bureaucracy, the size of the organization, its resistance to change occurred by systematic and technical shortcomings, lack of training, or overwhelming tasks can be restraining forces.

Checklist
  - Are possible ways fully explored?
  - Are both driving forces and restraining forces identified properly?
  - Did stakeholders develop a realistic change strategy?

Clarify Roles and Follow-Through Responsibilities

Involving stakeholders throughout the change efforts is key to the successful OD intervention, as mentioned earlier. In this regard, as a final step of the action-planning process, by clarifying the roles of the stakeholders and follow-through responsibilities, the goal of the desired outcome becomes associated with their roles and responsibilities, which are imprinted in their minds. The typical roles that should be covered are change agent (OD practitioner), change leader, change champion, and change team. For these roles, one person may play multiple roles depending on the available resources, and these roles may be changed during the change process.

Checklist
  - Do all stakeholders understand clarified roles and follow-through responsibilities?
  - Are stakeholders aware that at least one change champion is needed throughout the change process?

Step 5: Intervention

The intervention was delivered in a two-day off-site workshop. The venue was in the same city, but it had a nice view, and being away from their desks made the participants feel more refreshed and valued by the company. Group X and the new management were invited for the workshop.

As this was the very first workshop for Group X, Rachel facilitated the team-building exercises in the morning of Day 1 to break the ice among Team A, Team B, and Team C. The participants were mixed up and randomly assigned to five different teams. Rachel intentionally reassigned the teams for each exercise during the workshop to give everyone the opportunity to be able to talk to each other. The fun activities made the participants feel more comfortable with the workshop setting and made them feel closer to each other.

During the team-building exercises, the group members learned that there was a misunderstanding among the teams and recognized communication gaps within the group. Rachel asked the five teams to write down the important values of Group X in the Sticky Easel Pad. Each team was given opportunities to present the achievements of Group X and develop new ways of working for the remaining projects. The achievements and core values written by the five groups were posted around the walls.

The new management arrived in the afternoon of Day 1 with coffee and donuts. The new management acknowledged the achievements of Group X and appreciated the hard work and initiatives in innovation projects. The new management listened to the group's concerns about Group X being disbanded and the job security once all remaining projects were completed. The new management shared their vision for the company and future direction for innovation, and they left. Although the new management heard the group's concerns and answered the questions, the group members were left with more questions.

On Day 2, Rachel reassigned the groups to five teams and directed each team to develop new ways of working by incorporating the new vision shared yesterday and the ways to solve the internal group problems and also the organization's problems. The reassigned groups had time to develop action plans and milestones. Each group was asked to briefly make a presentation to others. Although all participants were tech-savvy, they were asked to use colored pens and the Sticky Easel Pad. In this way, they could collaborate better by reassigning the roles within the group. The person who was better at handwriting took the note-taking part. The person who was better at painting decorated the background of the pad. The one who was better at verbal presentation took the presentation part. Another who was better at presenting new ideas took the lead in the brainstorming part. Finally, the participant who was better at making summaries supported the note-taking group member. Everyone could do each role individually, but through this exercise, they could learn how everyone can collaborate better by understanding each other's different strengths.

At the end of the workshop, they were given a chance to share their thoughts and lessons learned. After the workshop, the group members said that they felt much closer to each other; realized the silos among Teams A, B, and C; shared their concerns to the management; and learned the new visions presented by the new management.

Step 6: Evaluation

A week after the workshop, Rachel sent an email to all group members with the summary of the workshop, pictures from the team-building exercises, and the new ways of solving internal problems and organizational issues developed by randomly assigned teams. The action plans developed by the five teams reflecting the new vision were also shared with the new management. Rachel conducted a post-intervention survey and shared the results with Richard. The survey response analysis indicated that the group members were more satisfied with their job, felt that they were valued by the senior management, were more engaged with the group and the company, and felt they collaborated better with the teams and the group members after the intervention. Rachel organized an online meeting with group members to present the summary report and post-intervention survey results. The group members welcomed her and shared how much the intervention improved their performance and how it changed their perception of the current situation.

Step 7: Adaption

As mentioned in other chapters, this is the time when the OD practitioner departs the organization. Before this separation, with the help and support of three team leaders, Rachel made sure the select a team leader as an Internal Change Agent (ICA). The ICA is entirely in charge of the change intervention in order to resume the work and maintain the change practices after she leaves. The ICA would support the team leaders for effective communication and implementation of the selected team's processes and procedures that were selected during the change intervention.

Step 8: Separation

Rachel recommended and guided Richard to facilitate follow-up sessions with his group on a regular basis. The workshop summary report was also shared with the new management, and the new management liked some of the creative ideas developed during the workshop. During the final session, Rachel guided them to celebrate their successful adaptation to the changes and close the intervention from her side but to continue their efforts for sustainable intervention in the company.

Results and Reflection

Table 9.3 represents a summary of step-by-step actions taken for conducting this intermediate-sized OD intervention by Rachel, the OD practitioner. This is an effective way to support OD practitioners in their approach to intermediate-size intervention; however, the length of intervention will vary depending on the size of the organization, the organization's structure, and the availability of the workforce.

Table 9.3   Summary of Steps for Implementing an Intermediate-Sized OD Intervention

Steps	*Actions*
Entry & Start-Up (Week 1)	■ Conduct the initial meeting and explain the intervention. ■ Submit and sign the contract. ■ Set a meeting with a group leader. ■ Build a rapport with group members by conducting a phone interview with them individually. ■ Share preliminary findings with the group leader.
Needs Assessment & Diagnosis (Week 2)	■ Select and start the relevant Needs Assessment. ■ Select and implement the selected diagnosis model. ■ Assess group members' genuine perception and thoughts on the changes and group dynamics. ■ Conduct an online survey. ■ Analyze the findings, and write a feedback report on the findings.
Feedback & Action Planning (Week 3)	■ Share the analysis with the senior management to secure their involvement and support. ■ Develop action plans with the partnership, with the group leader and some senior managers.

(Continued)

TABLE 9.3   Summary of Steps for Implementing an Intermediate-Sized OD Intervention (Con't.)

Steps	Actions
Intervention (Week 4)	■ Conduct activities and facilitate group work for bringing up the differences between the teams and group members. ■ Help group members get closer to each other through activities and effective communication. ■ Identify internal and external communication gaps. ■ Invite senior management to share the vision of the company. ■ Help group members develop action plans and milestones. ■ Help each group member share their thoughts and lessons learned.
Evaluation & Report (Week 5)	■ Share the intervention summaries indicating positive effects with stakeholders. ■ Conduct a post-intervention survey, and share the results with stakeholders. ■ Provide online wrap-up session with stakeholders, and recommend follow-up sessions for continued efforts for creating a healthier and more effective culture.
Adaption & Separation (Week 6)	■ Have a meeting with the internal change agent who will manage the maintenance of the intervention. ■ Guide facilitating follow-up sessions regularly. ■ Design a mentorship plan, and schedule follow-up with the internal change agent. ■ Celebrate the completion with everyone who was involved with the intervention.

Despite the successful OD intervention, higher performance of the group members, and Richard's efforts to convince the new management, the new CEO decided to disband the group and told the group to finalize all projects led by Group X. At least Richard appreciated the fact that the group members felt that their hard work was acknowledged by the management and that they learned how to better collaborate with each other, how to assign the roles within the group while respecting each other's strengths, and most importantly that their job security was guaranteed. Although Richard would no longer be their leader following the completion of the final projects, he decided to facilitate follow-up sessions on a regular basis to support the group members while projects were finalized to create a healthier workplace culture. He believed that once the culture is set, the positive effect would be built across the company as the group members would be assigned to other teams and groups.

Key Lessons Learned

Out of the work that has been done with organizations and their divisions or departments using intermediate-sized OD intervention, the following traits were found to be essential to the success of such an intervention:

Designing an Appropriate Approach

Any successful OD intervention starts with designing a relevant intervention approach to problems that would be discovered after a proper assessment and diagnosis. Initial assessments, data-gathering processes, and relevant analysis will prepare the OD practitioner to assist the client in designing an influential and useful action plan to complete the OD intervention.

Communication

Communication among management and leadership structure of the organization and key stakeholders is vital to the success of any intervention, especially the intermediate-sized OD intervention, which is designed for working inner-division issues. Clarity of communication, authenticity in communication, and being open to addressing issues among members are the backbone of a successful relationship, personally and professionally (Bakhshandeh 2015).

Building Relationships

Building relationships among people is one of the most important elements of any team or group work (Bakhshandeh 2009). This factor is real and includes any OD intervention that involves more than one person, and intermediate-sized OD intervention is not an exemption to this essential factor. One of the OD practitioner's unspoken responsibilities is to cause members to bond and have a trusting relationship in order to build a successful intervention among their teams, groups, divisions, or organization.

Trusting the Process

OD Practitioners should trust the proven process of an OD intervention and change efforts without changing the dynamics of any OD interventions of any level or size. OD processes, models, and methods are the cornerstones of successful OD intervention deliveries.

Discussion Questions

In the end, we are inviting you to look into the following discussion questions and scenarios about intermediate-sized OD intervention:

1. From your point of view, when is the use of intermediate-sized OD intervention most appropriate and useful to an organization?
2. What elements or characteristics of an organization make you select an intermediate-sized OD intervention over a team-building intervention?
3. Has your organization used an intermediate-sized OD intervention? If Yes:
   • What were the circumstances that made it appropriate for intermediate-sized intervention?
   • What was the role of the OD practitioner for a successful intermediate-sized intervention?
4. Have you, as an OD practitioner, conducted an intermediate-sized OD intervention? If Yes:
   • What were the important elements that needed to be considered when you designed an intermediate-sized intervention?
   • Did you encounter any resistance from the management before and/or during the implementation of the intervention? If you did, how did you resolve the resistance?
5. As a decision-maker in your organization, what type of behavior or attitude did you notice among your groups that directed you to choose an

intermediate-sized OD intervention for that division or section of your organization?

6. From your point of view, what are the most important values or principles that would strengthen an intermediate-sized OD intervention process?

7. As a member of one of the groups, how do you describe relationships among your groups and other related groups after the intermediate-sized OD intervention?

References

Anderson, Donald L. 2015. *Organization Development: The Process of Leading Organizational Change* (3rd ed.). Thousand Oaks, California: SAGE.

Bakhshandeh, Behnam. 2002. *Executive Coaching: For those of you who have arrived*. Unpublished workshop on coaching executives. San Diego, CA: Primeco Education, Inc.

Bakhshandeh, Behnam. 2008. *Bravehearts; Leadership Development Training*. Unpublished training and developmental course on coaching executive and managers. San Diego, CA: Primeco Education, Inc.

Bakhshandeh, Behnam. 2009. *Conspiracy for Greatness; Mastery on Love Within*. San Diego, CA: Primeco Education, Inc.

Bakhshandeh, Behnam. 2015. *Anatomy of Upset: Restoring Harmony*. Carbondale, PA: Primeco Education, Inc.

Cater, J. K. 2011. "Skype a Cost-effective Method for Qualitative Research." *Rehabilitation Counselors and Educators Journal* 4(2): 10–17.

Check, Joseph, and Russell K. Schutt. 2012. "Survey Research." *Research Methods in Education*. Thousand Oaks, CA: Sage Publication. 159–185.

Civera, Chiara and R. E. Freeman. 2019. "Stakeholder Relationships and Responsibilities: A New Perspective. *Symphonya* 1: 40–58. doi: 10.4468/2019.1.04.

Connelly-Jones, Maureen, and Willian J. Rothwell. 2018. *Evaluating Organization Development*. Boca Raton, FL: CRC Press; Taylor and Francis Group.

Cummings, T. G. and Christopher G. Worley. 2015. *Organization Development and Change* (10th ed.). Stamford, CT. Cengage Learning.

Deterding, N. M., and M. C. Waters. 2018. "Flexible Coding of In-depth Interviews: A Twenty-first-Century Approach." *Sociological Methods and Research* 1–31. doi: 10.1177/0049124118799377

DiCicco-Bloom, B. and B. F. Crabtree. 2006. "The Qualitative Research Interview." *Medical Education* 40(4): 314–321. doi: 10.1111/j.1365-2929.2006.02418.x

Freeman, R. Edward. 2010. *Strategic Management: A Stakeholder Approach*. Cambridge, England. Cambridge University Press.

Goodson, Melissa. 2019. "How to Create an Effective Online Seminar Using Organization Development." *Organization Development Journal* 37(4): 89–96.

Harrison, M. I. 2005. *Diagnosing Organizations; Methods, Models, and Processes* (3rd ed.). Applied Social Research Methods Series, 8. Thousand Oaks, CA. Sage Publication.

Janghorban, R., R. L. Roudsari, and A. Taghipour. 2014. "Skype Interviewing: The New Generation of Online Synchronous Interview in Qualitative Research." *International Journal of Qualitative Studies on Health and Well-being* 9(1): 1–3. doi: 10.3402/qhw.v9.24152

Jones, Brenda B and Michael, Brazzel. 2014. *The NTL Handbook of Organization Development and Change: Principles, Practices, and Perspectives* (2nd ed.). San Francisco: Wiley.

Levi, Daniel. 2017. Group Dynamics for Teams. Thousand Oaks, CA: Sage Publications, Inc.

Lewin, Kurt. 1951. *Field Theory in Social Science.* New York, NY: Harper and Row.

Rothwell, William J. 2015. *Beyond Training and Development* (3rd ed.). Amherst, MA: HRD Press, Inc.

Rothwell, William J., Jacqueline M. Stavros, and Roland L. Sullivan. 2016. *Practicing Organization Development: Leading Transformation and Change* (4th ed.). Hoboken, NJ: John Wiley and Sons, Inc.

Sleezer, Catherin M., Darlene F. Russ-Eft, and Kavita Gupta. 2014. *A Practical Guide to Needs Assessment* (3rd ed.). San Francisco, CA: John Wiley and Sons, Inc.

Spencer, Maria. 2017. Unintended Outcomes of Leadership Sensemaking in a Continuously Reconfigured Business Model Change Initiative. (Unpublished doctoral dissertation in workforce education and development). The Pennsylvania State University.

Stopper, Angela L.M. and L. Jennifer Myers. 2017. "Collecting and Analyzing Data for Organization Development (Chapter 6)." In *Assessment and Diagnosis for Organization Development: Powerful Tools and Perspectives for the OD Practitioner*, edited by W. J. Rothwell, A. L. Stopper, and J. L. Myers, 54–79. New York, NY: CRC Press; A Chapman and Hall Book.

Sullivan, J. R. 2012. "Skype: An Appropriate Method of Data Collection for Qualitative Interviews?" *The Hilltop Review* 6(1): 54–60. Retrieved from https://scholarworks.wmich.edu/hilltopreview/vol6/iss1/10/

Tenkasi, Ramkrishnan. 2018. "Re-Visiting the Past to Re-Imagine the Future of Organization Development and Change." *Organization Development Journal* 4 (36): 61–75.

Trochim, William M. K. and James P. Donnelly. 2008. *The Research Methods Knowledge Base* (3rd ed.). Mason, OH: Cengage Learning.

Yoon, H. J. 2017. "Diagnostic Models Following Open Systems (Chapter 3)." In *Assessment and Diagnosis for Organization Development: Powerful Tools and Perspectives for the OD Practitioner*, edited by W. J. Rothwell, A. L. Stopper, and J. L. Myers, 54–79. New York, NY: CRC Press; A Chapman and Hall Book.

Chapter 10

Large-Scale Interventions

S. Ron Banerjee

Contents

Overview

Large-scale intervention (LSI) is more an art than a science. The organization development (OD) practitioner who orchestrates a large-scale change intervention must be an artist. Their craft is in that they must use whatever tools they have available. When used together, they lead organization members and stakeholders to generative results and solutions that the organization requires. Today's world increases in complexity with each significant development in healthcare treatments or technologies. The way goods and services are delivered and consumed changes daily. This constantly morphing organizational backdrop of unplanned change requires OD practitioners and change leaders to meet change head-on. OD practitioners help stakeholders examine their organizational systems to understand better and predict how their organizations will react to a pre-identified change event or a future change event before it occurs. This chapter focuses on the following:

- Identify key terms and phrases associate with LSIs
- Discuss types of LSIs typically used by OD practitioners
- Why use LSIs?
- When to use LSIs
- Illustrate the application of LSIs to a business case study
- Introduce an LSI-focused tool

Typical Large-Scale or Whole System Interventions

According to Jacobs (1994), whole system change is used in conjunction with different large-group methods to explore organization change at a specific time (Arena 2009). As Dannemiller et al. describe it, the purpose is working to create pivotal moments throughout the organization system while developing a "one-brain, one-heart" mantra that permeates the entire organization at every level (Arena 2009, 49). Therefore, OD practitioners help in the sensemaking process for primary stakeholders. Sensemaking is "the creation of reality as an ongoing accomplishment that takes form when people make retrospective sense of the situations in which they find themselves when shaping organizational culture and behavior" (Weick 1995, 231). Yabome Gilpin-Jackson reminds us that "large-scale and similar organization development (OD) interventions work to generate meaningful conversation, connection and deepened relationships between partners in change, as well as alignment to action and organization effectiveness outcomes" (Gilpin-Jackson 2017, 419). Gilpin-Jackson indicates that the number of types of LSIs jumped from 18 to 61 in a decade (Holman et al. 2007). The following list is by no means an exhaustive list of those, but a list of a sample of LSI's (also called large-scale OD interventions, or LODI's).

Three Different Strategies to Large-Scale Change—An Integrated Approach

OD has grown and evolved since its beginnings, as has the perspective on how to effectuate and manage change. An OD strategy is a "plan of action defining how an organization will use its resources to gain a competitive advantage in a larger environment" (Cummings & Worley 2015, 791). An OD intervention is "any action on the part of a change agent—OD interventions require valid information, free choice, and a high degree of ownership by the client system of the course of action" (Cummings & Worley 2015, 788). "Large-Scale Interventions (LSI) are an approach for organizing sustainable changes with the active involvement of stakeholders throughout the whole system" ("Large Scale Interventions English" n.d.). LSI is an integrative, systematic approach to managing change that integrates three critical aspects of an organization into a coordinated change effort strategy. According to Brown (Brown 2011, 148), there are three basic strategies to change: structural, technological, and behavioral. The sociotechnical systems approach to change is an approach that is a matrix of connections between all three change approaches. Figure 10.1 captures the flow between the OD practitioner and improved performance while integrating the three different change strategies, the responses to the strategies, and the goals of each. Note the simultaneity of each of the strategies working in concert toward improved performance (see Figure 10.1).

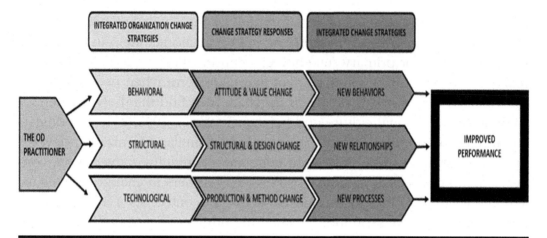

Figure 10.1 An Adapted Integrated Approach for Large-Scale Change. Adapted from (Brown 2011, 151).

LSI for Strategic Planning for the Organization

SWOT Analysis

Change leaders use SWOT analysis, a brainstorming technique, as a strategic planning tool. According to Phadermrod et al., "It helps the organization to gain a better insight of their internal and external business environment when making strategic plans and decisions by analyzing and positioning an organization's resources and environment into four different categories (regions): Strengths, Weaknesses, Opportunities, and Threats" (Phadermrod et al. 2019, 194). SWOT analysis is one of many tools in a strategic planning process. SWOT's advantage is its simplicity. However, what makes it attractive (simplicity) can be a disadvantage, suggesting that most vocal stakeholders receive the most credence.

SOAR Analysis

SOAR is another innovative strengths-based analytic, strategic planning approach. SOAR engages the whole system and integrates Appreciative Inquiry (AI) within the strategic planning framework. SOAR becomes a part of a transformational process that focuses on inspiring organizations to envision a future version of itself that is much better than it is currently. Intentionally omitting the negative, deficit-based Weakness and Threat categories featured in SWOT, SOAR focuses on Strengths, Opportunities, Aspirations, and Results (forming SOAR). By focusing solely on these positive quadrants, the intervention builds dynamic, sustainable relationships among stakeholders while envisioning today's organization and the future. SOAR, as part of the strategic planning process, can be the basis for an organization's mission, vision, and values statements creation or editing. Additional SOAR applications focus on strategic and tactical planning as a conduit to higher stakeholder engagement to yield transformational change. Holman et al. (2007) identify the SOAR process to include:

- Inquiring into strength and opportunities
- Imagining the best pathway to sustainable growth
- Innovating to create initiatives, strategies, structure, systems, and plans; and
- Inspiring action-oriented activities that achieve results (Holman et al. 2007, 379)

Whole System Transformational Change

Whole System Approach (WSA) coordinates and integrates multiple organizational change initiatives into one structured, collaborative change initiative focusing on the whole. Seeking organization-wide change, WSA is a platform for large-scale employee engagement to generate peak employee performance and highly effective leadership. Unique to WSA, the system focuses on stakeholders and potentially engages external stakeholders, including customers, vendors, suppliers, contractors, and others who might be impacted by the potential change or currently being impacted by the presenting problem. According to Holman et al. (2007), organizations that invest in WSA can anticipate:

- Accelerate the speed of change implementation
- Stimulate cooperation, engender commitment, and reinforce teamwork
- Generate organization-wide ownership of efforts with all stakeholders
- Produce results that could not have been accomplished using traditional methods
- Develop organizational self-reliance and resiliency for sustaining a thriving organization

- Achieve successful fundamental change and corporate re-invention (Holman et al. 2007, 443)

ERP Implementation

"Because they are designed to fit the needs of many organizations, enterprise systems are built to support generic business processes that may differ quite substantially from the way any particular organization does business" (Markus & Tanis 2000, 177). Enterprise Resource Planning (ERP) enables and simplifies complex organization (usually business-related) activity information sharing between different parts of the organization into smoother flows. Often referred to as ERP systems, ERP applications guide business activities across organizational boundaries such as departments or divisions. Large-scale ERP interventions generate solutions directed at resource efficiency and structural changes to improve workflows.

Markus and Tanis' four-phase model focuses on the importance of these critical success factors across ERP implementation and upgrade phases. The importance of these factors across the ERP implementation stages and upgrade is very similar to tasks associated with a traditional OD process. The Chartering step prompts similar activities found in OD entry and start-up where practitioners develop a "business plan and vision" and lobby to secure "top management support and championship" (Nah & Delgado 2006, 1). Nah and Delgado go on to describe "'ERP Team Composition, Skills and Compensation,' 'Project Management' and 'System Analysis, Selection and Technical Implementation'" as being a critical part of the Project phase (Nah & Delgado 2006, 1). Next, Nah and Delgado describe "'Change Management,' and 'Communication' as essential during the Project and Shakedown phases" (Nah & Delgado 2006, 1). Finally, Nah and Delgado describe the fourth stage of Markus and Tanis's ERP change model as "'Change Management' and 'Communication'" as essential to the Project and Shakedown phases (Nah & Delgado 2006).

Search Conferences

The search conference intervention is a highly participative strategic planning and policymaking tool. Practitioners use search conferences to develop and establish strategic and tactical goals for the organization. The search conference objective is to create action plans for the integration of ideas generated during the process. Search conferences focus on issues that impact conference participant invitees. According to Holman et al. (2007), search conferences are best with groups of no more than 35 people and typically occur over two days. Holden indicates that search committee interventions can also lead to new systems to manage future issues or issues that remain unaddressed from the past. Search committee interventions are based on open systems theory and consider the entire organization system and its operating environment. Search committee interventions integrate both system-related observations and environmental element observations when formulating action strategies. By considering these two system boundaries, the impacted community of stakeholders can gradually use the generated information as the basis for growth in other areas of the system and organization (Holman et al. 2007, 351).

Open Space Technology/Open Space Meetings

Stakeholders "self-organize" around everyone's conference theme-related interests. There is little structure, so the intervention is free-flowing within the OD practitioner/practitioner's boundaries. Cummings and Worley (Cummings & Worley 2015, 313) indicate that there are two sets of norms that, though mutually exclusive, are at the heart of the intervention's success. If these norms are not followed, the intervention is destined to fail. Cummings and Worley identify the first of the two norms as the "law of two feet," which prompts participants to take responsibility and be accountable for their behavior. These behaviors include attending meetings and going to discussions, which are the centers for collaboration, engagement, and learning. The authors describe different participants as either "butterflies" or "bumblebees." Butterflies attract others to engage in informal conversations that would probably not occur in formal settings such as meetings. Bumblebees move from group to group, contributing knowledge and new ideas to each of the conversations in which they participate.

Cummings and Worley (2015) refer to the next set of norms as the "four principles." The first principle accepts that whoever participates in the discussion is the right type of person to be involved. Next, the second principle features the concept of personal responsibility into the discussion mix and that participants should remain flexible and prompt others to action. The third principle focuses on the intervention's temporal nature, suggesting that things develop in their distinctive way, at their unique pace, in their own time. The fourth and final principle of open space focuses on the finality of the session. The discussion is done when it is done. This principle states that there is no obligation to continue discussions or meeting to satisfy any other requirement once the initial time requirement and debate or brainstorming is concluded (Cummings & Worley 2015, 317).

World Café

The World Bank defines the World Café technique as a "format of collaborations designed to yield deeper insights into pressing collective issues" (Watkins et al. 2012, 132). OD practitioners invite stakeholders to share conversations in group settings to generate ideas and opinions to formulate actions and solutions to address troubling needs. The World Café intervention is a popular, highly collaborative, generally, quick, and fun approach. The ability to use World Café is advantageous when dealing with large and diverse groups, promoting collaboration and transparency toward decision-making. World Bank change leaders state "(World Café) lends itself well to needs assessment because it can provide unique opportunities for gathering information when other techniques would not be appropriate, viable, affordable, or useful" (Watkins et al. 2012, 132).

Although this technique is extremely flexible and often yields more "nuanced data and findings than structured interviews or focus groups," (Watkins et al. 2012, 133), this approach requires substantial advanced planning. It is only as good as the number of and the type of stakeholders that participate in the discussions. In one creative version of this intervention referred to as "Speed Dating," OD practitioners change the typical World Café set-up from hosting the usual 20-minute conversations (generally held in small groups) and adjust it for a version similar to speed dating. In speed dating, single adults meet to interview each other when searching for a suitable romantic match. In this case, the twist is that stakeholder pairs have 5–8 minute problem-focused brainstorming sessions together before moving on to their next partner. After several rounds of these dyads, the practitioner begins to facilitate discussions and share ideas generated from the many conversations with the rest of the group.

Appreciative Inquiry Summits

Pioneered by David Cooperrider and Suresh Srivastava, AI has gained momentum as a proven intervention technique. The summit is an opportunity to introduce the concept of asset-based thinking, which in and of itself is a celebration and to celebrate the successful development of the future forward-looking action plan. By celebrating success, the organization creates a stronger foundation for sustained change. Appreciative inquiry summits engage as many stakeholders as possible in a real-time change effort based on creating deep, asset-based conversations through inquiry. Designed around the 4-D approach (Discovery, Dream, Design, Destiny), AI moves individual stakeholders through each phase. AI generates positive outcomes as possible solutions to what the organization is experiencing. AI helps to identify what stakeholders are doing correctly and what the organization will look like in a future state based on the stakeholders' preferences and opinions. Once the preferred future state is identified, the OD practitioner leads stakeholders in designing an action plan to realize these organizational aspirations.

Four Structures for Organizing Change Efforts on a Large-Scale (Banerjee n.d.)

There are four different structures or approaches that an organization navigates when dealing with an LSI. The organization often shifts between each throughout the large-scale change effort. The practitioner may believe that the structure to adopt is one way, but it quickly morphs into another approach. The awareness of this constant interaction between different structures differentiates a large-scale change specialist from the change management generalist. Figure 10.2 provides a brief description of four structures I previously referenced (Banerjee n.d.):

The Shadow Organization	Change efforts requires organizations to create separate organization charts of various specialized teams, i.e., training & development, physical plant, where teams engages the change effort based on required milestones, but only those that are focused on their specialization. These specialized teams still operate within their existing, respective overall work-groups or divisions targeting the required change milestones for their specific areas (Banerjee n.d.).
The Embedded Effort	Responsibilities of required change are built into the job employees' descriptions. By embedding the responsibilities of change into the job descriptions, this mandates attention to any change effort as a part of job performance. Change-related performance is added as the list of KPI's to be assessed as part of overall job performance. By mandating change responsibilities at the individual level, no additional organization structures are necessary to effectuate change (Banerjee n.d.).
The Dream Team	This is a change structure can also be referred to as the star approach. The change consultant works with the organization to identify superstars from within the organization. Once these stars are identified, a change task force is created comprised of these stars. The sole purpose of this task force is to generate a proposal for change implementation based on the stars' opinions and observations, which are ultimately presented to the C-level executives for disposition. It is a known fact that in talent management circles that an organization's "stars" are as much as 20% more productive than the average rank and file employee. This change structure builds on that high level of engagement and performance (Banerjee n.d.).
Institutionalized Structured Change	This change structure is when the organization chart is modified to create specific departments that handle a change aspect. For example, organizations are increasingly establishing departments that focus exclusively on Diversity and Inclusion-related change. In contrast, other departments might be created to manage change impacting production or quality, or safety. In all cases, the organization is augmented by the creation of separate change-focused departments as recognized parts of the overall organization. These change silos only focus on the parts of the large-scale change that impact those within their silo's boundary (Banerjee n.d.).

Figure 10.2   Four Structures for Organizing Change Efforts on a Large-Scale—(Banerjee n.d.).

Business Case Study

The following case study is based on an actual company. The names of the company and specific stakeholders have been changed for illustrative purposes.

Case Background

"Company A" is a U.S.-based, privately-owned, and specialty lighting manufacturing company located in the Midwest. Company A has 300 employees.

The leadership structure is similar to most individually owned, private companies with the owner, Bill Lighthouse, situated at the top of a matrix. Though an authoritarian leader, he is a servant leader and is loved by his employees. Critical managers and leaders from different silos within Company A form the remaining parts of the matrix.

There are six silos at Company A. The first silo is the owner (Bill Lighthouse). Chief Relationship Officer Elizabeth Montgomery is the administration/customer service team, while Chief Financial Officer Jessica Gold runs the financial division. The technical design/engineering team lead is Vice-President Tim Dezyne, who works closely with sales team lead Vice-President Garret Gray. Finally, the production/distribution team leads are 20-year veteran supervisors, Jim Major and Christine Senior.

Company A's challenge is that employees who worked under the previous owners are questioning the direction and the culture of the company. This lack of trust creates inefficiency. Mistrust is a distraction and undermining the facility's productivity and the ability for Company A to meet the increased demand for its highly innovative specialty products.

The organization has a history of profitability and success, resulting in significant company growth with major human capital implications. The owner and leadership team understands that change capability is critical to reaching Company A's overall goals. However, the leadership realizes that part of the organization is not prepared to achieve this capability.

The OD practitioner was contacted by the company's owner to "do some team-building exercises to create a better culture and new focus" to improve efficiency and ultimately increase Company A's ability to meet the increasing demand. The owner believes that if this mistrust can be mitigated, increased revenue for the company is inevitable.

Intervention Preparation

Rothwell (2010) indicated that the start of any change effort is where the OD practitioner must "enter the organization, to build a platform for engaging in change work with the client, and to contract for work, methods, relationships, and exchanges" (Rothwell 2010, 206). Due to large organizations' complexity, the OD practitioner must make considerable efforts in completing the "front-end work" (Rothwell 2010, 207), whose quality directly translates into success probability. The planning and preparation phase is where the OD practitioner established his relationship with the organization and gathered information to formulate the people-focused infrastructure for the LSI.

Step 1: Entry/Contracting

The OD practitioner set up a time to meet with the owner to explore the presenting problem using a prepared question list that included items like "In your opinion, what is the presenting issue, and how have you determined what the organizational problems and issues are?" The OD practitioner queries establish what the owner, a key influencer, believes regarding his organization's current status, what the problem is, and who is impacting that problem. The OD practitioner then asked the owner (primary stakeholder) to identify influencers in the company and to what degree they are equipped to lead the change at the local level. The OD practitioner should note the degree of influencer readiness described for each and used the notes for the first series of intervention interviews.

The OD practitioner exited the meeting reiterating the necessity of building and maintaining trust throughout the whole process. The owner had to be present, communicative, visible, and accessible during all change intervention stages. The OD practitioner pointed out that a 2016 Prosci study on change initiative effectiveness shows that over 70% of change initiatives failed because the primary sponsor was not engaged, nor was they visibly involved in the process. Regular communication was a core responsibility of the primary sponsor, integral to developing and supporting the subordinates' desire for change success (Creasey et al. 2018, 199–208).

The practitioner stated that in his role, he would remain ethical in his dealings with company employees and be free from conflict, saying that unequivocally, he would stay true to these important guidelines. The OD practitioner concluded by ensuring that if the right change team could be assembled enhanced by the owner's visible presence and commitment to the process, a high-level of employee engagement towards achieving Mr. Lighthouse's goals was probable.

The OD practitioner finalized the logistical, legal, and financial arrangements of the LSI. Additionally, the OD practitioner completed the psychological contract with Bill Lighthouse, the owner of the company. The psychological contract is a mutual commitment and comfort between the practitioner and Mr. Lighthouse. The psychological contract combines a shared understanding of why the OD practitioner was being engaged, how the OD practitioner would conduct the change intervention, and why the primary sponsor must be highly visible and engaged throughout the whole process. Being explicit about their mutual expectations built a high-level trust relationship. This comfort between the practitioner and the primary sponsor is a solid foundation for moving forward. In summary:

GOAL: Achieve an understanding of crucial influencers and sponsors' presenting problems and perspectives while establishing a consulting relationship between the OD practitioner and the primary sponsor/organization.

Step 2: Start-Up

The OD practitioner set up a second meeting with the owner not much later. The purpose of this meeting was to establish the parameters of the change project with details regarding the following (Rothwell 2010, 201–2; Foster n.d.):

- The goals for the LSI project
- The scope of the LSI project
- Mutual expectations
- Anticipated results
- Logistics and "rules of engagement"
- Dealing with and maintaining confidentiality
- Practitioner responsibilities
- Client responsibilities
- Project calendar
- Expected costs and payment arrangements
- Concluding steps towards sustaining the change
- Feedback and how to handle the feedback
- Termination procedures

GOAL: Articulate the parameters above. Gain permission and support from the primary sponsor beginning with the end in mind and start the generative LSI.

Step 3: Feedback and Assessment

As the initial foray into the organization, the OD practitioner gathered initial base information about the problem, the people most impacted, and generated feedback from sponsors, stakeholders, and decision-makers. In some instances, the OD practitioner may include feasibility studies and other assessments that might provide base data to assist in designing and planning the change project (Holman et al. 2007, 303).

GOAL: Identifying Who Should Be Involved—The Stakeholder
Community Map

Stakeholder analysis is the systematic identification, evaluation,
and prioritization of everyone who can influence or interest in a
project, program, or business. It assists with the development of
an effective stakeholder communication and engagement strategy.
It is a fundamental element of an organization's stakeholder
management plan ("Stakeholder Analysis, Stakeholder Mapping
Template - GroupMap," n.d.)

The OD practitioner needed to identify Company A's most influential
members. These members are the infrastructure that will drive the necessary
change to meet the owner's objectives. Stakeholder mapping is the process
that the OD practitioner used to identify stakeholders, the interested parties
impacted by the change initiative. Once stakeholders are identified, the OD
practitioner maps their names on either two axes, interests, and influences.
By establishing which stakeholders have the most significant interest in
change while also having the most influence, the OD practitioner was able
to identify critical influencers who would have the most profound impact on
the success of the change initiative. Stakeholder analyses can prioritize resources based on the highest representation in both categories and utilized
for information dissemination as per the communication and engagement plan.

Stakeholder analysis can be completed at the beginning of the change
initiative. However, it is recommended to revisit the matrix regularly
throughout the intervention to confirm that the most interested and influential
organization members are still contributing to initial expectation levels, critical
to project success. The OD practitioner understands that not engaging influential stakeholders "in the right way at an early stage can have disastrous
results for a project" ("Stakeholder Analysis, Stakeholder Mapping Template -
GroupMap" n.d.).

The following list shows individuals who are critical to any LSI's success
and why each is essential to move a change intervention forward successfully
and to successful completion. The OD practitioner considers several definitions when developing his stakeholder map. They are:

- *Primary Change Sponsor*—"The primary sponsor is the person who
  charters and authorizes the change. For large changes, this person is

typically a senior manager or officer of the corporation. For smaller changes, this person could be a supervisor or department manager" (Creasey et al. 2018). However, typically the primary sponsor has the authority to authorize the change initiative and has access to resources that will support the change initiative.

- *Change Executive Team*—Company A executives who are members of a change "task force," who deliver change by providing oversight and accountability to those change personas/sponsors who influence the change.
- *Change Team/Sponsor Coalition*—the group of sponsors who support change and promote change with their actions, behaviors, and conversations. Creasey et al. (2018) point out that sponsors can be from anywhere in the organization, but in particular, middle managers and supervisors are generally the most powerful sponsors of change. Note here that sponsors can be stakeholders, but not all stakeholders are sponsors as not all stakeholders support or advocate for change.
- *Change Personas/Sponsors*—influencers within the organization who assist in delivering the change through their actions or message sender and receiver when dealing with rank in file stakeholders.

When building his sponsor coalition, the OD practitioner decided that in identifying these influencers, before assessing their sponsor competencies, it was imperative that he:

- Knew influencers/sponsors by name
- Knew influencers/sponsors by position
- Knew influencers/sponsors by power/level of authority
- Knew background of influencers/sponsors and previous change experience
- Knew influencers/sponsors' perceptions of change

The OD practitioner was able to administer a Sponsor Competency Assessment to establish which sponsors would be good stewards of the change initiative. It helped identify those who potentially could harm the initiative with either their change resistance or lack of ability to drive change from their position of influence.

Step 4: Action Planning

Generating feedback through assessments and action planning is often used informally in OD preparation phases. Both may be used informally in the pre-launch and launch phases of various OD efforts (Rothwell 2010, 234).

Significant, radical change provides the OD practitioner the context for assessing and action planning for organizations. Often the OD practitioner's philosophy toward both guides them in these action planning and assessment activities. For example, in this case, the OD practitioner had a positive, asset-based, or appreciative philosophy toward change. The OD practitioner chose the AI approach. AI captures positive stories about Company A. These stories are then used to identify some of the processes and practices that give life to Company A. In this case, the choice for AI was natural for the practitioner. He noticed immediately that throughout his dialogues with stakeholders and sponsors, their view of Company A and Bill Lighthouse was significantly positive and favorable. Given the nature of positive comments received about Company A and Bill Lighthouse's leadership, it made sense to opt for a positive, asset-based action plan such as AI.

The OD practitioner collected data by examining existing data provided by the organization. Additionally, he conducted unstructured, open-ended interviews with key people who could reveal the strengths and weaknesses of Company A (the real power of using AI. The OD practitioner followed up with questionnaires used to evaluate sponsor competence, live observation of Company A workers, and live assessments through workshops and training. In this case, many of the workshops and training sessions had to be online,

The OD practitioner viewed action planning as an opportunity to energize and mobilize people at Company A to accelerate the time needed to create buy-in from the change resistors by focusing on the "What's In It For Me (WIIFM)" aspect of the change initiative. Following Beckhard and Harris's four-step process, the OD practitioner was able to ascertain:

- The level of change acceptance
- Where there needed to be additional change-related guidance or info
- Determine where change leaders or the OD practitioner needed to intervene
- Choose the technologies to be used in the intervention

"Because action plans most often include change, and change is scary and hard, it is helpful to create launch phases with different time frames to address short, medium, and long-term goals" (Rothwell et al. 2017, 148)

Step 5: Intervention

Company A LSI Appreciative Inquiry Summit

In Chapters 1 and 2, we already discussed AI. In this chapter, we view AI again, but from the perspective of Large Scale Intervention. The OD practitioner began to review initial base data for Company A. Based on conversations he had with different sponsors, he decided to choose AI as the LSI that would best fit the circumstances. Although there were some instances when the practitioner came across accounts of conflict, problems, or stress, it was clear that positive change was of interest to many. The OD practitioner viewed the AI intervention through the lenses of various goals that form the infrastructure for an LSI change initiative. As AI flows through a cycle of 4-Ds (see Chapter 2), the OD practitioner's intervention path looked like the following:

- **Discovery**—by mobilizing the whole system, the organization finds its positive core through inquiry of the change practitioner. The OD practitioner began interviewing key sponsors regarding the current and future states of Company A. In the end, the OD practitioner was able to form a core team to assist in the AI process. During this phase, the OD practitioner began to implement the SOAR analysis described earlier.
- **Dream**—long before the emergence of AI, Beckhard and Harris focused on the importance of including a vision of a preferred or "future state" of the organization (Beckhard & Harris 1987, 56). The OD practitioner spoke to internal groups for 20 minutes at a time to build enthusiasm toward the change process and helped them envision the Company A of the future. The OD practitioner was able to complete the SOAR analysis to this effect.
- **Design**—the OD practitioner facilitated final discussions in small groups of 20, creating propositions of what the future Company A would look like to the stakeholders. In this phase, the OD practitioner used action learning and such tools like nominal technique to gain consensus on critical features of the preferred future Company A.
- **Destiny**—in this final part of the AI cycle, the OD professional was able to strengthen the focus on the positive and affirmative to build a hopeful workforce focused on high performance (Holman et al. 2007, 77–78).

Before starting the AI-based change strategy, the change practitioner was involved in briefing line managers and influencers to assemble an internal change team. The OD practitioner developed "a series of questions focusing on affirmative topics for their interviews, developing an interview protocol, practice interviews, and best practice stories" as described by (Holman et al. 2007, 80). Just before the three-day planned AI Summit, the OD practitioner team focused on seven guiding questions that were germane to Company A's situation:

1. Who in the organization would be responsible for promoting this change?
2. How could the OD practitioner help sustain and improve executive/management buy-in?
3. What parts of the organization could support the change process as it moves forward?
4. What opportunities are there to promote and develop the change strategy even further?
5. What obstacles might be counterproductive or undermine the change initiative?
6. What resources will the internal change team and sponsor coalition need to foster the change initiative?
7. Who could best help with the execution of the change strategy and manage future-focused change without external assistance?

GOAL: Identify Impact Points of the Change Initiative: Heat Maps

The OD practitioner knew that a heat mapping process could do several things within the intervention context. From his previous sponsor identification assessment (a form of a heat map), the OD practitioner recognized that heat mapping was not a quick process. However, the OD practitioner considered a heat map to be a powerful tool to foster further discussions with the sponsor coalition. The new heat map would help facilitate better communication, decision-making, and planning for the change.

The OD practitioner used the heat map in local, more intimate discussions to set the stage for exactly what was to happen regarding the change initiative and when it was expected to occur. Much as when the tool was used when building the sponsor coalition, the new heat map gave a clear vision of each change's impact, but this time, showing the front-line stakeholder impact. The

OD practitioner also knew that heat maps could help identify how much change resistance could be expected and from whom. By identifying those possible trouble points early on, the OD practitioner can target specific areas to mitigate change resistance. This resistance was the core issue that Bill Lighthouse believed was causing the inefficiency, so it made sense to map not only the two supervisors whose resistance was potentially to blame but also those around the supervisors who might also resist.

Based on the stories told through AI interviews, the OD practitioner confirmed the need for improvement and efficiency within Company A, and using the heat map, was also able to identify the depth of the change resistance. The heat map was also used to develop the communication and reinforcement plans, especially targeting those who received additional coaching and interaction in Company A's resistance mitigation efforts.

GOAL: Managing Expectations Presenting the Change Strategy

Now that the OD practitioner had identified critical impact points for the change initiative, the focus shifted to aligning those impact points. More substantial organizations require many hands to do the "heavy lifting" of the change initiative. Whether refurbishing/re-inventing a division to take charge of change or assembling a "dream team," it was important that the change group presented the change strategy to all stakeholders, not the OD practitioner.

The Kick-off Summit: The OD practitioner decided on a multi-day "kick-off" whose sole purpose was to share the Strategic Change Initiative and how it came about. It was an opportunity for the OD practitioner to facilitate discussions on the implementation steps and discuss what was happening in the future. Note that smaller organizations may not require a multi-day event but can host a single-day change event open to stakeholders company-wide and using large-group facilitation.

The OD practitioner's challenge was to create stakeholder value identified in the change mandate communication that the OD practitioner helped develop. The OD practitioner noted an identification and acceptance process that each stakeholder goes through, which in and of itself is contextual and temporal. The process must be informed by the organization's change mandates, which ultimately establishes the boundaries and procedures that the consulting team considers when looking at the stakeholder matrix and impacts of the change systemically. By anticipating stakeholders' reactions to the change process and how those reactions affect other stakeholders in the matrix system, The OD practitioner could temper the resistance to change. Managing expectations is mission-critical in the intervention design process.

Managing client expectations is vital to establishing a trusting relationship between practitioner and client. By discussing and framing the intervention with clients based on reasonable expectations, the OD practitioner bolstered his credibility and the probability of success in meeting those reasonable goals. If the OD practitioner exceeded those reasonable goals, he knew it was a more significant opportunity to celebrate. In large-scale change initiatives, OD practitioners must recognize that reasonable expectations are essential to initiative success. If expectations are unreasonable, then the enterprise is already struggling before it is even out the gate. Overpromising combined with underdelivering is a recipe for disaster. By spending the extra time considering stakeholder expectations, the OD practitioner made the proposed change more palatable and reasonable. It is human nature to view change with either fear or skepticism. OD practitioners understand that those are innate defense mechanisms to status quo comfort zone challenges. Through his communication strategy, the OD practitioner established that the proposed changes would benefit Company A and stakeholders alike and that Company A recognized the anxiety and stress that often accompanies change. The OD practitioner knew that he and change sponsors must act to show compassion and understanding by establishing some reasonable expectations of the stakeholder. By setting reasonable expectations, the shock to the system was minimized, thereby lessening fear, stress, and anxiety that might be disruptive to a perfectly good change strategy.

Equally essential, transparency and disclosure of relevant information would build trust. The OD practitioner reiterated that downplaying serious issues or setting unrealistic milestones, goals, and timelines damages credibility immediately and undermines confidence in the change strategy that was being introduced.

The OD practitioner knew that one aspect of expectation management that practitioners often forget is that once an expectation is established, it is vital to keep the stakeholders in the loop regarding where the stakeholder is on the change timeline at the moment of communication. Change leaders must keep stakeholders posted in detail relevant to the stakeholder position (again, consider the organizational change structures from early on in this chapter).

GOAL: Organization Alignment

Targeted Training—Targeted training is when the change initiative must be delivered. Rather than the practitioner offering training organization-wide from the beginning, the practitioner identifies different constituencies impacted by the change the most or immediately. These constituency-focused change gatherings might focus on specific people who will be affected. The target then extends to other work groups or teams, then shifts again to larger entities like departments or divisions. The OD practitioner conducted the LSI in such a manner that he reserved the ability that in special cases, particularly when mitigating change resistance, to use targeted training for the maximum positive benefit and immediately aligning the needs and desires of the change sponsor with those of the front-line stakeholder.

The Communication Plan—As a practitioner, it is vital to the change initiative's success to recognize and communicate to the stakeholders that the new change process is an essential part of the organization's future. As such, recurring, effective, detailed communication must be the standard of communication from the very start.

The "Be On The Look Out (BOLO)" Technique—The OD practitioner decided to engage Company A stakeholders following a few different mantras. The first mantra was to communicate early in the process. OD practitioners should view a large-scale change initiative to be dependent on a conglomerate and matrix of relationships that must be maintained and informed for the effort to be successful. As a result, clear communication from the onset of the change was essential. Early communication needed to be detailed and concise. Early communication needed to indicate that the change process was about to occur. It was essential for stakeholders receiving the communication to "be on the lookout" (BOLO) for things related to the forthcoming change initiative.

Communication plugs directly into the structure that is being put in place by the organization to accomplish the change. However, there must be a balance between communicating with a purpose and communicating just for the sake of communicating.

Communicating without purpose and detail could fuel change resistance as stakeholders could start using words like "inundated" or "overload" or "death by memo." How the information that was being shared was relevant to the stakeholder audience receiving the information was essential. The OD practitioner tailored communication to a particular audience.

By communicating with all stakeholders regarding the anticipated benefits, the communication plan stumbled when Company A focused on the proposed changes and how they would benefit the organization and not the stakeholder. Painfully absent was how the person receiving the communication would benefit from the proposed change. By being inclusive in communication, it prevents any particular constituency from being or feeling left out. Unfortunately, when stakeholders felt overlooked, those forgotten or omitted stakeholders inevitably became a source for rumor and partial truths regarding the past's change efforts, which were extremely disruptive. It was equally problematic when communications dumbfounded stakeholders with unnecessary and extraneous details that had nothing to do with the stakeholder or the stakeholder's position.

So, the OD practitioner decided to communicate early and to everyone organization-wide. However, the OD practitioner purposefully focused on communicating only as often as necessary, always considering communication volume. The OD practitioner and change sponsors agreed to be detailed in their communication and remained open to adjusting the core information by tailoring aspects to specific silos or audiences.

> GOAL: Creating a Personal Change Commitment—A typical failure of LSI results from looking past the individual's inherent change powers and only focusing on the group as a whole. Large-scale change is focused on the entire group. But, there is a big HOWEVER. Failing to acknowledge that the ultimate power to change lies in the larger organization's individuals dooms the change initiative to fail. Each person's ability to process change is hard-wired into who they are. Many different psychometric tools are available to measure the way an individual responds to different change situations.

The OD practitioner decided to integrate a strategy where personalization to the change initiative established connectivity between Company A and an individual's commitment to change. By eliciting personalized feedback through targeted, deliberate opportunities for individual engagement, the OD practitioner created a foundation of collaboration and cooperation from the beginning.

Step 6: Evaluation

According to Brown, "Just as organizations are in continuous change, so too OD is a continuing process" (Brown 2011, 396). It is easy, especially in large-scale work, to watch as while sets of the organization's objectives are achieved, other new goals arise and along with them a new, fresh set of challenges. Nevertheless, Brown continues, " As a result, the OD practitioner has two primary criteria for effectiveness" (Brown 2011, 396). Brown believes that the effectiveness of an OD effort boils down to the stability of the OD effort after the practitioner exits the relationship and the organization system's ability to sustain the change and maintain the innovation it just went through it follows a recurring cycle of self-renewal. The OD practitioner must assess the level to which the intervention has yielded the intended results and outcomes. "The metrics used should have been identified and agreed before the intervention taking place" (Foster 2013). The following are more detailed lenses through which the OD practitioner viewed the success of Company A's LSI:

- Outcome-based evaluation determined whether the LSI had a material impact on stakeholders and the performance of Company A.
- Goals-based evaluation verified the AI intervention's real outcomes compared to Bob Lighthouse's goals that were part of the original contracted plan. A goals-based assessment identifies and promotes successful processes while discontinuing or realigning the ineffective ones.
- Process-based evaluation was utilized in conjunction with the outcomes-based assessment as the OD practitioner explored how and why the AI intervention produced the results that it did.

As indicated, because OD is an ongoing process, the OD practitioner decided to use a previously developed assessment of whether the undermining undertones that had once permeated the workspaces of Company A from veteran employees were still present even after the intervention engaged them. The OD practitioner used his AI protocol again with the production/distribution team leads, 20-year veteran supervisors, Jim Major, and Christine Senior. Both supervisors had been identified as change resistors and negative influencers. They had been positioning themselves and their subordinates between the state that Mr. Lighthouse wanted to see and where the two veterans were comfortable based on their previous loyalties. Using the final AI interview, the OD practitioner determined that the AI intervention had been a success. Not only were both veteran supervisors highly engaged and "wired into" the positive change direction for Company A, but they were also accepting of their ongoing roles, not just as supervisors, but change leaders in their own right.

Step 7: Adoption

During the adoption step, the OD practitioner must determine whether the company members accepted ownership and responsibility for the change that was addressed by the intervention and executed by the organization. The OD practitioner reviewed the action plan success metrics agreed to by Mr. Lighthouse and his Executive Change Team. Mr. Lighthouse and the Executive Change Team, along with the stakeholders and leadership, determined that the intervention had been effective and that they were going to adopt AI and asset-based philosophies for Company A's future. They would include AI as part of their onboarding process for all new and existing employees.

Step 8: Separation

During the separation stage, the OD practitioner must exit the organization after ensuring that the implemented change intervention will continue to work after he leaves. The OD practitioner established a final AI Summit to showcase the AI—Company A's success story.

> GOAL: Time to Celebrate—The Success Summit

Changing an organization's culture to embrace change is difficult. The organization is only as good as its people. The organization needs to recognize those stakeholders who are highly engaged in the change process and celebrate their stories with all stakeholders. By celebrating others' successes and rewarding those involved, the practitioner has effectively recruited advocates for the change initiative within the organization. With a network of recognized advocates, the change practitioner can build a stronger rapport with various constituencies focusing around the change "superstars." These superstars can be extremely useful in further communication or improving morale that might be struggling under the pressures of uncertainty due to the change initiative.

However, these celebratory gatherings, or summits, should not signify the end of the change initiative. Great care should be taken that the impression of premature finality does not take hold from the summit. A common mistake would be to end communication and eliminate the ongoing feedback fundamental to change initiative success long after the change effort has supposedly ended (Figure 10.3).

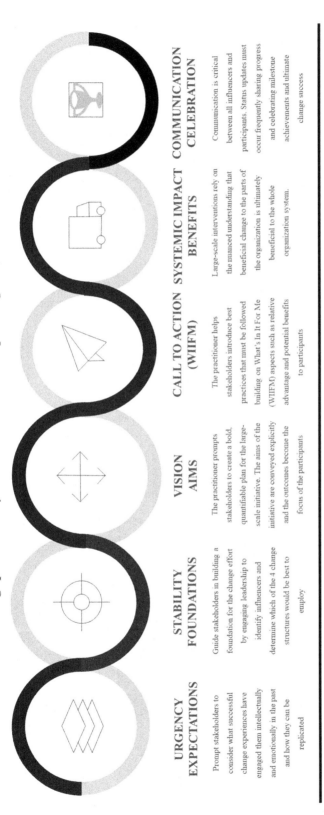

LARGE SCALE CHANGE PLANNING

The change process is only as successful as excellent planning and excellent execution

URGENCY EXPECTATIONS

Prompt stakeholders to consider what successful change experiences have engaged them intellectually and emotionally in the past and how they can be replicated

STABILITY FOUNDATIONS

Guide stakeholders in building a foundation for the change effort by engaging leadership to identify influencers and determine which of the 4 change structures would be best to employ

VISION AIMS

The practitioner prompts stakeholders to create a bold, quantifiable plan for the large-scale initiative. The aims of the initiative are conveyed explicitly and the outcomes become the focus of the participants

CALL TO ACTION (WIIFM)

The practitioner helps stakeholders introduce best practices that must be followed building on What's In It For Me (WIIFM) aspects such as relative advantage and potential benefits to participants

SYSTEMIC IMPACT BENEFITS

Large-scale interventions rely on the nuanced understanding that beneficial change to the parts of the organization is ultimately beneficial to the whole organization system.

COMMUNICATION CELEBRATION

Communication is critical between all influencers and participants. Status updates must occur frequently sharing progress and celebrating milestone achievements and ultimate change success

Figure 10.3   Large-Scale Change Planning—Original author creation © S. Ron Banerjee (2020).

Large Scale Intervention Planning Question List

Urgency Expectations	Stability Foundations	Vision Aims	Call to Action What's In It For Me (WIIFM)	Systemic Impacts and Benefits	Communication and Celebration
What about previous change initiatives have been a part of, inspired you to change?	Do current change leaders have the expertise and confidence to be able to lead this change initiative?	What is the aim of this change initiative and what is the level of urgency for its completion?	What is the nature of the change that is expected and how will it impact various constituencies in ways that are unique to each?	The success of large-scale initiatives requires a structured process for developing change throughout the system concurrently?	What forms of evaluation and assessment will be available to capture data in order to assess the impact of the change initiative?
What is it about this change initiative would prompt high levels of participation?	Is this change initiative a part of a larger change effort? Is it an initial step, middle step, or concluding step in the change process?	Is the aim ambitious yet actionable?	How do prospective participants currently feel about change? Is there a possibility that a resistance or change has grown due to the previous change initiatives?	How does the primary stakeholder plan to establish learning mechanisms to share information among participants?	How will the organization celebrate the experiences of change participants and the generative breakthroughs that have occurred during the large-scale intervention process?
Consider the scale of your proposed change initiative. What level of change is being sought, a system-wide transformation or an improvement to a current system?	What is the ideal series of reactions that you believe will occur and who will be involved in achieving your desired results?	What can you do as a primary stakeholder to create a shared sense of ownership towards achieving the desired outcomes?	Is there a possibility that the participants impacted by the change will feel overwhelmed or lethargic when it comes to participating in the initiative? What can you put in place to mitigate change resentment and dissent?	What mechanisms might be utilized to reach participants and particular targeted constituencies?	What can be done to make data not only easy to submit, but also easy to access and review by all parties?
As a primary stakeholder, are you committed to the levels of engagement this change may require to maintain the level of participant engagement necessary for change success?	Who can you engage that will have significant influence who can compel others to participate in the process? Who is a respected leader who can attract talented individuals to actively support and engage in the change initiative?	What is the timeframe for achieving the aims of the change initiative?	Consider resource availability. What amount of resources can be directed toward constituencies which require "extra attention" and where will those additional resources be taken from to mitigate these needs?	What are WIIFM benefits that will create value from the change initiative and does the primary stakeholder plan to foster that learning and value every day?	How can the primary stakeholder make the data useful and translate it into actionable knowledge which can improve ongoing learning and can facilitate performance improvement?
Is there an obvious performance lapse or a different need that creates a sense of urgency?	Who among those influencers is best suited to communicate effectively regarding the change initiative, the vision of the initiative, and the desired goals of the initiative?	Are there tacit goals that can be accomplished towards meeting the overall objective? (These are local goals and objectives that by their completion contribute to the overall success of the change initiative)	Are there other previous successful initiatives from which the constituency directly benefited with which the new initiative can be aligned?	Whether the whole system can be reached simultaneously or sequentially, what existing and potential communication changes are available to disseminate critical change related information?	What can the primary stakeholder do to regularly maintain the presence in the field to support and learn from participants?
What actions can you take that will make clear why the organization is seeking the change?	Who are the essential leaders who will be able to maintain and create relationships that are necessary for the success of the change initiative, even through there might be risk to work relationships with others?	What is the nature of the large-scale intervention? Is the intent of the LSI to help make participant free better by compliance? Is the proposed change a challenge to the existing organizational culture? Can certain elements of the LSO be introduced gradually and systemically leading to full implementation?	What external factors can contribute to participants being averse to change (media, regulations, compliance etc.)	What are the constraints that the primary stakeholder anticipates that might interrupt or preclude the distributed learning from taking place (This can often be time, limited resources, or geographic considerations)?	When faced with inevitable challenges, how can the primary stakeholder remain poised to address these situations while projecting an image of confidence and steadfastness while at the helm? How can the primary stakeholder establish a level of confidence and trust by generating iterative learning from the change experience on one hand while fostering creativity and optimism for success on the other?
	Can these influencers support the initiative by removing barriers, mitigating change resistance while recognizing success?		What can be done to communicate the benefits of the change not only for the organization, but also for the individual? (change incentives)	How will date be collected from the rank and file? How will that information be distributed to other constituencies? How will the information and innovations created from the process be shared system-wide?	What is the most significant way of celebrating successful change completion establishing a solid foundation for future change?

Figure 10.4 Large-Scale Intervention Planning Question List—Original author creation © S. Ron Banerjee (2020).

Key Lessons Learned

Successful large-scale change requires excellence in planning as well as execution. Practitioners must guide stakeholders through a rapid process that creates a change intervention structure worthy of participant trust, which is the continuous learning and improvement mechanism. By spending the necessary time to develop explicit rules for operation while managing clear expectations, the OD practitioner can assist the organization in emphasizing the continuous learning necessary to navigate a successful change intervention. By following the agreed-upon, established protocols, the OD practitioner helps to ensure that primary stakeholders have been able to position themselves to face the inevitable challenges that come along with large-scale change initiatives.

The OD practitioner assists primary stakeholders in remaining solution-focused and recognizing the importance of managing large-scale change logistics. Furthermore, the practitioner helps ensure that participants can rely on essential influencers who relentlessly demonstrate attention to detail and effective communication while assisting the critical mass of participants by giving them a voice and a sense of ownership for the change. The most successful large-scale change interventions balance dedicated, high-level planning, successful delivery of the intervention to participants, and attention to the many details generated during the intervention process. Although there might not be clear answers to many of the questions asked in the Large-Scale Intervention Planning Question Checklist (Figure 10.4), taking the time to review these nuances with primary stakeholders positions the organization for early victories built on keystones for intervention success. Moreover, the iterative learning that occurs by going through the process helps generate confidence and optimism essential to successful large-scale change.

Discussion Questions

1. What is the primary objective of an OD practitioner when first approaching an organization about conducting an LSI?
2. What are some problems that an OD practitioner might face when introducing an LSI to an organization? What are some problems that organizations might have in implementing an LSI?
3. Consider your answers to Question 2. Identify several types of LSIs and

give examples where each would make sense to introduce and how you would introduce them.

4. Compare and contrast the reasons for successful and unsuccessful LSIs. What stands out as critical to the success of the intervention? To what can most LSI failures be attributed?

5. What is it about a communication strategy that is so integral to the success of an LSI? Identify and explain what communication processes you believe should be in place for a successful LSI.

References

Arena, Michael J, PhD. 2009. "Understanding Large Group Intervention Processes: A Complexity Theory Perspective." *Organization Development Journal* 27 (1): 49–64.

Banerjee, Soumitra. n.d. "How to Structure Large Scale Change Efforts - Forum." *12Manage.Com* (blog). Accessed August 11, 2020. https://www.12 manage.com/forum.asp?TB=kotter_change&S=29

Beckhard, Richard, and Reuben T. Harris. 1987. *Organizational Transitions: Managing Complex Change.* Addison-Wesley OD Series xii, 117 p. Reading, Mass.: Addison-Wesley Pub. Co.//catalog.hathitrust.org/Record/001293248.

Brown, Donald R. 2011. *An Experiential Approach to Organization Development.* 8th ed. Boston: Prentice Hall.

Creasey, Timothy J., Kent Ganvik, Susie Patterson, Robert Stise, and Prosci (Firm). 2018. *Best Practices in Change Management 2018: 1778 Change Leaders Share Lessons and Best Practices in Change Management.* 11th ed.Loveland, CO: Prosci Inc.

Cummings, Thomas G., and Christopher G. Worley. 2015. *Organization Development & Change.* (10th ed.). Stamford, CT: Cengage Learning.

Foster, Carrie. 2013. "The Evaluation Phase « Organisation Development. 2013. https://organisationdevelopment.org/about-od/the-od-cycle/the-evaluation-phase/

Foster, Carrie. n.d. "The Contracting and Entry Phase « Organisation Development." Accessed August 10, 2020. http://organisationdevelopment.org/about-od/the-od-cycle/the-contracting-and-entry-phase/

Gilpin-Jackson, Yabome. 2017. "Participant Experiences of Transformational Change in Large-Scale Organization Development Interventions (LODIs)." *Leadership & Organization Development Journal* 38 (3): 419–432. https://doi.org/10.1108/LODJ-12-2015-0284.

Holman Peggy, Tom Devane, and Steven Cady. (Eds.). 2007. *The Change Handbook: The Definitive Resource on Today's Best Methods for Engaging Whole Systems.* (2nd ed. rev. and expanded). San Francisco: Berrett-Koehler.

Jacobs, Robert W. 1994. *Real Time Strategic Change: How to Involve an Entire Organization in Fast and Far-Reaching Change.* San Francisco: Berrett-Koehler.

"Large Scale Interventions English." n.d. Accessed August11, 2020. http://www.largescaleinterventions.com/english%20version/index_English2.htm

Markus, M. Lynne, and Cornelis Tanis. 2000. "The Enterprise System Experience—From Adoption to Success." edited by Robert W. Zmud and Michael F. Price. *Framing the Domains of IT Management: Projecting the Future Through the Past*, 173–207. Pinnaflex Educational Resources.

Nah, Fiona Fui-Hoon, and Santiago Delgado. 2006. "Critical Success Factors for Enterprise Resource Planning Implementation and Upgrade." *Journal of Computer Information Systems* 46 (5): 99–113. https://doi.org/10.1080/0887441 7.2006.11645928

Phadermrod, Boonyarat, Richard M. Crowder, and Gary B. Wills. 2019. "Importance-Performance Analysis Based SWOT Analysis." *International Journal of Information Management* 44 (February): 194–203. https://doi.org/10.1016/j.ijinfomgt.2016.03.009

Rothwell, William J. (Ed.). 2010. *Practicing Organization Development: A Guide for Leading Change* (3rd ed.). Pfeiffer Essential Resources for Training and HR Professionals. San Francisco: Pfeiffer.

Rothwell, William J., Angela L. M. Stopper, and Jennifer L. Myers. 2017. *Assessment and Diagnosis for Organization Development: Powerful Tools and Perspectives for the OD practitioner*. Boca Raton, FL: CRC Press/Taylor & Francis Group.

"Stakeholder Analysis, Stakeholder Mapping Template - GroupMap." n.d. *GroupMap - Collaborative Brainstorming and Decision Making* (blog). Accessed August 10, 2020. https://www.groupmap.com/map-templates/stakeholder-analysis/.

Watkins, Ryan, Maurya West-Meiers, and Yusra Laila Visser. 2012. *A Guide to Assessing Needs: Essential Tools for Collecting Information, Making Decisions, and Achieving Development Results*. Washington, DC: World Bank.

Weick, Karl E. 1995. *Sensemaking in Organizations*. Foundations for Organizational Science. Thousand Oaks, CA: Sage Publications.

Chapter 11

Industry-Wide Interventions

Norm Jones

Contents

Overview

This chapter provides a contextual framework for industry-wide interventions. It examines the circumstances by which interventions are adopted through all levels of system within an industry. This chapter covers the following areas:

- Industry-wide interventions and why they matter
- Making the case for change
- Change interventions
- Identifying the need for industry-wide change
- Electronic health records: An example of industry-wide intervention
- Evaluating system-wide interventions

Industry-Wide Interventions and Why They Matter

Industry-wide interventions come about as a result of system-wide observations around the need for change. A critical mass of these observations moves planned change interventions from a localized level to and beyond the level of system to influence how an industry operates relative to a change effort. This might be defined as an industry-wide intervention.

Organization development (OD), despite its many definitions, has at its core a clearly articulated commitment to helping bring clarity and process to intentional, planned change. Whether one favors Beckhard, Burke, Cummings & Worley, Bennis, or any other change theorist, most would agree that all OD theory involves change.

The inevitable transcendence of change across time and space as well as organization-type would suggest that the study of change would advance beyond the systems level to further examine planned change at the industry level. With the exception of HR research, it does not appear that a great deal of research around industry-level interventions and change has occurred—at least not from the OD perspective. Many industry leaders would benefit from the opportunity to gain greater access to OD approaches that support better understanding of interventions situated in change efforts.

Making the Case for Change

Rothwell et al. (2010) identify eight levels of organization change, with the sixth being industry or community-based change. Despite an apparent or unapparent need for change at the industry level, many different stakeholders may see themselves as responsible for making the case for necessary change. At the organizational level of system, the responsibility to articulate necessary conditions for change is not likely to be a bottom-up proposition, identified by Rothwell et al. (2010) as one of three modes of managing change. Therefore, for industry-wide change to be possible, many different systems, all with different cultures, organizational structures, leadership teams, and histories in a competitive marketplace, must acknowledge a collective need for a particular kind of change which leads to a future desired state based on identified outcomes.

Change Interventions

Interventions, broadly defined, are key to any change process (Cummings and Worley 2009) and represent activities though which changes in elements of an organizational work setting are implemented (Robertson et al. 1993).

To the extent that we view organizational outcomes as byproducts of such changes, interventions operate as independent variables (1993). According to Rothwell et al. (2010), change interventions within large systems are distinguishable from other interventions based on the following characteristics:

- They are triggered by environmental jolts and internal disruptions.
- They provoke revolutionary or transformational change.
- They incorporate new organizing paradigms.

- They are driven and led by senior executives.
- They require an organizational learning system.
- They involve multiple organization levels and large numbers of members.

Given these distinctions, what would constitute an industry-wide change intervention? Consider key terms in the list of distinctions: triggered; environmental; internal; revolutionary; paradigms; led; senior learning; levels; large. These terms serve as important indicators of change elements that explain system readiness for change. While this is traceable at the team and organizational levels, it becomes much more difficult to track within and across an industry because the environment within which an industry exists is made up of many different organizational cultures.

Identifying the Need for Industry-Wide Change

Healthcare is an ever-evolving industry. As a system, it is filled with complexity related to its regulatory environment, variable funding structures, governance issues that impact both public and private sector services, and, most recently, an externally driven shift in focus imposed by a global pandemic. All of this fluctuation and complexity creates an internal and external environment that makes the inevitability of change all the more daunting to face.

Those individuals responsible for any aspect of managing change both inside and outside of any discreet healthcare system must do their work with an attentive eye toward what is shifting at the industry level. These shifts render the work of OD, and more particularly the work of managing interventions to and through the point of evaluation, more critical than ever.

Change at the industry level takes time to emerge from the systems level. The point at which an entire industry experiences an intervention deems that intervention a core part of an organization's narrative around change. An individual organization joins a community of organizations that, in the aggregate, constitute an industry.

Part of the tension created in a change process is the extent to which adopters of the change are able to shape and influence any aspect of the change itself. An ideal paradigm was illustrated in the 2012 America Speaks 21st Century Town Meeting where "Tough Choices in Healthcare" were discussed. Hundreds of participants contributed their thoughts and perspectives on community healthcare and its relationship to legislative processes.

Planned Change

The process of planned change (Rothwell et al. 2010) can be explained in seven stages: exploration, diagnosis and planning, commitment building, managed change, planned follow-through, evaluation, and renewal.

Change Beyond the Level of Organization

Organizations who develop their own models and checklists for change are well positioned to fold change management principles into everyday organizational culture (Rothwell et al. 2010). It is less so the case that this possibility exists at the industry level, when not only many organizations, but many different systems (and the cultures and sub-cultures contained therein) are involved.

What process is most effective when an entire industry is faced with the need for planned, systemic change? I would posit that even at the level of industry, the fundamental framework of planned change holds great value. It is a matter of scale to ascertain what each step involves and which stakeholders are best positioned to influence change through delegated role and authority.

What Constitutes an Industry?

As previously mentioned, it doesn't appear that the field of OD has a specific working definition for the term, "industry" I've turned to the field of Human Resources (HR) to define the term. The Society for Human Resource Management (SHRM) follows commonly agreed-upon definitions of "industry" and the various industrial sectors detailed throughout the literature. Though SHRM research has not specifically undertaken its own study to define "industry" or "industries," their work addresses the needs of organizations in the four recognizable sectors of industry, as they are categorized based on their primary business activities. Their research, products, and services cover that spectrum to serve organizations in intellectual services, services, manufacturing/construction, and industries specializing in raw materials, such as oil, gas, agriculture, etc.

Specifically, regarding industry-wide workplace interventions, SHRM has studied change management, the effects of change, how to manage change, people-related policies and interventions surrounding change, managing productivity during change interventions, and the like. Most recently SHRM studied second-chance hiring and other cross-industry interventions of interest to executives wanting to remain competitive within their respective industries.

On the matter of historic perspective of industry shifts and interventions regarding electronic medical records, evidence is plentiful and well-documented. However, with regard to industry shifts and interventions, conventional wisdom as supported by the literature also reveals a few interesting points that should be considered as it relates to the future state of EHR. First, if the industry is competition driven, as the medical industry has become, the effects of both market-driven and government-driven interventions can influence productivity and sector growth while increasing efficiencies, whereas interventions designed to overcome a failure in the marketplace are less relevant to the medical industry. Thus, competition appears to be driving introduction of new business approaches in the medical industry in order to remain competitive—especially technology-based solutions like electronic health records (EHR).

Despite the need to implement these types of technology-based solutions to solve business problems in the medical field, privacy provisions and regulations worldwide will affect the short-term and long-term effectiveness of these types of shifts in the industry.

In fact, privacy concerns dominate a list of growing concerns from both the industry and patient viewpoints. Certainly, topics like safeguarding personally identifiable information (as governed by relevant laws domestically and internationally) are emerging as at least equally important as the many and varied issues related to healthcare "gadgets" that help individuals and medical personnel manage individuals' healthcare informatics.

Couple this with the growing desire of an individual to completely control his or her own personal medical information, the use of it, who has access to it, etc., there are likely to be unexplored issues that will affect industry-wide shifts, interventions and their effectiveness both short-term and long-term—and many other relevant questions that have been raised over time.

All these issues taken in total are likely to have yet-untold effects on how particular shifts are universally embraced by social culture as well as organizational culture. We may discover that it is too soon to predict when normalization will occur, but a review of other major interventions and shifts in the medical industry [perhaps in the last two decades] will likely tell a compelling story of how quickly and how well technology-driven interventions in the medical industry have been accepted as the cultural norm.

Large-Systems Change

Rothwell et al. (2010) refer to conditions that shift ground rules for organizations as one reason for large-system change. In the case of EHR, among other variables, the requirement to engage in an increasingly-complex and evolving environment is core to the case for change (Boonstra et al. 2014).

Pettigrew's framework (1987) on strategic change serves as an important basis for understanding innovation in the healthcare space. The framework uses as its primary domains of analysis, context, content, and process. Taken together, these three domains constitute organizational change (Boonstra et al. 2014).

Context-Blindness

It is interesting to cross-reference the concept of context-blindness (Rothwell et al. 2010) wherein blindness to one's own context and/or the context of others can lead to misunderstanding at both the interpersonal and organizational level. In both the case of Pettigrew's framework and the concept of context-blindness, a change process can be fundamentally altered by the information one has and the way that information is interpreted in an organizational context. Boonstra, Versluis, and Vos believe that this context can be divided between internal and external components. The internal context is comprised of structure, culture, resources, capabilities, and the politics of an organization (2014). The external context is comprised of the social, economic, political, and competitive environment of an organization

Emergent Change

The theory of emergent change (Burnes 2011) describes change as continuous, open-ended, and unpredictable. These three elements are certainly at play and working simultaneously as the overall healthcare system adopts or rejects the implementation of EHR. The literature around EHR implementation reveals no consistent use of any theoretical framework (Boonstra et al. 2014); however, emergent change informs the approach that Arts and Berg believe to be at play in their reference to socio-technical methodologies used in EHR implementation.

The social and technical dimensions of EHR implementation are dynamic and reliant upon one another. Aarts and Bergl (9) see implementation processes as non-linear and unpredictable. These attributes add to the overall complexities of the implementation process. The way in which work process and information technology sync has significant influence on the success of implementation. This also means that in order for the overall intervention to be deemed successful from an implementation standpoint, there must be connection between (1) medical work practices, (2) the information system, and (3) the hospital organization. Aarts and Berg (10) go on to assert that this level of synergy is only possible when and if adopters are willing to enact changes in how they do their work.

Theory and the Practice of Change

The theory and practice of change are connected. Organizations often behave as if individuals must choose a side: the theoretical side having to do with validation through research and the establishment of evidence or the practical side which is validated by observation and behavioral analysis. The reality is that planned change is predicated upon both theory and practice. One important social science theory at play within the practice of change is the known as the diffusion of innovations. We've framed implementation of EHR as an intervention within the overall healthcare system but it could also be defined as an innovation inasmuch as it involves rearrangement of a system to introduce an intervention that will bring about different business results and involve different methods of practice (Schwartz and Davis 1981). The ability to disseminate information about an innovation is core to the intervention implementation process.

According to Dearing (2009), the requisite communications process which allows for innovation information to be disseminated through an organization is known as the diffusion process. This process depends on three enabling conditions: an individual's need to reduce uncertainty in the face of new information; the need for individuals to understand their perceptions of others; and the need to do what others have done (Dearing 2009). The foundation of the theory was put forward by Linton (1936), who believed that diffusion included three distinct elements: presentation of a new culture element to the society, acceptance by society, and integration of the accepted element into the preexisting culture. Rogers Diffusion of Innovation Theory substantiates the moment of the tipping point whereby innovation, communication, time, and a social system come together to form the basis for planned change.

The Innovation

Rogers (1995) describes the innovation as "an idea, thing, procedure, or system that is perceived to be new by whomever is adopting it (5)."
It is important to note that the idea itself need not be newly developed but new to the individual or groups adopting the idea. Five key characteristics: relative advantage, compatibility, complexity, trialability, and observability, help to explain rates of adoption. Table 11.1 above shows the relationship of each characteristic to the anticipated improvement.

Table 11.1   Innovation Adoption Characteristics and Rates

Characteristic	Anticipated Improvement
Relative advantage	Faster adoption based upon perceived advantage the innovation has over what exists.
Compatibility	Level of alignment with adopters' values, needs, and experiences.
Complexity	Innovation is understood and used. The simpler the idea, the faster the adoption.
Trialability	Faster adoption based on the ability to test and assess.
Observability	Faster adoption based on how visible the innovation is to others.

Communication

The second element of Roger's innovation theory focuses on communication. The theory correlates the source of information regarding the innovation with the rate of adoption. This particular dimension of the theory is crucial because it is predicated upon an interpersonal condition—the social contract between two or more people plays a role between people who see themselves as similar relative to adoption behaviors (Rogers 1995).

One could imagine that this element has a strong influence over the efficacy of EHR implementation. It is one thing for a healthcare organization to make a decision to implement EHR, but the precision with which nuances of the implementation are communicated is also a critical element of a successful intervention. When role and authority are taken into account this becomes an even more complex proposition. There are those who will use the record—likely end-users—and those who are responsible for implementation of the system. They are many stakeholders in between. Communication throughout the introduction of an intervention is key. Strength and clarity of message is often evidenced through the success of the implementation.

Time

The third element of Roger's innovation theory focuses on time. The element is comprised of three components: the innovation-decision process, adopter categories, and the rate of adoption (Rogers 1995). In the context of this theory, time should be viewed as a continuum spanning the point at which a potential adopter becomes aware of the innovation to and through the point of adoption or rejection. Between these points are five steps in between:

knowledge, persuasion, decision, implementation, and confirmation. There are also five stages *within* the innovation process: agenda-setting, matching, redefining/restructuring, clarifying, and routinizing. The first two stages constitute what is referred to as the initiation phase. By the end of this stage, one will have a clear sense of whether or not the innovation will be adopted or rejected. Assuming adoption, the last three stages constitute the implementation phase.

Adopter Categories and Rate of Adoption

Measurement of how inclined someone is to adopt is another important element of industry-wide intervention. Rogers (1995) defines these adopter categories as: "innovators, early adopters, early majority, late majority, and laggards" (2). Table 11.2 illustrates the traits of each adopter category.

Identifying the Need for Industry-Wide Change

This chapter uses the healthcare industry as an environmental backdrop for the intervention of medical records. When we think of think of Cummings and Worley's (2009) descriptions of an intervention as "planned, and deliberate" (750) the implementation of EHR certainly fits the bill. The difference between an organizational intervention and an industry-wide intervention is that the planning for implementation of the change effort cannot be co-ordinated across the entire industry. In the case of EHR, many different environmental conditions, both internal and external, influence the timing and scope of implementation. A hospital, for example, is typically better

Table 11.2 Adopter Categories and Traits

Adopter Category	Adopter Traits
Innovators	Actively seek innovation; venturesome; not afraid to take risks.
Early Adopters	Open to change; closely connected to social system.
Early Majority	Usually about one third of social system, adopt just before average member of social system; deliberate in making adoption decision.
Late Majority	Another third of the social system; slower to adopt; skeptical about the actual innovation.
Laggards	Traditionalists; last group to adopt; suspicious of new ideas, products, services, process, etc.

positioned to implement EHR than a community health clinic. The two organizations both exist within the same industry but also within very different contextual systems.

Even within hospitals, there are distinct forces at play which may lead to variable forms and levels of implementation. Boonstra and Govers (2009) offer three characteristics that distinguish hospitals within the healthcare industry: (1) they are working to meet multiple objectives, (2) they have complex structures, and (3) they have a workforce made up of varied positions with multiple levels of autonomy.

Consensus-Gathering Processes

Senge et al. (1999) in his framing of consensus-building, locates necessary conditions for establishing agreement, at the senior most levels of the organization. He says:

> "Building genuine consensus on governing ideas, on systems of checks and balances and on blocks against authoritarian drift does not require unanimity. It does require people willing to find common ground in principle and practical solutions that everyone can live with. It also requires a group of people who collectively have the power to take action in designing go variance systems. In a corporation, this means the CEO and some significant percentage of senior managers. Depending on how sweeping the changes are, it may require involvement of board members as well" (378–379).

Even within one organization, the process of gathering consensus, at least initially, involves many stakeholders, the majority of whom hold a great deal of power around decision-making and setting strategic direction toward a future, desired state. One can imagine how much more difficult consensus-building becomes when that consensus must be built across multiple organizations and organizational systems.

One might also argue that, in the case of EHR, building consensus is not a necessary activity, in order for the intervention to take place. While this may be true in the literal sense, the consistency with which EHR are implemented across various systems contributes to the overall narrative around its efficacy. In this context, the word "efficacy" is not referring to the meaning or value of the EHR system itself, but rather to the efficacy of its implementation within the overall healthcare system.

A key but complicating factor in considering the challenges of EHR implementation is the fact that the intervention took place amidst a contentious federal regulatory environment. EHR gained support at the federal level through the 2009 American Recovery and Reinvestment Act, which illuminated the shortcomings of the healthcare industry as it relates to medical recordkeeping. Atherton (2009) identifies the economic environment at the time of implementation as a driving force and background for the intervention.

The Role of External Influences

One study by Jha, DesRoches, Campbell, Donelan, Rao, Ferris, Shields, Rosenbaum, and Blumenthal (2009) on hospital-based EHR found that of the 63.1% response rate from surveyed hospitals (N = 3049), only 1.5% had a comprehensive EHR system. The study defines "comprehensive" by the presence of EHR "in all clinical units" (p. 1628). Of the responding hospitals, those in urban areas (which also tend to be larger hospitals) and teaching hospitals, were more likely to have EHR systems. Respondents also reported capital requirements (1628) and high maintenance costs (1628) as primary barriers to implementation.

Location of an organizational system, the environment around it, and the overall healthcare environment are but a few critical variables which determine the extent to which external forces may influence industry-wide intervention and change. In the case of EHR, there are also just as many (if not more) internal variables at play as well. As previously mentioned, there is no industry-wide set of standards guiding necessary conditions for implementation of EHR in hospitals. Even in an internal setting, this challenge could easily exacerbate challenges around buy-in and individual stakeholder investment.

Considering Force Field Analysis

Payne (2013) discusses her use of Force Field Analysis in analyzing the value of specific change frameworks during the introduction of electronic clinical documentation among nursing staff. Force Field Analysis requires change agents to consider what "field of forces," as Lewin puts it, are hindering a system from its desired future state through restraining forces, and which are strengthening the driving force necessary to achieve that future desired state. In the case of EHR, these forces are at play both within individual organizations, at every level of system (Payne 2013) and also outside of the organization in the system-environment, where culture and readiness for change are also influenced and implicated.

Identifying Industry Leaders

Cummings and Worley (2009) speak of interventions as change efforts that are "planned, deliberate, and presumably functional" (750). The vast nature of a system, and for this discussion, a healthcare system, makes the identification of industry leaders a complex proposition. There are those who hold positional leadership by virtue of function and title. The individuals matter greatly when it comes to the execution of change, specifically change that is carried out, in part, through one's vetted role and authority. It is important to note, however, that positional leaders are but a small fraction of the community of adopters and implementers involved in such a significant universe of stakeholders connected to adoption and implementation of EHR within an organization and system. It would be interesting to conduct a stakeholder mapping exercise that identifies the variety of roles and positions necessary for successful implementation of an intervention such as EHR at the systems level.

Management of Change in Teams

Perhaps one of the most effective ways to understand industry-wide interventions is to situate the salience of organizational learning to the overall change process. Inasmuch as change requires both individual and team-inspired shifts in behavior, it is useful to analyze the ways in which an organization both understands itself as a learning organization and, as a consequence, behaves in accordance with that imagination of itself.

Ambassadorship in a Change Process

Leaders of change have myriad opportunity to influence teams' and members' perception and engagement with the change process. One of the most critical moments for a leader to gauge psycho-emotional investment in planned change occurs during the phase Wheatley (2016) calls "the neutral zone." She goes on to describe this zone as "a lonely place" (53) wherein people are disconnected from one another but also disconnected from the change process itself. Groups and teams often lose identity in these moments.

The opportunity to strengthen a team during times of transition involves a great deal of communication. Opening lines of communication allows ambassadors of change efforts to gauge how groups and individuals are faring in the change process. Even if the change is not experienced as positive, the psychology of change can feel more positive when individuals feel less isolated during the change. Communication becomes a kind of 'glue' that holds and connects people during a time that can often feel uncomfortable and possibly even scary.

Ambassadors of change are those who accept, only as a baseline, particular competencies to successfully lead individual and teams through change. The deeper work of change leadership moves above and beyond these domains and seeks what is possible through observation during various moments of engagement with team members. Adapted from Boyatzis (1998), Table 11.3 illustrates what Rothwell et al. (2010) outline as effective leadership competencies during change (Table 11.3).

Table 11.3 Leadership Competencies to Effectively Lead Change

Competency	Competency Description
Efficiency Orientation	The ability to perceive input/output relationships and the concern for increasing the efficiency of action.
Planning	The ability to define goals/objectives, strategy, tactics, and resources to be used to meet the purpose (mission).
Initiative	The ability to take action to accomplish something, and to do so before being ask, forced, or provoked into it.
Attention to Detail	The ability to seek order and predictability by reducing uncertainty.
Flexibility	The ability to adapt to changing circumstances, or alter one's behavior to better fir the situation.
Networking	The ability to build relationships, whether they are one-to-one relationships, a coalition, an alliance, or a complex set of relationships among a group of people.
Self-Confidence	The ability to consistently display decisiveness or presence.
Group Management	The ability to stimulate members of a group to work together effectively.
Developing Others	The ability to stimulate someone to develop his abilities or improve his performance toward an objective.
Oral Communications	The ability to explain, describe, or tell something to others through a personal presentation.
Pattern Recognition	The ability to identify a pattern in an assortment of unorganized or seemingly random data or information.
Social Objectivity	The ability to perceive another person's beliefs, emotions, and perspectives, particularly when they are different from the observer's own beliefs, emotions, and perspectives.

Evaluating System-Wide Interventions

The Whole-Scale ® Change methodology is a whole systems approach used to create rapid and sustainable change in organizations and communities around the world. Founded on solid theory and robust models it is flexible enough to address a wide range of organizational issues. A Whole-Scale journey engages large and small microcosms of the organization as the key elements of the change process, groups as small as ten and as large as 1,000 face-to face or virtual. Whole-Scale is based on the belief that the wisdom needed to create successful change is in the people, and the role of the consultant is to help leadership uncover, combine, and apply that wisdom to accomplish the results they are seeking.

Any leader willing to adopt Whole-Scale change methodologies would be well-positioned to promote a systems-thinking framework to evaluate the efficacy of a system-wide intervention. Huz et al. (1997) propose a framework for evaluating interventions enacted at the systems level.

Tools/Activities

The EHR system implemented at Health System X is an example of an intervention involving evaluation of attitudes toward the introduced change.

Entry

As efficient as EHR systems may be on their face, consultative entry involves the challenge of coming into a system distracted by the perception of added responsibility precision of records, additional costs, steep learning curves related to the need to learn new systems, and physicians who believe it beneath them to enter data.

Start-Up

The intervention was clear in its scope—to examine the experience of implementing EHR in Health System X. Consultants gathered this information through semi-structured interviews.

Semi-structured interviews followed the following format:

- Explain background and rationale for the interview.
- Present question but allow the interviewee to lead the conversation.
- Be concise. The interviewee should do most of the talking.

- Be conversational in re-routing responses that don't answer presented questions.
- Address any contradictions from other interviews in the form of follow-up questions.

Assessment and Feedback

Data gathered through interviews focused on four specific issues related to implementation: critical events, organizational leadership roles, culture, and changes in clinical practice. Feedback revealed challenges in all four areas related to implementation problems, not only with the system itself but with communication around the efficacy of the system.

Example of Agenda for System-Wide Leadership Summit

Health System X held a leadership summit as part of a culminating effort to collect information about the implementation of electronic health records. Such a summit allowed a cross-section of critical stakeholders in the change effort to share feedback in a format that would generate discussion and new ideas for how change might be managed in the future.

I. Opening and statement of purpose
II. Review of aggregated data by organizational divisions
III. Small-group discussions (by department) on top five highest and lowest scores
IV. World Café Gallery Walk
    a. Using the word bank generated in the planning retreat, which words still resonate?
    b. What do the top five highest and lowest scores indicate about our shared culture?
    c. If you were to do a SWOT analysis of our training for EHR, what would you include?

Action Planning

After engaging with the data resulting from the interviews, Health System X was able to reimagine data-entry roles for medical assistants, nurses, and physicians; discuss methods of troubleshooting for technological issues related to system use and end-user training challenges, and innovative forms of telephone consultations.

Key Lessons Learned

Industry-wide interventions are dynamic in that they represent culminations of organization-wide interventions that were likely implemented in varied timeframes and under disparate sets of circumstances. Although every organization exists in a different internal and external system, an industry has, as its backdrop, multiple organizations which exist within it. This should be viewed as an asset and an opportunity to more proactively plan change which may move beyond the level of system. Below, is a list of four key lessons learned while compiling this chapter.

1. There are opportunities to study change *before* it moves beyond the organizational level.
2. Industry-wide interventions require assessment of organizational learning systems.
3. Most determinants of whether or not EHR will be implemented are environmental.
4. The final stage of planned change, renewal, informs future iterations of intervention evaluation.

Discussion Questions

1. Should the field of OD create a definition for the term *industry*?
2. Should Force Field Analysis become a standard evaluation process when change is driven or influenced by a legislative environment?
3. Has organizational culture reached a point whereby every hospital should be held accountable for implementing EHR?
4. Should the body of literature on systems thinking include more case studies on industry-wide interventions?
5. Are there competencies specifically tied to a person's ability to lead industry-wide change?

References

Atherton, G. 2009. *How Young People Formulate Their Views About the Future: Exploratory Research*. London, UK: Aimhigher Central London Partnership. University of Westminster.

Boonstra, A. and Govers, M. J. G. 2009. "Understanding ERP System Implementation in a Hospital by Analyzing Stakeholders." *New Technology, Work and Employment* 24 (2): 177–193.

Boonstra, A., A. Versluis, and J.F. Vos. 2014. "Implementing Electronic Health Records in Hospitals; a Systematic Literature Review." *BMC Health Services Research* 14 (370): 2–24.

Boyatzis, R. E. 1998. *Transforming Qualitative Information: Thematic Analysis and Code Development*. Thousand Oaks, CA: Sage Publication.

Burnes, B. 2011. "Introduction: Why Does Change Fail, and What Can we do About it?" *Journal of Change Management* 11 (4): 445–450.

Cummings, T. G. and Worley G. W. 2009. *Organization Development and Change* (9th ed.). South-Western Cengage learning.

Dearing, J. 2009. "Applying Diffusion of Innovation Theory to Intervention Development." *Research on Social Work Practice* 19 (5): 503–513.

Huz, Steven, D.F. Andersen, G.P. Richardson, and R. Boothroyd. 1997. "A Framework for Evaluating Systems Thinking Intervention: An Experimental Approach to Mental Health System Change." *System Dynamics Review* 13 (2): 149–169.

Jha, A. K., C. M., DesRoches, E. G. Campbell, K. Donelan, S. R. Rao, T. G. Ferris, A. Shields, S. Rosenbaum, and D. Blumenthal. 2009. "Use of Electronic Health Records in US Hospitals." *New England Journal of Medicine* 360 (16): 1628–1638.

Linton, R. 1936. *The Study of Man: An Introduction*. New York, NY: D. Appleton-Century Company.

Payne, S. 2013. "The Implementation of Electronic Clinical Documentation Using Lewin's Change Management Theory." *Canadian Journal of Nursing Informatics* 8 (1-2): 1–11.

Rothwell, William J., J. Starvos, R. Sullivan, and A. Sullivan. 2010. *Practicing Organization Development: A Guide for Leading Change* (3rd ed.). San Diego, CA: Pfeiffer.

Rogers, E. M. 1995. *Diffusion of Innovations*. New York, NY: Simon and Schuster.

Robertson, P.J., D. Roberts, and J. Porras. 1993. "Dynamics of Planned Organizational Change: Assessing Empirical Support for a Theoretical Model." *Academy of Management Journal* 36 (3): 619–634.

Schwartz, H. and Davis, S. M. 1981. "Matching Corporate Culture and Business Strategy." *Organizational Dynamics* 10 (1): 30–48.

Senge, Peter, A. Kleiner, C. Roberts, R. Ross, G. Roth, and B. Smith. 1999. *The Dance of Change: The Challenge to Sustaining Momentum in Learning Organizations*. New York, NY: Doubleday.

Wheatley, Margaret J. 1994. *Leadership and the New Science: Learning About Organization From an Orderly Universe*. San Francisco, CA: Berrett-Koehler Publishers, Inc.

Wheatley, T. 2016. "Psychology and Brain Science are Not Zero Sum: Comment on Klein." *Psychology of Consciousness* 3 (4): 387–389.

Chapter 12

Community-Based Interventions

Jamie Campbell

Contents

Overview

This chapter provides information and support for creating community-based interventions. According to Rothwell, Stavros, and Sullivan (2016), the sixth level of OD intervention is industry or community-based change intervention. This chapter focuses on the community change intervention part, also known as community development. Furthermore, this chapter provides insight into how to engage, process, and depart from the community as an organization development (OD) practitioner. Also, readers will be introduced to the following elements of a community change intervention:

- What are community-based interventions?
- Identifying the power structures within the community
- The stages of community-based change intervention
- Understanding the needs and wants of the community

OD practitioners are often called into work for many different types of organizations or groups. It is critical to remember that OD practitioners are systems-thinkers. They partner with the client to improve the organization (Wilson 2018). Safely advancing this idea one step further, and for this chapter, it is useful to consider individual communities as organizations. An OD intervention may be necessary when a community calls for someone with the necessary expertise or experience to respond to the groups' certain needs. Most importantly, the task of that someone will be to engage the community's majority of people and make them active members in identifying their own solutions. An OD practitioner can be that special someone with the necessary expertise and experience to help the community members through a community-based OD intervention.

Understanding Communities

It is crucial to understand and appreciate a community, the community's social fabric, and its background and history when assisting with any community-based intervention effort. A community is not just a series of interconnected buildings or landmarks or a group of people in a common area. A community is all these things, and in many cases, it can be the lifeblood of an area. Accepting the call for assistance can be a daunting responsibility, so it is best to understand the community with which the OD practitioners are working. According to Berns (2007), there are five major ways to interpret the idea of *community based*. These are:

1. **Production, Distribution, Consumption:** This is how the community members make their living doing various jobs within the community.
2. **Socialization:** This point refers to how the community instills norms and values upon the community members. To foster socialization, community members may create and follow traditions like tree lightings, large meal gatherings, etc. Community members can also establish rules and generally accepted norms amongst them.
3. **Social Control:** Here, the community enforces the established rules of law, norms, and values recognized by the community members.
4. **Social Participation:** This is how community members interact with each other to fulfill the need for companionship. Examples of social participation are religious services, neighborhood sports leagues, or group activities.
5. **Mutual Support:** Community members recognize that there could be issues too large or too complex for one member or one group in the community to handle alone. For example, raising funds for a municipal park or housing development may be too difficult for one person or group, but may be possible if others in the community also participate and help each other.

When invited to work with a community, OD practitioners will need to identify the *presenting problem(s)* and the *underlying problem(s)* first. The presenting problem is why they were hired. It is what the client or OD practitioners can see right up-front. Another way to look at a presenting problem is to perceive it as a symptom or a surface issue. In many cases, clients often only want to deal with the presenting problems because they can be fixed quickly or relatively easily.

An underlying problem is the root cause of the presenting problem. If the underlying problems are not addressed, the solutions that are provided to resolve the presenting problems can be temporary or short-term. Underlying problems can range from communication issues between groups to inequalities in socioeconomic status. Underlying problems are usually discovered after the data-collecting process, such as preliminary conversations and one-on-one or focus group interviews with the community leaders and local participants. There are two reasons why underlying problems may exist. First, the problems are well known and apparent, but the community has not effectively communicated their presence or how to deal with them. Second, the problems can cause pain and angst that people just do not want to deal with. These underlying problems can create opportunities for permanent resolutions to the presenting problems, which would not be solved without OD practitioners' careful intervention and interactive assistance from the community. Both types of problems can be powerful tools for understanding the complete problem facing the community.

Types of Community-Based Interventions

Just as it is crucial to understand the problems facing the OD practitioners in developing a community-based intervention, it is also essential to understand the resources at hand to help create sustainable community plans. There are several ways to approach a community-based intervention. The following are four types to assist OD practitioners in developing a community-based intervention while using the community itself as a part of that intervention (McLeroy et al. 2003):

- **Setting.** This refers to the boundaries in which the community intervention is going to take place.
- **Target.** This refers to the community locations that will be changed due to the systemic changes created by the intervention.
- **Resource.** This refers to financing, assets, and materials needed for implementing a successful intervention.
- **Agent.** This is the engagement of individuals within the community as the catalyst for change and engagement of the selected intervention.

According to McLeroy et al. (2003), electing from one of these categories allows OD practitioners to determine a way to include the actual community itself as an instrument in the successful creation and sustained implementation of a plan. Selecting one or a combination of these categories can formulate a plan of engagement to which each person can give full consent. For example, using the types and categories of setting and resource together can be quite effective. Positive outcomes can be achieved by using these categories together. Using the community's location and the businesses, churches, and schools embedded in the area can create a positive outcome for the intervention. Figure 12.1 shows how the community can be used as a resource and how the persons involved can impact the intervention.

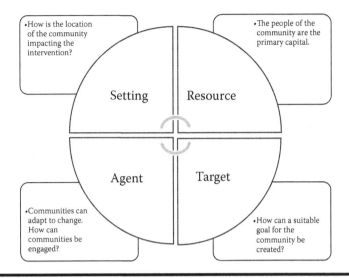

Figure 12.1   Using the Community as a Resource.

Identifying the Power Structures Within the Community

Figure 12.2 resembles a table with some seats around it. An OD practitioner can use this configuration and structure as a tool to begin community intervention. It might be helpful to think of this exercise as a major family dinner.

Figure 12.2   Community Intervention Table Setting.

Everyone at the table is related in some fashion, but everyone does not think the same and may have hidden agendas. Just like planning dinner seating, setting a meeting for a new intervention can be as difficult.

An OD practitioner may want to start asking some questions as below:

- **Who is the decision-maker?**
  Those who invited the OD practitioner into the community may not be the final authorities to approve the OD practitioner's intentions and action plan. This potential discrepancy can create a problem for payments to the OD practitioner or how the intervention moves forward.

- **Are there people who should not sit next to each other?**
  If possible, with some community members' assistance, the OD practitioner should determine who should not sit next to each other. The practitioner must consider that individuals have differing points of view. The OD practitioner may want to sit the individuals with different viewpoints on the same side of the table as a means for encouragement and to create an environment or mindset of "we are all on the same side."

- **Where is the influence coming from?**
  Those individuals with the most influence might not have any power at the table, but they could hold sway over the group.

- **Who are the naysayers?**
  It is common that some individuals might say "No" or "That's not going to work here" to a change intervention. But they could be an OD practitioner's most helpful contributors.

- **How many people does the OD practitioner need at the table?**
  Understanding the proper number of people and the correct people to have around the table can be difficult to accomplish. Knowing who should be at the first meeting could be an important start in creating a positive implementation. Speaking with the clients and other community members will provide some leads and the opportunity to speak with other community members at large. The selection of individuals invited to the table should also have some flexibility. If the right people are not there, even in the second meeting, it could impede progress. Making sure that the correct people are at the table can ensure acceptance of the proposed intervention.

- **Who is willing to buy into the message?**
  It is also common that some individuals are willing to hear an intervention message without a great deal of coercion or resistance. These individuals are likely to display an open, accepting, and engaging body

language. Therefore, they should always be in the line of sight of most of the people in the room.

- **Are there people who have not decided yet about the intervention?**
  When entering a community intervention, there will always be a sense of apprehension from community members about the intervention led by an unknown individual. However, they may be willing to give the benefit of the doubt to the OD practitioner.

Asking these questions will assist OD practitioners in the change intervention. Furthermore, it will help them find additional people to develop creative ideas that would serve the community in the change effort.

Business Case Example

Although this is a fictional case, the data represent an actual community. The actual data for the area can be found at City-Data.com (http://www.city-data.com/neighborhood/West-Farms-Bronx-NY.html). All the names used in this case example are fictitious.

The Purpose

The Mid-Bronx Development Association (MBD) has contacted Mr. Claude Brown to create a community intervention program that will get its residents to be tested and vaccinated for Coronavirus (Covid-19).

Mr. Brown was contacted by Ms. Sarah Brooks, who serves as the current director of MBD. As a respected OD practitioner with over 20 years of experience, Mr. Brown was contacted to help create a community-based plan to implement a procedure and get the newly created vaccine out to the community at large. MBD cannot seem to get buy-in from the community residents. Mr. Brown was aware of the background, history, and relationship between communities of color and the U.S government and medical industry. He knew that communities of color had considerable mistrust on government-proposed medical interventions (such as The Tuskegee Experiment in 1932 and the appropriation of cells from Henrietta Lacks without her consent in 1951). He also knew that there was some concern with the speed at which this vaccine was developed, and the residents of the community were concerned that they were the experimental test group.

Community Background

The community of the West Farms neighborhood of the Bronx, New York, covers just .15 square miles and has a population of 5,328 people, most of whom are from underrepresented communities. The majority population in the community are Latino (73.3%) and African American (20.4%). The community's median household income is $33,500, and the median rent is $900. The median age of the community is 33.3 years (30.6 years for males, 36.0 years for females). Seventy-two percent of residents use mass transit. There are two major hospitals in the area that serve in conjunction with several area clinics. The area is also serviced by several churches, two synagogues, and a mosque.

Participants

Before entering the community, Mr. Brown wanted to understand the situation better. Mr. Brown recognized that he needed to speak with the community members to determine their problems. He first contacted Ms. Brooks, the "contacting client," who initially reached out to him. He wanted to better understand who she was, how she fits into the community, and what she wanted to accomplish through his services. Through a few conversations, Mr. Brown discovered that Ms. Brooks had been in the community for five years after relocating from Albany's governor's office. She came into the current position after being selected over several local candidates. Mr. Brown assessed that she was a proven administrator but still must prove herself to this community. While she has won many residents over, she still has many detractors.

After developing a cordial working relationship with Ms. Brooks, Mr. Brown sought out the following community members to be involved with the change intervention process:

- Rev. Dr. John Burell has been in the community for over 30 years. His church has been a cornerstone for many residents. His father was also the pastor of this church.
- George Nevis was a prominent business owner. He had several stores in the community, but MBD felt that he charged the residents far too much for the products offered.
- Keshia Tims owned a daycare center in the area. While her facilities were

understaffed, she believed she needed to be in the community close to the center even though she was not turning a profit.

- Vincent James served as the Assemblyperson of the district. He was not as engaged as he once was and relied heavily on Sonny Vasconsellis to make many decisions for assembly vote and resident engagements in the community.
- Sonny Vasconsellis serves as Mr. James' chief of staff and primary point of contact. He also serves as Ms. Brooks' supervisor.
- Assemblyperson James was the "paying client". Mr. Brown attempted to meet with Mr. James several times, only to have a brief meeting with Mr. Vasconsellis. Mr. Vasconsellis told Mr. Brown what Mr. James thought the community needed and what Mr. Brown should be doing (with Mr. James' direction).

After contacting the above individuals, Mr. Brown then set meetings with other community leaders and those he thought might influence the community. He met with the following individuals;

- Rabbi David Saltzman leads a congregation in the shadow of Saint Barnabus Hospital. The Rabbi and the head physician Edward Phillips have clashed over the number of vaccinations that needed to be distributed.
- Dot Washington has been in the community since the early 1970s. Now retired, she has become the mother of her block and is not entirely sold on MBD or Assemblyperson James. She wants a better life and a brighter future for her grandchildren, but she cannot make it happen in the community by herself. After meeting her and learning of her concerns, Mr. Brown felt she would be an important voice at the table.
- Dr. Angela Samuels had two lucrative clinics in the area and viewed her offices as the best things for the residents even though she was not there often. Her physician assistant, Millie Reyes, ran the office and was responsible for all medications that were distributed. Residents went to her clinics because it was easy to get things done quickly. Nurse Reyes is trusted to help patients in their time of need.
- Dominga Hill was a civil rights activist and a local schoolteacher trying to get MBD to engage with the local elementary schools for health programs.

The OD Practitioner

There are four main reasons why organizations like MBD reach out to an OD practitioner like Mr. Brown (Andrade 2019):

> **First:** Organizations just want an outside opinion. Ms. Brooks reached out to Mr. Brown because she realized that she was in a difficult situation. Her most effective way to defuse this situation was to bring in an expert from the outside to give an unbiased opinion of what should be done to improve the organization. As an OD practitioner, Mr. Brown has developed a reputation for being neutral and clear in his responsibilities to the organization. He is known for making sure the most appropriate needs that are determined by the community are met (2019).
>
> **Second:** Members of the organization may not be qualified to provide a strong and competent OD engagement. These members of the organization may also feel better about talking with an outside person(s) due to trust issues already present within the organization (2019).
>
> **Third:** The employees do not have to stop any work or projects they are responsible for while the OD practitioner performs the intervention. The organization can continue to focus on its primary work functions (2019).
>
> **Fourth:** It may be easier to engage an OD practitioner with the organization through a contract. OD practitioners are hired for a specific period, and when the task is completed, the OD practitioner departs (2019).

Assemblyperson James wants the intervention done quickly and efficiently (meaning cheaply). He wants someone to come in and depart quickly while Ms. Brooks continues her relationship with the community (Staples 2016).

Step 1: Entrance

In this step, Mr. Brown wanted to identify the main individuals who were going to be able to represent the entire community so he could begin the intervention. Since he would not be able to speak to all the residents to find out their needs (Campbell 1998), he made sure to get a varied group of people around the table for the intervention. It is best to get a voice directly from members of the community. He recognized that he would be asking many questions to these individuals to get to the core of what they needed to implement this vaccine program. By asking the participants questions, Mr. Brown knew he would get a better feel for what the community needs. The following *needs statements* were important ones that he made sure to watch for in his questioning:

- *What this community needs…*
- *My people need…*
- *This is a real concern about…*
- *We do not have enough…*
- *This block/town/community could really use.…*

Mr. Brown knew that the second group of phrases, the *want statements*, would be just as important as the needs statements for a successful intervention (Campbell 1998). Understanding the want statements could help the participants negotiate in some areas when the conversation around the table slowed. The "want statements" can have the following phrases:

- *I want my people to have…*
- *We do not need it, but we would like…*
- *We could use…but only if we get…*
- *I need for my area to have…*
- *Look, we just need to give this area…*

As the table came together, Mr. Brown had to determine what intervention type would be the strongest tool for creating a sustainable and successful intervention. He used the STAR method to use the community as a tool for implementation (Hambrick & Fredrickson 2001). As it has been mentioned earlier in this chapter, the STAR acronym stands for the following:

- **S** (Setting): Location of the intervention and the possible places that people in the community can be gathered to meet and discuss issues and concerns.
- **T** (Target): Goals provided by and created by the collective group.

- **A** (Agent): Persons who can be considered as agents for the intervention and engage others for buy-in.
- **R** (Resource): Material(s) that will be needed to make this project succeed, such as monetary, talent, or hardline items.

In this step, Mr. Brown also began to prepare for his departure. OD practitioners know that organizations eventually outgrow, or the need for a particular consultant may cease to exist. The OD practitioners may also get a feeling that they have done all that can be done for this intervention (Weisbord 2012). Mr. Brown wanted the community to understand that when his work is completed through their leadership and active participation, he would not be in the community forever. By setting this expectation upfront, Mr. Brown wanted the residents to realize that the community work needed to go on even after his departure. However, he made it clear that the community should feel free to rehire him in the future if there is ever such a need.

Step 2: Setting the Table (Defining the Power Structure)

Please refer to Figure 12.2 earlier in this chapter to see how Mr. Brown viewed the table for his community intervention. When reviewing his table, Mr. Brown began to place his participants in buckets; the bucket titles are listed below. Mr. Brown also considered that all individuals around the table were going to require a different level of engagement and could not be randomly paired together.

- **Clients:** They are individuals who asked him to come to create the intervention. He must make sure they understand he is there to work with them and engage them as much as possible.
- **Naysayers:** These are the individuals who think they do not need Mr. Brown's help, and they can accomplish the goal better than him and his OD intervention.
- **Influencers:** They may not have a great deal of financial weight, but their word is gold. If Mr. Brown can get them to see his vision, they will help him in ways that will mean more than finances.
- **Early Adopters:** Excited for the help and the desire to be a part of the change, they can be paired with an influencer or naysayer.
- **On the Fence:** This group of individuals presents the toughest challenge for the OD practitioner. They want to hear what the OD practitioners

have to say and see what they are going to do, but the OD practitioners may not feel for their position right away. The OD practitioner will need to keep them away from the naysayers but close to the decision-makers or influencers.

- **Decision-Makers:** These are the persons with the final say. They may not have asked the OD practitioner to come into the community, but they will have a say whether the OD practitioner stays in the community.

- **OD practitioners:** Mr. Brown did not place a seat at the table for himself because he is a facilitator. He knew that he must be able to work across all lines and not be engaged with any one person (except the client) too much. He wanted to make sure even if the people around the table were not completely on his or Ms. Brooks' side, they would, at the very least, allow him to do his work.

Table 12.1 is a list that Mr. Brown created to talk with the residents about their needs during this implementation. He did inform all the individuals he spoke with that he would present their requests to the entire group in an anonymous fashion. This action allowed a safe environment for participants to speak freely and to develop processes for the implementation.

Table 12.1   Needs and Wants List

Individual	Needs	Wants
Client		
Naysayer		
Influencer		
Early Adopter		
On the Fence		
Decision-Maker		

Source: Adapted from Koonce and Harper (2005). Engaging African American Parents in the Schools: A Community-Based Consultation Model. *Journal of Educational and Psychological Consultation* 16(1–2): 55–74.

Step 3: Assessment and Feedback

This phase could be considered as a *listening tour*. Mr. Brown continued to check in with the individuals around the table. In this step, he reported the findings from the initial group meeting to the participants. Mr. Brown asked them for additional solutions that they did not have a chance to express during the initial meeting. He did not do this in a formal setting but in some type of casual setting where the community members could feel at ease. For example, he met many people at either a Starbucks or Krispy Kreme Doughnuts for morning coffee. He knew that he would not have many opportunities to engage community members one-on-one where they would feel completely comfortable. By meeting in a public space, he knew that they might feel more open to answering his questions and feel less constricted in giving him their unfiltered insights into what they thought was needed by the community. Mr. Brown gradually took this step with constructive intention, given he felt this would be a great way to gather information as he continued to push his change intervention process forward.

Step 4: Action Planning

After covering many points with the participants, Mr. Brown wanted to establish a plan of action. This action planning amounted to strategies developed on the earlier steps, such as reporting findings on problems and solutions raised from the interview processes for data gathering. To review his strategy plan, he referred to Hambrick and Fredrickson's (2001) article titled "Are You Sure You Have a Strategy?" and EV Genderen's article titled "What Is the Strategy: Back to Basics." Hambrick and Fredrickson (2001) identified the major elements of having a strategy. Mr. Brown took from this reading that he should be able to answer the following five main questions (Hambrick & Fredrickson 2001, 50):

1. **Arenas:** What is the working space? What is the location that is being engaged?
2. **Vehicles:** How are we going to reach our goal?
3. **Differentiators:** What makes our methods and practices stand out to establish this organization as a leader?
4. **Staging:** What takes place first? How will this effort conclude?
5. **Economic Logic:** Can the bottom line be increased?

Step 5: Intervention

Once Mr. Brown had a workable, productive, and effective strategy in place, he wanted to make sure that the community members could see both the short- and long-term goals based on the objectives they set from their first meeting.

- At the start of the intervention plan, Mr. Brown went to Ms. Brooks to go over the roundtable community meeting details. During the meeting with Ms. Brooks, he suggested that they meet with Assemblyperson James to clarify the vaccine's objectives. Mr. Brown worked with Rev. Burell and Nurse Reyes to get a ground-level approach to engage the residents about their distrust.
- This approach helped in creating a platform for most residents to meet with someone in charge. Mr. Brown continued this action for three weeks before the vaccine reached the offices of Dr. Samuels. Dr. Samuels had a few suggestions for him, but she assured him that Nurse Reyes would let him know what he should do. Mr. Brown had a phone meeting with Nurse Reyes the week before the arrival of the vaccine.
- Mr. Brown then approached Ms. Tims and Mr. Nevis at their businesses about continuing the community outreach. In meeting with Ms. Tims, he found that she was supportive, but many of her clients would still be hesitant to give this vaccine to their children. Ms. Tims wanted to know how to get more children involved in the process. When he met with Mr. Nevis, he still found some resistance in discussing the vaccine. Mr. Nevis felt that Assemblyperson James had not been given enough credit for this effort, and he did not feel the Assemblyperson had given his "true" blessing for this endeavor.
- Immediately after this meeting, Mr. Brown contacted Mr. Vasconsellis to see exactly what Assemblyperson James was thinking about the project because Mr. James was not communicating to Mr. Brown or Ms. Brooks.
- Lastly, Mr. Brown sought out Ms. Hill, who had been noncommittal in each of the prior meetings. During the meeting with Ms. Hill, she expressed distrust in both Ms. Brooks and Mr. James. Ms. Hill still had reservations, but based on the information, she felt that the residents needed to have the vaccine. She was preparing to meet with many community residents to seek out locations for vaccination.

- When the vaccines arrived, Mr. Brown went back to all participants to see how the vaccines were being accepted in the community. He found that all but Mr. Nevis were following and supporting the plan to distribute the vaccine to the community.
- The clinics agreed to give out 750 to 1,000 doses of the vaccine per week. The daycare centers were providing brochures and video links to the parents and caregivers. Ms. Washington had engaged the senior centers and had given several "community talks" at the local park about the vaccine.
- Mr. Brown also saw that Rev. Burrell's parishioners were going door to door in several neighborhoods. He approached Mr. Nevis to find out why he was not engaging with the intervention in the manner to which he agreed and found that he had a conversation with Assemblyperson James who told him that he did not have to comply with the chosen plan since everyone else complied.

Step 6: Evaluation

Mr. Brown met with all the community leaders to get their feelings before the vaccine arrived, after it arrived, and during its distribution. An example of the type of questions that he asked for an evaluation of the program can be seen in Table 12.2. Mr. Brown started with these questions and modified them as he moved through the process. He wanted to be sure he did not miss any potential pitfalls moving forward. Mr. Brown sought to hear about the problems in the process from the community members. Doing this type of continuous evaluation allowed him to shift and pivot as needed for a successful implementation.

The following sample bank of questions can be asked of community members:

1. What do you think of _____Program?
2. If you could change one thing about this program, what would it be?
3. Rate the status of _____ Program.
4. What effort is not needed from _____ Program?
5. Can you tell me the goal of _____ Program?

Table 12.2 asks community members to rate the program.

Table 12.2 Survey

Directions: On a scale of 1 to 5 with 5 being the best and 1 being the worst, please rate the following:					
Question	*1*	*2*	*3*	*4*	*5*
Your level of service					
Recommending this program to another resident					
Meeting your needs					
Helping the community					
Understanding by staff of your needs					
Would you be willing to participate in an interview for more detailed responses?	YES	NO			

Step 7: Adoption

According to Leseure et al. (2004), there are five primary rules for the adoption of successful practices in communities: 1) identification of the need for performance; 2) improvement of identification of best practices to address these needs; 3) prioritization of these best practices; 4) assessment of required predecessor practices, and 5) implementation. As the selected community leaders came to a consensus on what was needed to be done to ensure a positive outcome with the delivery of the vaccine, the community leaders recognized they would become the primary conduits for the vaccine program's success. This recognition came from the community leaders having buy-in and feeling responsible for making the program work with their constituents in the community to use the resources to solve the problem. Mr. Brown could see that the plan created at the table meetings was now a reality in the community.

Step 8: Separation

Finally, the time came for Mr. Brown to depart and separate from the client. He conducted four separation meetings as follows.

1. The first meeting was with Ms. Brooks to review the process and evaluate what did work and what could be done differently.
2. The second meeting with Assemblyperson James was to conclude the project and engage him about what he thought of the project's implementation.
3. The third meeting was with both Ms. Brooks and Mr. James to report his findings and to give them ideas on supporting their community efforts. Mr. Brown also wanted to report his findings to ensure that there was an understanding of the results and all their concerns were addressed after their individual conversations.
4. The last meeting was with the entire group to celebrate their success. Mr. Brown also wanted the entire community to continue working with MBD. At this meeting, Mr. Brown shared the results of the project and what the community leaders thought they should do to ensure all residents had the opportunity to receive the vaccine. He then asked them, as a group, what solutions they thought they should utilize. As a result of this closing discussion, it was determined that there would be an additional step (e.g., consequences such as removal from the community leaders' table) for members of the group who do not live up to the persons' agreed-upon commitment at the community table. Ms. Washington and Ms. Brooks were selected as the leaders for making sure the group kept the number of residents taking the vaccine high until all the community members had received the appropriate dosage. Before leaving, Mr. Brown reminded Ms. Brooks that he would be more than happy to assist her if she needs further assistance.

Mr. Brown had a chance to review his notes after the intervention was completed to see how far he strayed from his original intervention plan. A complete display of his intervention schedule is available in Table 12.3.

Table 12.3 Intervention Schedule

			Stage 1: Establishing the Contract (2 to 3 Weeks)			
		Who	Why	What Is the Importance	Where	Time Length
Primary Communication Plan		Sponsoring Client (S.C.)	Understanding what the job for the OD consultant will be. Establishing what the contract will be (pay rate, materials needed, who is responsible for what technology is being used).	Clarity on why your presence is needed, hearing the presenting problem in detail before agreeing to perform the intervention; everything needs to be discussed and engaged for the intervention. This will help cut down on surprises in terms of execution of the contract.	In-person preferably, but via Zoom or WebEx is a good secondary option, a phone being the last option. Technology gives us a more personal connection and shows you can use all tools at your disposal.	One to two weeks for the contract. (you will be talking to this person throughout the entire contract on other topics)
		Paying Client (P.C.)	Check to confirm that your sponsoring and paying clients are on the same page. Understand why you are being brought in from every angle.	There may be times where your sponsoring and paying clients are two different people which means you can have two different ideas for needs to be done during this intervention. Assess which opinion is the final decision.	In a separate meeting away from the sponsoring client (preferred) to ensure unburdened communication.	One to two days with follow up reporting periodically

(Continued)

TABLE 12.3   Intervention Schedule (Con't.)

Stage 2: OD Consulting Plan (3 to 26 Weeks)

	Who	Why	What Is the Importance	Where	Time Length
Secondary Communicati-on Plan	Community Members (C.M.)	Understanding what the community needs is just as important as understanding what the client wants.	The client(s) may have an idea of what the community needs which may differ from what the community members need.	This should be in the areas where community members reside, their offices, coffee houses, community centers, and eateries.	Three to six weeks (possibly longer depending on the size of the constituent group)
	S.C.	Finding out which community members should be contacted for the intervention.	See whom S.C. has determined to be vital to the project and who is not.	This can be done by email so that information (phone numbers, emails) can be accurate.	One to two hours
	P.C.	Finding out which community members should be spoken to for the intervention.	See whom the P.C. has determined to be vital to the project and who is not.	This can be done by email so that information phone numbers, and emails can be accurate.	One to two hours

(Continued)

TABLE 12.3   Intervention Schedule (Con't.)

Stage 2: OD Consulting Plan (3 to 26 Weeks)

	Who	Why	What Is the Importance	Where	Time Length
Intervention: Stage 1	C.M, S.C., P.C.	Everyone has had a chance to speak with you and give you unfiltered wants and needs. You are now going to have to distill these points into a presentable statement.	Creating a "wants and needs" list for the community can allow you to detail and engage the presenting and underlining problems that you are being brought in to help with. Length of time should be determined here and if longer than the original contract, revisit the contract with the S.C. and P.C.	This is an in-person team-building workshop to garner buy-in from the entire group and allow the group to come up with action items in which to engage.	Two to Three days
Intervention: Stage 2	C.M.	To present to the C.M. their specific area of focus with details from the larger group with an emphasis on their specific role in the intervention.	This step allows for the total transparency of the actions and expectations of each member. This meeting should also reaffirm the large-group meeting and reestablish deadlines and deliverables.	This must be in-person or video. This way you read body language and facial expressions.	One half day with each C.M.

(Continued)

TABLE 12.3 Intervention Schedule (Con't.)

Stage 2: OD Consulting Plan (3 to 26 Weeks)

	Who	Why	What Is the Importance	Where	Time Length
	S.C.	Progress updates in case any C.M. leader proves more difficult than expected,	Keeping S.C. will allow them to relay information to the P.C. and keep them aware of difficulties that you are encountering.	This meeting can be done over any communication medium that makes all parties comfortable.	Once a week at least, if not daily
Implementation	C.M.	Members should be encouraging the general community to now get involved with discussing a sanctioned intervention.	The implementation at this point should be laid out and put into action.	The C.M. will determine how this communication will be carried out; you will need to make sure you are a part of the community stream.	This can take 2 weeks to 3 months to complete depending on the project
	S.C.	S.C. should be just as engaged in the implementation as C.M. You should keep them engaged in the implementation process.	Keeping S.C. will allow them to relay information to the P.C. and keep them aware of difficulties that you are encountering.	This meeting can be done over any communication medium that makes all parties comfortable.	

(Continued)

TABLE 12.3 Intervention Schedule (Con't.)

Stage 3: Time to Go! (2 Weeks)

	Who	Why	What Is the Importance	Where	Time Length
Evaluation	C.M., S.C.	Get everyone back to the table to check in and discuss concerns, additional questions, and comments.	Make sure the agreed-upon path is being followed, and see what tweaks and strengthenings are needed or what can be effectively removed from the intervention plan.	This meeting should be conducted in person but over a different medium would be acceptable; however, conducting attendance is mandatory.	At the mid-point of the project and a week before the contract ends
Separation	C.M., S.-C., P.C.	Conduct exit interviews with all parties involved.	Find out what was missing and done well. Plan the set-up for a possible return for another project.	Hopefully in person, but Zoom is acceptable.	The final week of the project

Tools

The following chart provides several useful resources for understanding the OD intervention on a community level (Table 12.4).

Table 12.4   Additional Resources

Organization	URL	Overview
Creative Interventions	https://www.creative-interventions.org/about/ci-projects/community-based-interventions-project/	Intervention and prevention measures
Strategies for Social Change	https://strategiesforsocialchange.com/resource/	Community building tools
Management of Social Transformations (MOST) Program	https://en.unesco.org/themes/social-transformations/most	Interventions from a global perspective
The Winters Group	https://www.wintersgroup.com/	Assessment, survey, and focus group support
The Community Guide	https://www.thecommunityguide.org/tools	Budgeting to Interventions can be found here
Diversity Edu	https://get.diversityedu.com/workplace-diversity-climate-assessment/?gclid=Cj0KCQjw-uH6BRDQARIsAI3I-UdM_NiP7MZJ0q-QvxAwOi5FB-lKf1ioChXL-FyITZMyJ2PRQZFAUEYaAurwEALw_wcB	Assessment and focus group support
National Center for Biotechnology Information	https://www.ncbi.nlm.nih.gov/pmc/articles/PMC1447783/	Interventions from health and medicine point of view
Robert Wood Johnson Foundation	https://www.rwjf.org/	Resources from various fields

Key Lessons Learned

This chapter described community interventions and how to get community members engaged in creating their own solutions. As OD practitioners create community interventions, they need to remember this important point—the community itself can be an active member of the intervention. The chapter proposes using the STAR method to identify OD practitioners' first ally. The OD practitioners can use a metaphorical table to assist them in identifying members of the community and planning a stronger intervention for the community. Mr. Brown determined that assessing what the community needs, from their own words, could help clarify what is essential to the success of a sustainable community intervention instead of the simple wants of one or two community leaders.

Discussion Questions

After reading the chapter, think about a community intervention that you would like to implement. Then, answer the below questions:

1. Which community-based intervention, using the community as an active participant, works best for your work?
2. How many people need to be at the table?
3. What characteristics can be helpful at the table?
4. What characteristics can be harmful?
5. Which person at the table should be focused on the most?
6. What is the role of the OD practitioner in community intervention?
7. Name the five purposes for which communities come together?
8. What could Mr. Brown have done better?
9. Which participant was the most significant impediment?

References

Andrade, Greg. 2019. *Here's Why Companies Really Hire Consultants*. April 30. https://www.graphite.com/blog/why-companies-really-hire-consultants/.

Berns, Roberta M. 2007. *Child, Family, School, Community: Socialization and Support*. Belmont, CA: Wadsworth Publishing Company.

Campbell, Colin. 1998. "Consumption and the Rhetorics of Need and Want." *Journal of Design History* 11(3): 235–246.

Hambrick, Donald, and James, Fredrickson. 2001. "Are You Sure You Have a Strategy?" *Academy of Management Executive* 15(4):151–153.

Koonce, Danel A, and Walter, Harper. 2005. "Engaging African American Parents in the Schools: A Community-Based Consultation Model." *Journal of Educational and Psychological Consultation* 16(1):55–74.

Leseure, Michel, Joachim, Bauer, Kamal, Birdi, Andy, Neely, and David, Denyer. 2004. "Adoption of Promising: A Systematic Review of the Evidence." *International Journal of Management Reviews* 5-6(3-4): 169–190.

McLeroy, Kenneth R., Barbara L. Norton, Michelle C. Kegler, James N. Burdine, and Ciro V. Sumaya. 2003. "Community-Based Interventions." *American Journal of Public Health* 93(4): 529–533. doi: 10.2105/ajph.93.4.529

Rothwell, W. J., Jacqueline Stavros, and Roland L. Sullivan. 2016. *Practicing Organization Development: Leading Transformation and Change* (4th ed.). Hoboken, NJ: John Wiley & Sons, Inc.

Staples, Lee. 2016. *Roots to Power: A Manual for Grassroots Organizing*. ABC-CLIO.

Weisbord, Marvin. 2012. "The Organization Development Contract." *Handbook for Strategic HR* 53–60. New York, NY: AMACOM.

Wilson, A. 2018. *Why Government Needs Organization Development*. https://www.govloop.com/community/blog/why-government-needs-organization-development/.

THE FUTURE
IV

Chapter 13

The Future of Organization Development Interventions

William J. Rothwell

Contents

The future of organization development (OD) interventions hinges on the future of work, workers, workplaces, and work environments. How will people perform their work in the future? Who will do the work? Where will people work? And what conditions outside organizations in the work environment will affect work, workers, and workplaces? (See Figure 13.1.) This chapter addresses these important questions, offering thoughts on the future of OD interventions as they are affected by trends (Lawler & Boudreau 2015; Surkutwar 2017).

Work in the Future

Work in the future will not occur in so-called "full-time jobs," defined as jobs packaged in timebound units such as 5 days a week, 40 hours, for 50 weeks per year. Consider three predictions for work in the future.

Work Prediction 1: Work Will Be Performed as Tasks or Projects

Work will not be packaged in "jobs." Instead, work will be performed in projects. Few, if any, people will have traditional full-time jobs. Most work will be done in the context of a project or even tasks within projects. A shift

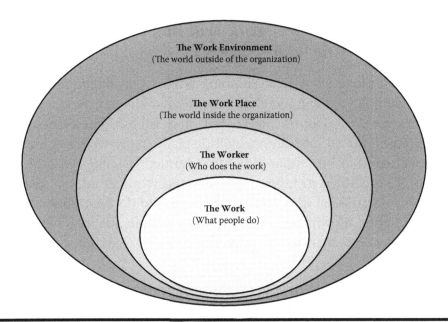

Figure 13.1   The Future of OD Interventions.

will occur from paying for time to paying for work products and results. That shift will occur due to increasing global competition, greater parity in wage rates internationally occurring over time, and differences in national policies regarding taxation, tariffs, and employee benefits such as healthcare insurance and national policies on childcare and eldercare.

The transformation from timebound jobs to results-based tasks and projects will be accompanied by creative efforts of organizations to minimize the amount of human contact that will be necessary. In short, there will be a move away from thinking of filling job vacancies to find creative approaches to get the work done. As many as 100 different ways have already been identified to get work done without hiring or promoting workers (see Rothwell et al. 2012).

In the future "agile work" will be the order of the day. Much work will be posted online on sites like guru.com, and workers will compete for tasks or projects. Low-cost but high-value vendors will be most competitive.

Helping employers and workers adapt to future "agile work" will be a future challenge for OD practitioners. OD interventions will be needed to facilitate change in converting from "time-based" to "results-based" approaches. OD interventions may also be needed to help managers change how they interact with workers, since "results-based" employment systems usually rely on many vendors rather than employees.

Work Prediction 2: More Work Will Be Performed by Robots and Artificial Intelligence

Employers will move away from defining work as packaged in human jobs. Increasingly employers will focus on how the work is performed. Much work will be performed by sophisticated robots and artificial intelligence.

Robots and artificial intelligence will displace many workers, and those workers will need to be retrained or cross trained for other work. OD practitioners will be needed to help employers and workers interact effectively with robots and artificial intelligence. How people do their jobs affects their productivity, and OD will be needed to help people adapt to new kinds of interaction between smart technology and workers (Steghofer 2017).

Work Prediction 3: Work Will Benefit from Crowdsourcing Logic

The creative potential of large groups will be tapped by applying crowdsourcing logic to solving organizational problems or leveraging organizational strengths. OD principles will be combined with technology applications to reach optimal decisions across very large groups quickly (see Cancialosi 2015). The same methods may also be used to fund new work projects and to source talent best equipped to implement solutions or leverage strengths.

Workers in the Future

Workers of the future will be older and better educated, and many will be retirees. Consider three predictions for workers in the future.

Worker Prediction 1: Fewer Young Workers Will Be Available in Many Countries

Birth rates decline after periods of economic slumps. Not surprisingly, then, birth rates dropped after the global financial crisis of 2008. Flash forward 20 years, and it should become apparent that there is a projected reduction of college-age students in 2025 and college graduates in 2030. Employers will compete for a dwindling supply of traditional entry-level-age workers. That may spur increased efforts to substitute alternatives to younger workers—such as automation, artificial intelligence, and telework methods that can diminish labor shortages that are intensified by geographical distances. These efforts will pose special change intervention challenges for OD practitioners as well as workers and managers alike.

Worker Prediction 2: Organizations Will Compete for Retirees and Disabled Workers

The drop in available and traditional young workers may also spur efforts to make better use of traditionally overlooked labor groups—such as retirees or disabled workers. Tapping new workers and new work methods will create challenges. That will prompt sweeping changes in organizations, necessitating major change efforts.

When different generations are present in workplaces, employers may face special challenges in dealing with varying expectations—and stereotypes—about people in different age categories. One big problem is the mistaken view that "old dogs can't be taught new tricks," a viewpoint that has been disproven by research about human learning (Rothwell 2020). OD practitioners will be needed to facilitate change efforts designed to dispel mistaken beliefs.

Worker Prediction 3: Employers Will Compete for Talent Using Childcare and Eldercare Benefits

Everyone knows that the U.S. does not have adequate childcare or eldercare policies. Young parents must pay an average of $15,000/year for each child to be taken care of while the parents work (McClure 2020). If the same parents have elderly relatives, the costs can be outrageous (Paying for Senior Care 2019). If employers are willing to subsidize some costs for those squeezed by these costs, then the employers will enjoy a distinctive competitive advantage in attracting and retaining talent. But implementing such policies will require major change efforts, necessitating OD interventions to help address the perceptions, feelings, and beliefs associated with these efforts.

Workplaces in the Future

Workplaces of the future will be "anywhere." More people will work from home—or other venues such as coffee shops or automobiles—and fewer will work in offices located in major urban areas. Consider three predictions for future workplaces.

Workplace Prediction 1: More People Will Work from Home—or from Alternative Venues

For some time there has been a trend toward working from home full-time or part-time.

According to GlobalWorkplace Analytics (2019):

- 5 million employees (3.6% of the U.S. employee workforce) currently work at home half-time or more
- 62% of employees say they could work remotely
- 80% of employees want to work from home at least some of the time

But working from home is itself a change effort—for workers and for managers. It requires corporate culture change efforts using methods such as OD. OD practitioners of the future will need to help people adapt to changing work settings and the new demands that these new work settings may create.

Workplace Prediction 2: People Will Grow to Prefer Virtual Workplaces

In many cases, workers prefer working virtually than working in residential offices.

According to GlobalWorkplace Analytics (2019), "more than a third of workers would take a pay cut of up to 5% in exchange for the option to work remotely at least some of the time; a quarter would take a 10% pay cut; 20% would take an even greater cut." That suggests workers already prefer virtual to residential workplaces.

There are many reasons why people prefer virtual settings (Global Workplace Analytics 2019). By working virtually, workers can avoid tiresome and expensive transportation costs to central office locations. They can be safer, since travel can attract criminals. They can also save money and time, since it is costly to travel from suburbs to inner cities. It can be time-consuming and uncomfortable to make those commuting trips as well. And those who work virtually can enjoy the comfort of working in loose clothing such as pajamas rather than in tight-fitting business suits.

Working virtually, which has grown more popular due to the necessity imposed by the Covid-19 virus, will be an increasingly dominant form of work. That will lead to major change efforts. After all, managers and workers alike will need to learn how to work somewhat differently in virtual settings.

Workplace Prediction 3: There Will Be Less Foreign Travel but Increased Use of Videoconferencing

Many people have grown accustomed to the ease of international travel. But, after the Covid-19 virus, travel has grown more restrictive. It is likely to remain restrictive, though perhaps not so much as during the worst of the pandemic. More international business will be conducted by videoconferencing and other technologically assisted means. That will mean more attention must be devoted to cross-cultural issues that can stem from communication by technology-assisted means (Blank 2020). OD interventions may be needed to help people work together in virtual sessions more effectively.

Work Environments in the Future

Work environments of the future will be more turbulent and more prone to black swan events that start out small and seemingly inconsequential but eventually grow into earth-changing situations. Consider three predictions for future work environments.

Work Environment Prediction 1: More Natural and Manmade Disasters Will Influence Work, Workers, and Workplaces

Global warming will lead to many more natural disasters. Examples of that include an increased incidence of hurricanes, tornadoes, and other weather-related events. Some experts predict that natural disasters, and other issues associated with global warming, will make it harder to raise crops and animals, which will in turn stimulate competitive conditions leading to wars.

When people worry about food, they find it more difficult to do business. For that reason, OD interventions may be needed to address conflict resolution and diplomacy. OD interventions may also be needed to help workers and employers deal with the work-related impacts of natural disasters and human conflicts.

Work Environment Prediction 2: Taken-for-Granted Resources Will Grow Scarce

In the future, there is an increased likelihood that fresh water will grow into a scare resource (Thirst Project 2020). Oil may run out (Lindgren n.d.). Fish and other natural food sources, such as wild game, may grow scarce (Vince 2012). Sea levels are rising (Lindsey 2019). In the U.S., there is a long-term predicted shortage of physicians (see AAMC 2019).

When people are worried about finding food and water for themselves and their families, they will find it difficult to concentrate on work. For that reason, OD practitioners in the future may need to help organizations address change efforts designed to help workers cope with resource shortages. That may need to happen on a tactical, day-to-day level rather than long-term strategic change efforts.

Work Environment Prediction 3: Technology Will Create New Ways to Work and Interact

The barrier between personal and work life is falling. People are always expected to be available. One reason for that is the ubiquitous nature of electronic devices such as iwatches, cell phones, tablets, laptops, and others. These devices always make it possible to reach people and in almost all locations. As work moves from time to results-based efforts (see above), technology will create new ways to work and interact. Teleworkers experience that now. But the more devices and the more platforms or software exist, the more ways workers must interact. And imagine what happens when people begin to work in virtual worlds where a simulated environment exists for interaction. It is already possible to do that, but 3D virtual interaction is in its infancy.

OD interventions in the future may be needed to help employers adapt to new ways to use technology to interact. It may also be needed to avoid cyberbullying and cyberharassment, well-known problems with technology-based methods (Sarasota County Sherriff's Office 2019). Organizations will need to establish policies and procedures to deal with abuses of telework in the future, and OD practitioners will be needed to facilitate change by using those policies and procedures. OD will also be needed to facilitate the long-term change needed to reduce racial tensions and sexual harassment.

Other Trends in OD Interventions

While work, worker, workplace, and work environment trends will most definitely affect OD interventions in the future, there will also be other trends worthy of mention. Among them: (1) Big Data will be used for assessment and feedback; (2) OD interventions will become well-integrated with daily conversations and with business meetings; (3) blockchain methods will affect OD interventions; and (4) diversity, inclusion, equity, and globalized efforts will increasingly be regarded as OD. Each is worthy of brief discussion.

Additional Trend 1: Big Data and OD Interventions

Interest in so-called Big Data has swept the business world. Big Data are defined, of course, as the burgeoning amount of information available to organizations. When carefully analyzed, Big Data can be used in assessing organizational problems and strengths and can provide the basis for valuable information that can be fed back to workers—and to possible users, such as artificial intelligence. In the future, Big Data will be readily available—and often instantly available. It can used in OD interventions to provide continuous data to shape and inform decision making. But human users will often be tasked to make sense of Big Data, and OD methods will be needed to do that.

Additional Trend 2: OD Interventions Will Be Integrated with Conversations and Business Meetings

Time has become the key to competitive advantage. Organizations that can beat their competitors to market with new products or new ways to serve customers will often capture market share. As a result of this emphasis on speed, OD interventions will be forced to move into real time. To that end, more interest in the future will center around change as it can be stimulated by conversations and questioning. More interest will also focus on coaching business leaders on how to intervene in human systems in real time—and more effectively—than in the past. OD practitioners will need to focus attention on real-time interactions among people—and that includes crucial and meaningful conversations (Patterson et al. 2011; Stavros & Torres 2018).

Additional Trend 3: Blockchain Methods Will Affect OD Interventions

Blockchain has emerged as a trend that has taken the business world by storm (Tapscott & Vargas 2019). Initially used as a recordkeeping method for digital currencies such as bitcoin, blockchain can be applied to many transactions above and beyond the financial. Implementing blockchain can be done using OD interventions, and finding other applications for blockchain beyond financial ones can also be performed using OD interventions. Consequently, blockchain may be a trend that affects OD interventions in the future.

Additional Trend 4: Diversity Efforts Will Increasingly Be Regarded as OD Interventions

Too many people who have been tasked to formulate and implement diversity, inclusion, equity, and multicultural programs in organizations have had limited success (Dobbin & Kalev 2016). One reason is that these efforts are not always regarded as OD interventions; rather, many are treated as training interventions. It is not possible to change an organization using training alone. For that reason, and due to the continuing need to address diversity issues in organizations, many OD interventions in the future will focus on diversity-related issues (Holvino et al. 2004).

Table 13.1 Worksheet on OD and the Future	
Directions: In the left column below, list some trends you have read about in this chapter or that you have found on the web. Name the trend and briefly describe what it is and what it means. Then, in the right column, indicate what OD interventions may be needed by your organization in the future to help people in your organization deal with the change. There are no right or wrong answers to this activity, but some answers may be better than others.	
What is the name of the trend, and what brief description can you offer of what the trend is and what it will mean for your organization?	What OD interventions may be needed by your organization in the future to help people in your organization deal with the change?
1	
2	
3	
4	
5	
6	
7	
8	
9	
10	

Discussion Questions

1. What trend studies can you find on the web? Using at least two recent trend studies, offer your own predictions about the future of OD interventions.
2. What special competencies may be needed by OD practitioners in the future to address the future challenges described in this chapter?
3. What opinions do you have about future trends and the competencies that operating managers will need to help workers deal with, or anticipate, the trends unfolding over time? How do the competencies of operating managers differ from, and overlap with, those needed by OD practitioners?

References

AAMC. 2019. "New Findings Confirm Predictions on Physician Shortage." Retrieved from https://www.aamc.org/news-insights/press-releases/new-findings-confirm-predictions-physician-shortage

Blank, Steve. 2020. "What's Missing from Zoom Reminds Us What It Means to Be Human." Retrieved from https://steveblank.com/2020/04/27/whats-missing-from-zoom-reminds-us-what-it-means-to-be-human/

Cancialosi, Chris. 2015. "Crowdsourcing: Your Key to a More Effective, Engaged Organization." Retrieved from https://www.forbes.com/sites/chriscancialosi/2015/08/03/crowdsourcing-your-key-to-a-more-effective-engaged-organization/#51a140d8eaef

Dobbin, Frank, and Alexandra, Kalev. 2016. "Why Diversity Programs Fail." *Harvard Business Review*. Retrieved from https://hbr.org/2016/07/why-diversity-programs-fail

Global Workplace Analytics. 2019. "Latest Work-at-Home/Telecommuting/Mobile Work/Remote Work Statistics." Retrieved from https://globalworkplaceanalytics.com/telecommuting-statistics

Holvino, Evangelina, Bernardo, Ferdman, and Deborah, Merrill-Sands. 2004. "Creating and Sustaining Diversity and Inclusion in Organizations: Strategies and Approaches." In *The Psychology and Management of Workplace Diversity*, edited by M. S. Stockdale and F. J. Crosby, 245–276. London: Blackwell.

Lawler, Edward, and John, Boudreau. 2015. *Global Trends in Human Resource Management: A Twenty-Year Analysis*. Redwood City, CA: Stanford Business Books.

Lindgren, Gunnar. n.d. "Impending World Oil Shortage." Retrieved from http://www.imc-cim.org/mmap/pdf/prod-lindgren-oil-e.pdf

Lindsey, Rebecca. 2019. "Climate Change: Global Sea Level." Retrieved from https://www.climate.gov/news-features/understanding-climate/climate-change-global-sea-level

McClure, Robin. 2020. "How Much Your Family Should Expect to Pay for Daycare." Retrieved from https://www.verywellfamily.com/cost-of-daycare-616847

Patterson, Kerry, Joseph, Grenny, Ron, McMillan, and Al, Switzler. 2011. *Crucial Conversations Tools for Talking When Stakes are High* (2nd ed.). New York: McGraw-Hill.

Paying for Senior Care. 2019. "Senior Care Costs/Aging Care Calculator." Retrieved from https://www.payingforseniorcare.com/costs

Rothwell, William J. 2020. *Adult Learning Basics* (2nd ed.). Alexandria, VA: Association for Talent Development.

Rothwell, William J., Jim, Graber, and Neil, McCormick. 2012. *Lean but Agile: Rethink Workforce Planning and Gain a True Competitive Advantage*. New York: AMACOM.

Sarasota County Sherriff's Office. 2019. "Cyber Safety." Retrieved from https://www.sarasotasheriff.org/programs_and_amp_services/crime_prevention/cyber_safety.php

Stavros, Jacqueline, and Cheri, Torres. 2018. *Conversations Worth Having: Using Appreciative Inquiry to Fuel Productive and Meaningful Engagement*. San Francisco, CA: Berrett-Koehler.

Steghofer, Jan-Philipp. 2017. "The Next Generation of Socio-technical Systems." Technology and Society. Retrieved from https://technologyandsociety.org/the-next-generation-of-socio-technical-systems/

Surkutwar, Preeti. 2017. *Current Trends in Human Resource Management*. Balti, Moldova: Lap Lambert Academic Publishing.

Tapscott, Don, and Ricardo, Vargas. 2019. "How Blockchain Will Change Construction." *Harvard Business Review*. Retrieved from https://hbr.org/2019/07/how-blockchain-will-change-construction

Thirst Project. 2020. "Water Crisis." Retrieved from https://www.thirstproject.org/water-crisis/?gclid=Cj0KCQjw_ez2BRCyARIsAJfg-ksHVQAn_p41zL_5qwbDAE_-zqO_zZRTiScpKUuV0EXdusjQ8d5v8QsaApZhEALw_wcB

Vince, Gaia. 2012. "How the World's Oceans Could Be Running Out of Fish." Retrieved from https://www.bbc.com/future/article/20120920-are-we-running-out-of-fish

Chapter 14

What Unique Issues Surface When Implementing OD Interventions?

William J. Rothwell

Contents

Overview

Implementing organization development (OD) interventions is about *executing* change efforts, change projects, or change initiatives. As many observers of the contemporary business scene have noticed, many grand change plans flounder in the challenges posed by daily execution (Bossidy & Charan 2002). But what are some of the major challenges posed by daily execution in an OD intervention? How can those challenges be overcome by careful daily change facilitation? What unique challenges are posed by the implementation of OD interventions ranging in scope from those geared to individuals, teams or work groups, intergroup, organizational, industry, community, or larger scale changes and those ranging by time frame such as short-term to multi-year? This chapter addresses these important questions.

Challenges in Implementing OD Interventions

There are many reasons why OD interventions fail during implementation. In many cases, they are the same reasons why all change efforts fail. Those include:

- The change goals or objectives are not clear or are not measurable.
- Managers and/or workers have not been convinced that the change should be made, and appeals to convince managers and workers to change have not been made to both the rational (head) and emotional (heart) reasons for change.
- No provision is made to modify goals or objectives as changes outside the organization influence the desired results during implementation.
- It is not clear who should do what in the change effort and what results are desired from those change efforts.
- Workers and managers are not adequately involved in setting change targets and in implementing the change.
- Managers and/or workers do not agree among themselves what new behaviors or results are desired during the change effort or after successful implementation.
- Confusion exists over the role(s) of any consultants who are there to help make the change.
- The action plan for the OD intervention is unclear or not well-communicated.
- Inadequate communication exists as the change is implemented so that people eventually forget what they are doing, why they are doing it, how they are doing it, and what results have been obtained from actions taken in the change effort.
- Organizational policies, leadership, structure, and rewards have not been modified to support the change.
- Insufficient resources have been provided for implementation—such as inadequate people, money, or time.

- Management loses commitment to the change during the implementation.
- Obstacles to change implementation are not identified, and steps are not taken to address the obstacles so that the root causes of resistance to change are never addressed.
- Key stakeholders are not consulted, or their concerns are not addressed during implementation.

Appendix A at the back of this book provides resources that can help you overcome these—and other—challenges. *Appendix A* includes selected articles, books, research studies, videos, web links, and other resources that address issues related to implementing change efforts.

Overcoming Challenges Posed by Implementing OD Interventions

Relatively few organizations have established standards for change implementation, though such standards do exist, as established by the Association of Change Management Professionals (2014). Such *standards*, understood to mean requirements to be met during the implementation of change efforts, would address—but go beyond—all the requirements of the guidelines and standards governing best practices in project management (Ilies et al. 2010). Of course, OD interventions have unique requirements that go beyond traditional project-oriented change management.

Standards for OD may include those for change management, and standards for good change projects include the following (Salapatas 2000):

- A defined life cycle and milestones
- Clear project requirements that are stable and scoped
- Clear authorization and ways to modify the project
- Clear organization (structure), systems, and roles
- Planned commitments from key stakeholders
- Clear ways to take corrective action as needed
- Ways to check work quality
- Ways of tracking actions taken against actions planned
- Identified ways to address special issues or challenges as they arise

Additional and overlapping standards are set forth in the research conducted by the Project Management Institute as the basis for certification in project management (Project Management Institute 2017 and 2020).

But implementing OD interventions often goes beyond simple projects to encompass complex projects and/or encompass many simultaneous change efforts at once. As a simple example, implementing self-directed work teams in an organization might require simultaneous change projects geared toward making modifications in the physical setting (e.g., seating arrangements), in technology (e.g., scheduling software used by the team), training (on team requirements), communication methods (to ensure team members communicate with each other), and many other change projects. They must be orchestrated to best effect, and that may require temporary structures such as task forces, committees, steering groups, or other temporary groups to ensure that many components of a change effort are coordinated and integrated as they are implemented. At the same time, the organization's leaders or OD practitioners may need to facilitate reviews of organizational HR policies and procedures to ensure that efforts to recruit, select, manage, appraise, train, develop, reward, and promote workers are aligned with the OD intervention.

At the same time. Many organizations today have many strategic change efforts underway simultaneously. While one major OD intervention can be effectively managed with project management approaches, there is a crowding out effect when an organization is undergoing 100 or more major strategic change efforts simultaneously. When that happens, managers and workers alike grow confused about what change projects they are working on, what goals are to be achieved, what progress has already been made, what next steps might be, and how to evaluate results. It is for that reason that Whole Systems Transformational Change was invented to bring together all the key stakeholders and participants in one planned event to reunify all change projects under a Grand Strategy (Bunker & Alban 1996).

See the tool at the end of this chapter to rate how well OD interventions are managed in your organization.

Unique Challenges Posed by the Scope of Change

The OD practitioner's role can change, depending on the scope of change. To be clear, the scope of change answers the question "How many people are affected by the change effort?" Small-scope OD interventions affect individuals (through instrument-guided development, coaching, and similar interventions), teams or work groups (through team building, T-groups, process consultation, and similar interventions), departments or divisions (through intergroup development such as cross-team confrontation meetings or HR transformation), entire organizations (e.g., strategic planning, implementation of Enterprise Resource Programs), whole industries (e.g., changing how auto companies make money through electric rather than petroleum-based cars), communities (e.g., social activist efforts, workforce or economic development efforts), or even diplomacy (e.g., applying OD principles at the United Nations, World Bank, or nongovernmental organizations).

In small-scope change efforts, the OD practitioner's role is akin to that of a clinical psychologist. OD is a helping relationship focused on one person and/or one person and his or her immediate social network. Interactions between OD practitioner and client can occur formally (planned meetings), informally (unplanned get-togethers), or some combination of planned and unplanned. When OD practitioners work with one person at a time, it is a straightforward transaction with immediate give-and-take. Building trust and rapport is essential, and that is carried out over time through working together.

The larger the group with which the OD practitioners must deal, the more they will need to use combinations of mass media (e.g., websites, help lines, and town hall meetings), targeted communication (e.g., scheduled meetings with teams and/or individuals, focus groups, and surveys), and meetings with managers and workers who exercise influence over groups. Applying project management methods is important, but large-scale change efforts will require more attention to efforts segmented to different internal groups within the organization.

Unique Challenges Posed by the Timeframe

Short-term OD interventions—such as team-building experiences occurring in a retreat over a weekend—will require prework, real-time work, and postwork. As prework, OD practitioners may need to assess team-building needs before the group meets to identify and feed back to the team perceptions from the team about what group dynamics need improvement. As real-time work, OD practitioners need to work with the whole group but also interact with subgroups (e.g., managers, workers, union leaders) and individuals (e.g., known change skeptics).

Longer-term OD interventions will require more structured modes of interaction to support change efforts. OD practitioners may need to establish task forces, action teams, steering committees, and other groups to focus on specific tasks in the change effort. (Tasks associated with the change effort may include training, communication, physical settings, technology, and so forth.) OD practitioners will then need to ensure continuing ways of interacting with these groups and facilitating cross-group communication.

Key Lessons Learned

OD interventions can vary by duration. Some interventions can be short; some can stretch across many years. During long-term implementation, much can change: the people involved in the OD intervention can leave; the goals of the intervention may change; the external environmental factors and the internal organizational factors affecting the intervention can be dynamic and subject to fluctuations; the resources available for the intervention can change over time; and much more.

Many OD interventions fail (Mirvis & Berg 1977). While there are many reasons why they fail, it is important to manage the change journey during the roll out and implementation.

That can be done by establishing guidelines or by following research-based standards on change in general. Alternatively, the organization can establish standards for implementing OD interventions. Follow through is critical. The goal is to avoid common reasons for failure in execution.

Discussion Questions

1. What should OD practitioners do during the implementation of an OD intervention? List as many action steps or action ideas that you can think of.
2. Why might the role of OD practitioners differ by the scope of the OD intervention? For instance, why would the role of an OD practitioner in implementing a team-building intervention differ from the role of an OD practitioner in implementing a large-scale organizational change?
3. Why might the role of OD practitioners differ by the duration of an OD intervention? What are some differences between what an OD

practitioner should do in a short-term change effort (e.g., weekend retreat offsite) and a long-term change effort (e.g., facilitating the implementation of a five-year strategic plan using OD)? (Table 14.1)

Tool

Table 14.1 An Assessment of OD Intervention Implementation

Directions: Use this assessment instrument to determine how well an OD intervention is implemented. For each OD intervention standard listed in the left column below, rate how well you feel that has been implemented in an OD intervention.
Use this scale: **0 = Not applicable; 1 = Very ineffective; 2 = Ineffective; 3 = Neutral; 4 = Effective; 5 = Very effective.**
Then, in the right column, make notes about improvements needed. If you wish, ask other stakeholders to use this instrument to rate the implementation of the OD intervention separately from OD practitioners. When finished, compare scores and note areas for improvement.

OD Intervention Standard		*Rate How Well the Implementation Has Been Facilitated*						*Notes for Improvement*
	Scores	**0**	**1**	**2**	**3**	**4**	**5**	
1	The OD intervention's purpose is clear.	0	1	2	3	4	5	
2	The OD intervention's goals are measurable.	0	1	2	3	4	5	
3	Managers have agreed on the OD interventions goals among themselves.	0	1	2	3	4	5	
4	The tasks to be completed for the OD intervention have been clearly listed.	0	1	2	3	4	5	
5	The people involved in the OD intervention have been identified.	0	1	2	3	4	5	
6	The OD consultant's role in implementing the OD intervention is clear.	0	1	2	3	4	5	

(Continued)

TABLE 14.1   An Assessment of OD Intervention Implementation (Con't.)

7	The OD intervention has a clear timeline.	0	1	2	3	4	5	
8	The OD intervention has clear milestones.	0	1	2	3	4	5	
9	The stakeholders (i.e., those who have a stake in the change) have been identified.	0	1	2	3	4	5	
10	A clear communication plan has been prepared over time for each stakeholder group.	0	1	2	3	4	5	
11	It is clear what role OD practitioners should play during the OD intervention implementation.	0	1	2	3	4	5	
12	Organizational structures have been established to support the OD intervention.	0	1	2	3	4	5	
13	OD practitioners facilitate regular meetings to discuss intervention progress.	0	1	2	3	4	5	
14	OD practitioners facilitate ways to collect data about intervention progress and feed that information back to stakeholders.	0	1	2	3	4	5	
15	OD practitioners document successes and communicate them to stakeholders.	0	1	2	3	4	5	
16	OD practitioners facilitate efforts to celebrate intervention successes.	0	1	2	3	4	5	
17	OD practitioners monitor the external environment and point out to stakeholders any trends that affect the OD intervention.	0	1	2	3	4	5	
18	OD practitioners monitor changes inside the organization that may affect the successful implementation of the OD intervention and points them out to stakeholders so that they may address what modifications may be necessary to the OD intervention.	0	1	2	3	4	5	

(*Continued*)

TABLE 14.1   An Assessment of OD Intervention Implementation (Con't.)

19	OD practitioners regularly gather evaluation information– particularly as it may relate to the organization's strategic goals/Balanced Scorecard and feed it back to decision-makers.	0	1	2	3	4	5	
20	OD practitioners continuously monitor best practices and other information relevant to the OD intervention and feed it to stakeholders for their attention.	0	1	2	3	4	5	
Score *Add up all numbers in the middle columns (rates) and place in the box to the right.*								

References

Association of Change Management Professionals. 2014. *Standard for Change Management.* Winter Springs, FL: ACMP.

Bossidy, Larry, and Ram, Charan. 2002. *Execution: The Discipline of Getting Things Done.* Redfern, NSW: Currency.

Bunker, Barbara, and Billie T. Alban. 1996. *Large Group Interventions: Engaging the Whole System for Rapid Change.* San Francisco: Jossey-Bass.

Ilie, Liviu, Emil, Crisan, and Ioana N. Muresan. 2010. "Best Practices in Project Management *Review of International Comparative Management* 11 (1): 43–51.

Mirvis, Phillip H., and N. David Berg. (Eds.). 1977. *Failures in Organization Development.* New York: Wiley-Interscience.

Project Management Institute. 2017. *A Guide to the Project Management Body of Knowledge* (6th ed.). Newtown Square, PA: PMI.

Project Management Institute. 2020. *Project Management Handbook.* Newtown Square, PA: PMI.

Salapatas, J. N. 2000. *Best Practices—The Nine Elements to Success.* Paper presented at Project Management Institute Annual Seminars & Symposium, Houston, TX: Project Management Institute.

Appendix A

Selected Resources to Support OD Intervention Implementation and Related Topics

OD Intervention Implementation

Articles

- Aarons, Gregory A., Mark G. Ehrhart, Laura R. Farahnak, and Michael S. Hurlburt. 2015. "Leadership and Organizational Change for Implementation (LOCI): A Randomized Mixed Method Pilot Study of a Leadership and Organization Development Intervention for Evidence-Based Practice Implementation." *Implementation Science* 16(10): 11. 10.1186/s13012-014-0192-y
- Almasaeid, Turki F., and Suhaib A. Anagreh. 2020. "Organizational Development Interventions to Solve Performance Management Challenges." *Journal of University of Shanghai for Science and Technology* 22(1): 1744–1760. Retrieved from: https://www.researchgate.net/publication/346402868_Organizational_Development_Interventions_to_Solve_Performance_Management_Challenges
- Bartunek, Jean M., and Michael K. Moch. 1987. "First-Order, Second-Order, and Third-Order Change and Organization Development Interventions." *Journal of Applied Behavioral Science* 23(4): 483–500.

- Hornstein, Henry. 2008, January/February. "Using a Change Management Approach to Implement Programs." *Ivey Business Journal.* Retrieved from: https://iveybusinessjournal.com/publication/using-a-change-management-approach-to-implement-it-programs/
- Romme, Georges L. 2011. "Organization Development Interventions: An Artifaction Perspective." *Journal of Applied Behavioral Science* 47(1): 8–32. doi:10.1177/0021886310390864

Books

- Argyris, Chris. 1970. *Intervention Theory and Method: A Behavioral Science View.* Reading, MA: Addison-Wesley.
- Tearle, Ruth. 2020. "Organizational Development: How to Choose the Right Intervention." Retrieved from: https://changedesignsportal.worldsecuresystems.com/announcements/Organizational-development-how-to-choose-the-right-intervention

Websites

- Association for Change Management Professionals (ACMP) Standard for Change Management. Retrieved from: https://www.pmservices.ru/downloads/acmp_standard_change_managem.pdf
- Tearle, Ruth. (no date). "Organization Development: What Type of Organizational Development or OD Intervention Do You Need?" *Change Designs.* Retrieved from: https://changedesignsportal.worldsecuresystems.com/public/team/teamstrategy/Team-intervention.html
- "What Is Organizational Development? A Complete Guide." AIHR Digital. Retrieved from: https://www.digitalhrtech.com/organizational-development/

Videos

- Carmazzi, Arthur. "Creating Sustainable Organizational Culture Change in 80 Days." *TEDxMaitighar.* Video File. June 21, 2019. Retrieved from: youtube.com/watch?v=r2XE87EoI7M
- Gautam, Vinayshil. "Intervention Strategies for Organization Development-Individual/Group." *NPTEL.* Video File. April 10, 2012. Retrieved from: youtube.com/watch?v=_y3Q6oAOud0
- Comey, Teresa. "OD Interventions and Teams." BCODN. Video File. February 26, 2012. Retrieved from: youtube.com/watch?v=5KNaY-nXnTY

- "Organization Development Interventions." EDU WALA. Video File. July 14, 2012. Retrieved from: youtube.com/watch?v=3Onti2XMtyI
- Aggarwal, Shashi. "Organization Development Interventions (Techniques of OD)" Monday.com. Video File. December 18, 2019. Retrieved from: youtube.com/watch?v=X2WqmCK1u1A
- "Organization Development Intervention Techniques." Dynamic Study. Video File. October 27, 2018. Retrieved from: youtube.com/watch?v=qQJ1HNEMpi4

Software

- Project Management Software. Capterra: https://www.capterra.com/sem-compare/project-management-software?gclid=Cj0KCQiAqo3 BRDoARIsAE5vnaKjdpAwOEpHmzzR9AZIZ59qcDY_0O5 AI6dLUMQuHB3M6B9vHRYhtVwaArTFEALw_wcB
- Decision Support Software. Capterra. Retrieved from: https://www.capterra.com/decision-supportsoftware/

Executing Change Efforts

Articles

- Cândido, Carlos. J. F., and Santos P. Santos. 2015. "Strategy Implementation: What Is the Failure Rate?" *Journal of Management and Organization* 21(2): 237–262. doi.org/10.1017/jmo.2014.77
- Dandira, Martin. 2011. "Involvement of Implementers: Missing Element in Strategy Formulation." *Business Strategy Series* 12(1): 30–34. doi.org/1 0.1108/17515631111100386
- Donald, Mathew. 2019. *Leading and Managing Change in the Age of Disruption and Artificial Intelligence.* Wagon Lane, Bingley: Emerald Publishing. doi.org/10.1108/9781787563674
- Dumas, Colette, and Richard H. Beinecke. 2018. "Change Leadership in the 21st Century." *Journal of Organizational Change Management* 31(4): 867–876. doi.org/10.1108/JOCM-02-2017-0042
- Franken, Arnoud, Chris Edwards, and Rob Lambert. 2009. "Executing Strategic Change: Understanding the Critical Management Elements that Lead to Success." *California Management Review* 51(3): 49–73. doi.org/ 10.2307/41166493

Books

- Harvard Business Review. 2011. *Harvard Business Review on Inspiring and Executing Innovation.* Boston, MA: Harvard.
- Morgan, Mark, I., Andrew B. Cole, David R. Johnson, and Robert J. Johnson. 2010. *Executing Your Business Transformation: How to Engage Sweeping Change Without Killing Yourself or Your Business.* San Francisco, CA: John Wiley & Sons.

Reports

- Hawker, James, R., and Richard S. Dali. 1988. "Anatomy of an Organizational Change Effort at the Lewis Research Center." *NASA Contractor Report 4146.* Retrieved from https://core.ac.uk/download/pdf/42831886.pdf

Websites

- Johnston, Alasdair, Frederic Lefort, and Joseph Tesvic. (n.d.). Secrets of Successful Change Implementation. McKinsey & Company. Retrieved from: https://www.mckinsey.com/business-functions/operations/our-insights/secrets-of-successful-change-implementation

Videos

- McChesney, S. Covey, and J. Huling. "The 4 Disciplines of Execution." Productivity Game. Video File. July 17, 2017. Retrieved from: youtu.be/2HKn49r3-Ko
- "5 ways to Lead in an Era of Constant Change." TED. Video File. November 3, 2016. Retrieved from: https://www.youtube.com/watch?v=urntcMUJR9M

Making Corporate Culture Change

Articles

- Deal, Terrence E., and Allan A. Kennedy. 1983. "Corporate Cultures: The Rites and Rituals of Corporate Life." Addison-Wesley. *Business Horizons* 26(2): 82–85.
- Hassard, John, and Sudi Sharifi. 1989. "Corporate Culture and Strategic Change." *Journal of General Management* 15(2): 4–19. doi.org/10.1177/030630708901500201

- Kono, Toyohiro. 1990. "Corporate Culture and Long-Range Planning." *Long Range Planning* 23(4): 9–19. doi.org/10.1016/0024-6301(90)90148-W
- Maull, Roger S., Peter Brown, and R. Cliffe. 2001. "Organizational Culture and Quality Improvement." *International Journal of Operations & Production Management* 21(3): 302–326. doi.org/10.1108/014435701103 64614
- Peters, Thomas J., and Robert H. Waterman. 1984. "In Search of Excellence." *Nursing Administration Quarterly* 8(3): 85–86.
- Sadri, Golnaz, and Brian Lees. 2001. "Developing Corporate Culture as a Competitive Advantage." *The Journal of Management Development* 20(9): 853–859. doi.org.10.1108/02621710110410851
- Schein, Edgar H. 1990. "Organizational Culture." *American Psychological Association* 45(2): 109. doi.org/10.1037/0003-066X.45.2.109
- Bolboli, Seyed A., and Markus Reiche. 2014. "Culture-Based Design and Implementation of Business Excellence." *TQM Journal* 26(4): 329–347. doi.org/10.1108/TQM-01-2014-001
- Woods, III, George I. 2008. *Organizational Change: Its Impact on Identity, Commitment, Interorganizational Perceptions, and Behavior* (Order No. AAI3336150).

Books

- Cameron, Kim S., and Robert E. Quinn. 2011. *Diagnosing and Changing Organizational Culture: Based on the Competing Values Framework*. San Francisco, CA: John Wiley & Sons.
- Cummings, Thomas G., and Christopher G. Worley. 2014. *Organization Development and Change*. Stamford, CT: Cengage Learning.
- Kotter, John P. 2008. *Corporate Culture and Performance*. New York, NY: Simon and Schuster.
- Kotter, John P. 2012. *Leading Change*. Boston, MA: Harvard Business Press.
- Martin, Joanne. 2001. *Organizational Culture: Mapping the Terrain*. Thousand Oaks, CA: Sage Publications.
- Bate, Paul. 1994. *Strategies for Cultural Change*. Woburn, CA: Butterworth-Heinemann.
- Schein, Edgar H. 2009. *The Corporate Culture Survival Guide*. San Francisco, CA: Jossey-Bass.
- Scharmer, Otto C. 2009. *Theory U: Learning from the Future as It Emerges*. San Francisco, CA: Berrett-Koehler Publishers.

- Weick, Karl E., and Kathleen M. Sutcliffe. 2011. *Managing the Unexpected: Resilient Performance in an Age of Uncertainty.* Vol. 8. San Francisco, CA: John Wiley & Sons.

Websites

- "You Can Consciously Change Your Organization Culture" (n.d.). The Balance Careers. Retrieved from: https://www.thebalancecareers.com/how-to-change-your-culture-1918810

Videos

- Carmazzi, Arthur. "Creating Sustainable Organizational Culture Change in 80 Days." TEDx. Video File. June 21, 2019. Retrieved from: youtu.be/r2XE87EoI7M
- Pennington, Randy. "Creating a Culture-Change." www.penningtongroup.com. Video File. July 20, 2012. Retrieved from: youtu.be/-XQjzCiRzn4

Implementation Science

Articles

- Bauer, Mark S., Laura Damschroder, Hildi Hagedorn, Jeffery Smith, and Amy M. Kilbourne. 2015. "An Introduction to Implementation Science for the Non-specialist." *BMC Psychology* 3(1): 32. doi.org/10.1186/s40359-015-0089-9
- Eccles, Martin P., and Brian S. Mittman. 2006. "Welcome to Implementation Science." *Implementation Science* 1 (1). doi.org/10.1186/1748-5908-1-1
- Hunsley, John, and Eric J. Mash. 2007. "Evidence-Based Assessment." *Annual Review of Clinical Psychology* 3(1): 29–51. doi.org/10.1146/annurev.clinpsy.3.022806.091419
- Lewis, Cara C., Sarah Fischer, Bryan J. Weiner, Cameo Stanick, Mimi Kim, and Ruben G. Martinez. 2015. "Outcomes for Implementation Science: An Enhanced Systematic Review of Instruments Using Evidence-Based Rating Criteria." *Implementation Science* 10(1): 155. doi.org/10.1186/s13012-015-0342-x
- Ogden, Terje, and Dean L. Fixsen. 2014. "Implementation Science." *Zeitschrift Für Psychologie* 222(1): 4–11. doi.org/10.1027/2151-2604/a000160

- Rabin, Borsika A., Peyton Purcell, Sana Naveed, Richard P. Moser, Michelle D. Henton, Enola K. Proctor, Ross C. Brownson, and Russell E. Glasgow. 2012. "Advancing the Application, Quality and Harmonization of Implementation Science Measures." *Implementation Science* 7(1): 119. doi.org/10.1186/1748-5908-7-119

Report

- Fixsen, Dean, Michael Dennis, Ken Martinez, and Jennifer Wisdom. 2015. "The Current State of Implementation Science: The Critical Role of Research Education." Institute for Translational Research in Adolescent Behavioral Health. 28th Annual Research & Policy Conference. Child, Adolescent, and Young Adult Behavioral Health. Retrieved from: http://cmhconference.com/files/presentations/28th/s44-1.pdf

Videos

- Fixsen, Dean. "Implementation Science Speaker Series: Applied Implementation Science." Johns Hopkins Bloomberg School of Public Health. Video File. February 24, 2014. Retrieved from: youtube.com/watch?v=MsMh1y3xd7o
- "What Is Implementation Science." IRL-Research and Science Course. University of Minnesota. Video File. August 30, 2019. Retrieved from: youtu.be/Cvk-cpDptOc
- "Introduction to Implementation Science." Massachusetts Department of Elementary and Secondary Education. Video File. February 25, 2020. Retrieved from: youtube.com/watch?v=eJoNkAavMEY

Using Evidence-Based OD

Articles

- Aarons, Gregory A., Mark G. Ehrhart, Lauren R. Farahnak, and Michael S. Hurlburt. 2015. "Leadership and Organizational Change for Implementation (LOCI): A Randomized Mixed Method Pilot Study of a Leadership and Organization Development Intervention for Evidence-Based Practice Implementation." *Implementation Science* 10(1): 11. doi.org/10.1186/s13012-014-0192-y

Books

- Daugherty, Alice. 2015. *Organizational Assessment, Restructuring, and Evidence-Based Management*. Emerald Publishing Limited.
- ten Have, Steve, Wouter ten Have, Anne-Bregji Huijsmans, and Maarten Otto. 2016. *Reconsidering Change Management: Applying Evidence-Based Insights in Change Management Practice* (1st ed.). New York, NY: Routledge, Taylor & Francis Group.
- Jones, Maureen Connelly, and William J. Rothwell (Eds.). 2017. *Evaluating Organization Development: How to Ensure and Sustain the Successful Transformation*. Boca Raton, FL: Productivity Press. doi.org/1 0.1201/b21877
- Leonard, H. Skipton, Rachel Lewis, Arthur M. Freedman, and Jonathan Passmore. 2013. *The Wiley-Blackwell Handbook of the Psychology of Leadership, Change, and Organizational Development*. Wiley-Blackwell.
- Scandura, Terri. A. 2019. *Essentials of Organizational Behavior: An Evidence-Based Approach* (2nd ed.). Thousand Oaks, CA: Sage Publications.
- Schultz, Randall L., and Michael J. Ginzberg (Eds.). 1984. *Management Science Implementation*. Vol. 1. New York, NY: JAI Press.
- Scott, John. C., and Douglas H. Reynolds (Eds.). 2010. *Handbook of Workplace Assessment: Evidence-Based Practices for Selecting and Developing Organizational Talent* (1st ed.). San Francisco, CA: John Wiley & Sons, Inc.

Videos

- Woods, Dabrow. "Evidence-Based Practice: Improving Practice, Improving Outcomes." Wolters Kluwer. Video File. June 3, 2014. Retrieved from: youtu.be/OvenUa3Ww8o
- Wilkinson, David. "6 (Evidence Based) Guidelines for Organizational Change." The Oxford Review. Video File. April 18, 2016. Retrieved from: youtu.be/qLij_l4tFB8
- Gnall, Kathy. "How Organizations Implement and Sustain Evidence Based Practices Strategies, Tips, and Tools." CSG Justice Center. The National Reentry Resource Center. Video File. June 19, 2013. Retrieved from: https://youtu.be/5F0Zpy9cRfg

Index

Note: *Italicized* page numbers refer to figures, **bold** page numbers refer to tables

Printed in the United States
by Baker & Taylor Publisher Services